Hong Kong Media and Asia's Cold War

Hong Kong Media and Asia's Cold War

PO-SHEK FU

OXFORD
UNIVERSITY PRESS

Oxford University Press is a department of the University of Oxford. It furthers
the University's objective of excellence in research, scholarship, and education
by publishing worldwide. Oxford is a registered trade mark of Oxford University
Press in the UK and certain other countries.

Published in the United States of America by Oxford University Press
198 Madison Avenue, New York, NY 10016, United States of America.

Library of Congress Cataloging-in-Publication Data
Names: Fu, Poshek, 1955- author.
Title: Hong Kong media and Asia's cold war / Po-Shek Fu.
Description: New York, NY : Oxford University Press, [2023] |
Includes bibliographical references and index.
Identifiers: LCCN 2022053498 (print) | LCCN 2022053499 (ebook) |
ISBN 9780190073770 (paperback) | ISBN 9780190073763 (hardback) |
ISBN 9780190073800 | ISBN 9780190073794 (epub)
Subjects: LCSH: Mass media—China—Hong Kong. | Mass media—Taiwan. |
Cold War—Social aspects—Asia. | Motion pictures—Political
aspects—China—Hong Kong. | Motion pictures—Political aspects—Taiwan.
Classification: LCC P92.H6 F8 2023 (print) | LCC P92.H6 (ebook) |
DDC 302.23095125—dc23/eng/20221207
LC record available at https://lccn.loc.gov/2022053498
LC ebook record available at https://lccn.loc.gov/2022053499

DOI: 10.1093/oso/9780190073763.001.0001

Paperback printed by Marquis, Canada
Hardback printed by Bridgeport National Bindery, Inc., United States of America

In Memory of my
Father 傅明燊 *and Father-in-law* 金堅

"People with training in historical craft
may now try to write a history of
émigrés in Hong Kong."

Historian Qian Mu
Zhongguo lishi yanjiufa (1970)

"My parents escaped from China after the
war. They basically went to Hong Kong
and restarted their lives. In Hong Kong in
the fifties was pretty strange. It's like
'Casablanca.' Everyone from all over
China went there, and there were
people from all over the world. My
dad was always saying, 'So-and-so is
probably a spy.'"

Filmmaker Wayne Wang
New Yorker, June 5, 2022

Contents

Preface

This book is about Hong Kong and the Cold War in Asia. The British seized Hong Kong militarily from China in 1842. After a century, with the outbreak of the Pacific War, the colony fell to Japan. After the war, the British took back Hong Kong. In 1949, when Mao defeated Chiang Kai-shek in the civil war to establish the People's Republic of China (PRC), he did not liberate the colony. Under British colonial rule, Hong Kong became a clandestine battleground of ideological contest between China and the United States during the Cold War. Vowing to "retake the mainland," the Nationalists ensconced on Taiwan (Republic of China; ROC) fought with the Communists for legitimacy as the sole government of China. The Cold War and an extended civil war converged, and influenced each other, in British Hong Kong as the Communists, the Nationalists, and the United States struggled to mobilize the refugees and exiles to battle for the hearts and minds of ethnic Chinese in Asia. This book tries to understand how Hong Kong became the crossroads in Asia's Cold War and the ways in which the global conflicts affected the British colony.

The fall of the Berlin Wall in 1989 and the demise of the Soviet Union two years later, along with increasing access to source materials in both East and West, have given rise to much new scholarship on Cold War history. Its breath and diversity is amply demonstrated in the *Cambridge History of the Cold War*, which assesses the changing field in international and global dimension.[1] The three-volume collection covers many different approaches and viewpoints—such as Jessica Gienow-Hecht's study of European intellectuals, Rosemary Foot's discussion of human rights, and Nicholas Kull's chapter on popular culture, that went beyond the conventional emphasis on the diplomacy and security conflicts of the superpowers. It brings up, especially, two key themes of recent research on the Cold War. The first is an interdisciplinary approach that places the East-West tension "in the larger context of chronological time and geographical space," with increasing focus on the roles of ideas, culture, and mentality. This new research agenda goes a long way toward bringing our attention to the complex synergy between foreign policy and domestic changes, state mobilization and social consciousness, and the impact of international conflicts on everyday life that made up the twentieth-century history of which the Cold War was an important part.[2] Another theme is broadening the geographical scope of research to the Third World. To use Federico Romero's phrases, it marked a shift from "a primarily Euro-Atlantic focus to the complex heterogeneity of the global south," and for some of its best works, from an emphasis on policymakers of the superpowers to "the agency of a variety of actors in Latin America, Asia, or Africa."[3] The important point here is giving prominence to the dynamic, multifaceted interaction between the US and Soviet interventions and local actors—be they political elites, social movements, or intellectuals and artists—who struggled to shape and appropriate the Cold War tension in pursuit of their own causes.[4]

While greatly expanding and complicating our understanding of the Cold War and its significance in the twentieth century, there are also historical phenomena left overlooked or obscured by this new global research agenda. As most, if not all, of the "hot wars" and major flashpoints took place in Asia and other Third World countries—including the Korean War, the Vietnam War, and Angola's War of Independence—which suffered huge loss of human lives and vast physical damages, the bulk of the new Cold War literature has given prominence to military conflicts and crisis-ridden encounter with decolonization in this part of the globe. This explains, at least in part, the scant attention paid to the British colonial outpost along China's southern coast, Hong Kong, which had experienced no hot war or organized movement for independence. The Communist leadership decided it was more valuable in view of US hostility to leave it to British rule. British governor Alexander Grantham (and his successors) tried to hold on to its colonial rule by maintaining neutrality in the Great Power conflicts while misleadingly calling the city the "Berlin of the East" in an attempt to court US support. The Soviets attacked China for allowing its territory to be controlled by imperialist powers despite its claim for leadership in world revolution. Surrounded by anticolonial movements in the region, Hong Kong was a historical anomaly.[5]

Hong Kong Media and Asia's Cultural Cold War argues that British Hong Kong was a crossroads in the Cold War where the global, the regional, and the local intersected. It functioned as a nerve center of the contest for hegemony in the region between the Communists, the Nationalists, and the United States. Each took advantage of the colony's political neutrality, convenient transportation and communication, established media environment, and huge concentration of émigré intellectuals and artists to launch propaganda and psychological warfare that targeted Chinese diasporic communities in Southeast Asia and around the globe. In an effort to put the Cold War conflicts under control and to maintain its legitimacy, on the other hand, the colonial government did its best to regulate, commercialize, and depoliticize media and cultural life by means of censorship and political surveillance, often in coordination with other parts of the British Empire. The cultural Cold War in Hong Kong became, therefore, intertwined, closely and ambivalently, with a society giving relentless primacy to profits, apolitical entertainment, and global expansion.

Like other countries, myriad types of entertainments and information sources were brought into play in the cultural battle in British Hong Kong: art, literature, music, radio broadcasts, newspapers, stage drama. This book focuses on film and magazines. With its mass popularity and cultural salience, as Tony Shaw and Denise Youngblood discuss in *Cinematic Cold War*, cinema served a powerful shaping role in the cultural Cold War conducted "from the East, West, North, or South." It prompted a sizable literature on the Cold War film propaganda in Europe and the United States.[6] In comparison, attention to Hong Kong and other Asian cinemas from a Cold War lens has emerged only relatively recent.[7] Mid-twentieth-century Hong Kong cinema was multilingual, containing various dialect productions catering to various audience groups. Although the overwhelming majority of the local population were Cantonese speakers, standing at the center of the Communist-Nationalist–US propaganda warfare was the Mandarin cinema, which was largely created by refugees and exiles who had fled from the mainland since 1946 and especially 1949. It was divided along ideological lines into two cinematic blocs: pro-Communist "Patriotic" studios vs pro-Nationalist "Free China" studios. The dividing line was constantly in flux, even as Taiwan officials took various steps, overtly and covertly, to rigidify and institutionalize it in an effort to block off Communist influences. US intervention in support of a cinematic "free Asia" complicated and expanded the inter-bloc conflicts.

The extant literature places emphasis on Cantonese films and "Patriotic" studios in part because of the assumption that, as a part of the underground Communist propaganda machinery, they were political and, thereby, illustrative of the Cold War politics in Hong Kong filmmaking. It should be clear from the following pages that I am deeply indebted to their works. I choose instead to focus on pro-Nationalist or US-sponsored Mandarin production.

This cinema produced films that have been mainly considered popular entertainment with little political relevance. But filmmakers on both sides of the ideological divide actually encountered the politics of the hearts-and-minds contest under a similar set of business conditions and colonial censorship, and with an array of film genres and subjects that often influenced each other. As we can see, most of the pro-Communist films were wholesome, family-friendly, light-hearted entertainment (with no sex, nudity, or bloody violence), and some of their rivals' productions, such as US-funded Asia Pictures' *Long Lane,* Cathay-owned MP&GI's *Air Hostess,* or Shaw Brothers' *Love Eterne* contained messages that were subtly but evidently sympathetic to a "free China" and "free world" agenda.

Despite numerous online and print anecdotal materials available, there is no systematic research devoted to print media. Actually, the British colony boasted the largest and most dynamic marketplace of news outlets and periodicals in the Sinophone world, thanks largely to the cultural Cold War. With their reputed cosmopolitan experiences and long-honed Mandarin-based writing skills, émigré journalists and intellectuals from Shanghai, especially, played a dominating role in the print media industry. Beijing and Taiwan, respectively, openly and secretly controlled a large number of newspapers (such as *Ta Kung Pao* and the *Hong Kong Times*) and magazines, and the United States Information Services (USIS) and the Asia Foundation (TAF; a CIA-funded nongovernmental organization) covertly supported a similarly large number of print materials and publications. One of them was *Chinese Student Weekly,* a flagship publication of the Union Press founded in the early 1950s by a group of young émigré intellectuals on the fringe of the liberal "third-force" movement active in republican Beijing and especially Shanghai. The weekly was arguably the most influential youth magazine in mid-twentieth-century overseas Chinese communities around the globe, with branch offices in Macao and urban centers across Malaya and Singapore, Thailand, and Indonesia. Antagonistic to one-party dictatorship on both sides of the Taiwan Strait, the group was silent, however, on the repressive rule and social inequality of colonialism. In the 1960s, the weekly went through a generational change. Its new film section opened many young readers' eyes (including future auteurs Ann Hui and John Woo) to new waves of European and American film aesthetics while calling into question the messaging of local filmmaking, contributing to the revitalization of Cantonese cinema in the 1970s, along with an increasing local consciousness among the new postwar generation.

I write this book on the basis of empirical research that draws from contemporary sources—that include newspaper accounts, film studio publications, and memoirs—and largely untapped materials at the Hong Kong Public Record Office, the Hong Kong Film Archive (especially its unclassified materials), and the Asia Foundation collections at the Hoover Institution. In addition, my favorite part of writing this book was having the opportunities to meet and interview men and women who lived the Cold War history as filmmakers, editors, student activists, or simply audiences. Their reminiscences give intimate voices as well as provide much-needed balance (as a cross-referencing tool) to archival documents and other historical materials, which are fraught, as is well known, with partisan bias, especially for a highly politicized period such as the Cold War.

In my previous book on Chinese cinema under Japanese occupation, *Between Shanghai and Hong Kong*, I proposed the idea of a "Shanghai–Hong Kong nexus and its ramifications in the popular cultures and entertainment business" between the two cities between 1935 and 1950.[8] *Hong Kong Media and Asia's Cultural Cold War* extends the chronology to the 1980s (which saw the adoption of the Basic Law guaranteeing the principle of "One Country, Two Systems"). This book can therefore be seen as a sequel. Unlike the refugees who had escaped Japanese rule, who never thought of settling in, those who fled to Hong Kong after 1949 were there to stay. Many of them became, wittingly or unwittingly, involved in the cultural Cold War as they found jobs in the expanding business networks of film studios and magazine publishers on both sides of the ideological divide. Indeed, the ideological battles fostered a politicized and antagonistic atmosphere, but it also, as we can see, drove rapid expansion and industrial transformation of the media ecosystem. They accelerated movement of money, new technique and technology, new management and professional standards, and cultural innovation (such as new-styled opera and martial arts films), and spurred market expansion and region-wide cultural exchanges and coproduction (through such mechanisms as the USIA- and TAF-backed Asia Film Festival, Taiwan's Golden Horse Film Festival, and Beijing's Asian Film Week and series of various "film weeks"). All these cultural dynamics contributed to the modernization, energy and heterogeneity of British Hong Kong's film and print media industries. Hong Kong was a strategic crossroads in the Cold War in Asia, and at the same time, Asia's Cold War played a significant, facilitating role in shaping its twentieth-century modernization and cultural dynamics.

Acknowledgments

I wrote this book during the COVID-19 pandemic. Working on the book was for me a labor of love. It gave me moments of joy and discovery at a time when the world was in isolation and experiencing many painful moments. My special gratitude goes to Jia LeeNi, Robert Hsi, Loke-Ley, and especially Law Kar, all in their eighties or nineties, for their resilience and generosity in sharing their amazing life experiences. I am also grateful to other artists and activists for granting me many hours of personal interviews.

Writing this book, as evidenced in the numerous citations, I stand on the shoulders of many other scholars, and I want to express my debt to their pioneering works. I am indebted to colleagues who gave me critiques of individual chapters in different versions: Margaret Blair, Antoinette Burton, John Carroll, Chan Koon Chong, Kai-wing Chow, Nicola Di Cosmo, Kirk Denton, Gary Fine, Kristen Hoganson, Christina Klein, Perry Link, Andrew Nathan, Odd Arne Westad, Yu Wang, and John Wong. I am also thankful to Mian Chen, He Qiliang, Hui Kwok Wai, Kwok Ching Ling, Kenny Ng, Su Tao, Stevenson Upton, Wang Meng, Lanjun Xu, and Kenneth Yung for sharing research tips and materials with me.

For their encouragement and help, big and small, over the years, my gratitude to Thomas Bedwell, David Bordwell, John Burns, Chen Jianhua, Chen Zishan, Stephen Chu, Parks Coble, Law Kar, Leo Ou-fan Lee, Li Daoxin, Li Kwok Wai, Qin Yameng, Stanley Rosen, Shi Chuan, Elizabeth Sinn, David Der-wei Wang, Wen-hsin Yeh, and Man Fung Yip. I also want to thank the many hardworking archivists in Hong Kong, Stanford, and Shanghai, especially the Hoover Institution Library and Archives and the Hong Kong Public Records Office. I had the fortune to start thinking about this book project at the Institute for Advanced Study in Princeton. Its serene setting and celebration of intellect is an ideal place for giving one's imagination free rein. I must also thank my many amazing students at the University of Illinois who have made my Hong Kong cinema classes so enjoyable.

This book would not exist without the dedicated and talented people at Oxford University Press. My special thanks to Zara Cannon-Mohammad,

Hinduja Dhanasegaran, and my wonderful editor Norman Hirschy, who asked me to give him a proposal that literally started the making of this book.

My most special and important acknowledgement is to my family. I haven't seen my 87-year-old mother, Liu Yuk Chun, since the pandemic began. Thanks to my younger siblings for keeping her company. In this difficult time in Shanghai, it is fortunate to have my incredibly generous brother- and sister-in-law, Jin Yong and Jin Wen, taking care of my mother-in-law, Zhu Liangzhi. Her big heart and lifelong love for learning means a great deal to me. My wife, Qiang, always sensible, makes sure I put things in perspective. Our two sons, Benjamin and Jefferson, a scientist and a ux strategist, believe in my work and are always ready to save me from yet another computer mistake. They inspire and motivate my efforts more than they know. I lovingly dedicate this book to my wife and to our sons.

1

East Meets West

Crossroads in the Cold War

Squeezed between giant antagonists crunching huge bones of con-
tention, Hong Kong has achieved within its own territories a coexistence which is baffling, infuriating.

Han Suyin[1]

The greatest danger which the world is suffering from is this Cold
War business. . . . It creates barriers of the mind which refuses to understand the other person's position.

Jawaharlal Nehru[2]

Hong Kong was a British colony on the southeastern coast of China.
Bordering the southern province of Guangdong, it is surrounded on three
sides by the South China Sea. Within a day train's ride to South China and
famed for its large, deep seaport, it had long served as China's major link to
global trade and movement of people and ideas.[3] "That clock tower over there
is the train station." An American diplomat was brought by a colleague to the
Tsim Sha Tsui waterfront near the iconic clock tower, which was built in 1915
as part of the old Kowloon-Canton railway station. "Walk a minute you could
get on a train to China, if only we were allowed to. Right behind where we
came from, you're on the ship back to San Francisco or you could go around
the world. Looks like we'll be on the *Radiant Star* to weave between more
ships than you can count on the way across the most beautiful harbor in the
world."[4] Its strategic location and convenient transportation links between
China and the rest of the world made British Hong Kong what a US intelligence officer calls a "crossroads for Chinese people of different stripes" in the
Cold War. Coexisting in it, along with an international business community,
were agents and officials from Communist China, Nationalist-ruled Taiwan,

Hong Kong Media and Asia's Cold War. Po-Shek Fu, Oxford University Press. © Oxford University Press 2023.
DOI: 10.1093/oso/9780190073763.003.0001

and Chinese émigrés working with American government agencies. "It was one of the few places where the [opposing] sides could rub elbows and," he continued, "if situations called for it, pass on communications to each other's government."[5]

The Cold War and the Chinese civil war converged in the crossroads of British Hong Kong. It became a base for the opposing powers' cultural and propaganda war to win the hearts and minds of members of the Chinese diaspora scattered across Asia, especially Southeast Asia. Their struggles to shape and influence public attitudes and opinions in other territories, as US historian Kenneth Osgood argues, were part of the intensifying psychological warfare that demonstrated the Cold War "was a political, ideological, psychological, and cultural contest as well as a military and economic one."[6] Mass media was a major front in the cultural Cold War in Hong Kong. And film as a visual medium was one of the potent weapons political leaders, foreign policymakers, and cultural officials of Communist China, Nationalist-ruled Taiwan, and the United States utilized in the contest for allegiance from the ethnic Chinese communities in the region. Indeed, the colony's cinema industry during the early Cold War, from around 1949 to the mid-1960s, was divided along a pro-"free China" (Taiwan), pro–"free world" versus pro-Communist "Patriotic" binarism. As we can see, the binary divide was itself a political rivalry. While Taiwan tried to reinforce it by institutionalizing the boundary, the Communists made it porous in pursuit of United Front interests, and the British weakened and depoliticized it with media censorship and surveillance.

Mandarin was the official language of nationhood of the Chinese governments on both sides of the Taiwan Strait. It was no surprise that despite the long history of Cantonese film production in Hong Kong and that the overwhelming majority of the local population were Cantonese speakers, it was the Mandarin cinema, created by mostly refugees and exiles from Shanghai—the pre-1949 Chinese-language film capital—that stood front and center in the cinematic warfare and synonymous with the colony to audiences in many parts of the world. The émigré Mandarin film industry brought into focus British Hong Kong as the crossroads of political coexistence and confrontation, and its entanglement of film and media production, contents, and distribution constituted a key agent in Asia's cultural Cold War. This chapter tries to help readers understand the confluence of propaganda and psychological warfare, colonial surveillance and censorship, and industrial and business environment that shaped the multivalent history of the Communists, Nationalists, and the United States' contest for overseas Chinese in the region. The discussion focuses on the émigré Mandarin film world, which started with the migration of filmmakers and political exiles from the mainland on the eve of the Communist victory, and which was to cast a long shadow of uncertainty and political antagonism over the British colony.

A Borrowed Place Living on Borrowed Time

Twentieth-century China was in constant crisis. No more than a year after Japan's surrender did the civil war between the Nationalist state (Kuomintang [KMT]) and the Chinese Community Party (CCP) forces erupt. The Chinese conflicts took place at the time of a rapidly deteriorating relationship between the United States and the Soviet Union. Despite Washington's massive assistance, the Nationalists, hobbled by incompetence and corruption, quickly lost ground to Mao's forces. The chaos and violence drove hundreds of thousands of exiles and refugees to Hong Kong, and the "loss of China" sent shock waves to Washington. Shortly after establishment of the People's Republic of China (PRC), in June 1950 Kim II-sung invaded South Korea. The Truman administration responded by landing troops as part of the United Nations–led police action and ordering the US Navy's Seventh Fleet to neutralize the Taiwan Strait, breathing new life into Chiang Kai-shek's exiled regime on the island. "It was the fortress of our hope, the citadel of our battle against an alien power which is ravaging our country," Madam Chiang proclaimed in 1950 as she tried to link the Chinese civil war to the global Cold War. "China's struggle now is the initial phase of a gigantic conflict between good and evil, between liberty and Communism."[7] In October, the Chinese People's Volunteer Army crossed the Yalu River to enter the war. The Cold War had extended to Asia.

The majority of refugees to Hong Kong were peasants and poor laborers from neighboring Guangdong, but there were also economic and cultural elites from Shanghai and its environs, whom the local press referred stereotypically as "White Chinese" (白華), playing on the term for the wealthy white Russians fleeing the Bolshevik Revolution. It is well known that Shanghai émigrés generally felt out of place in the small Cantonese-speaking colony, where living standards were lower and cultural norms and values far less modern than where they had come from. However, they represented a wide spectrum of political beliefs and socioeconomic status. While there were business tycoons and former Nationalist officials who had arrived with money and business connection, most were middle-class intellectuals and professionals struggling to make do with limited resources.

Among these White Chinese were old hands in the film business. They followed what can be called the Shanghai–Hong Kong nexus of border-crossing movement of cinematic capital and people that had started, on a smaller scale, during the War of Resistance against Japan.[8] Now, in the chaotic period of 1947–1949, some entertainment businessmen tried to take advantage of the British colony's financial stability to make movies for the mainland market. Seeing it as a transient base, they stayed away from politics and stuck to tried-and-true plots to ensure quick returns. T. Y. Lee (李祖永), however, an American-educated scion of a Shanghai business magnate, took a different approach. With the assistance of S. K. Chang (張善琨), the legendary producer who was accused of collaboration with the Japanese, he founded Yung Hwa (永華影業) in 1947, a Hollywood-styled studio said to be the largest in Chinese film history. Believing that technological modernization was what China needed to rebuild its film industry and to go global, ultimately he invested huge capital in big names in the industry and state-of-the-art film technology in its debuts, *National Spirit* (國魂, 1948), which tells the story of a Song dynasty (960–1279) loyalist's refusal to surrender to the Mongol conquerors, and *A Secret History of the Qing Court* (清宮秘史, 1949), a sympathetic portrayal of the Qing emperor Guangxu's (1871–1908) failed modernization reform.[9] Lavishly made, both historical epics came out as the Communists were routing Nationalist forces from Manchuria to Shanghai. Although popular among audiences and having received Chiang's commendation, these films created a cash-flow crisis for Yung Hwa because of China's crumbling banking and foreign currency systems (see later in the chapter for details). The films were also attacked by leftist critics in Hong Kong, who were plotting to seize control of Lee's well-equipped studio for the Communist cause, for subservience to the moribund "Chiang [Kai-shek] dynasty" with the "reactionary values of loyalty."[10]

In fact, some left-wing filmmakers and writers fled to the colony to escape the Nationalist reign of terror. They endeavored to rebuild the CCP cultural apparatus (mostly destroyed during the Japanese occupation) and mobilize popular support for Mao's revolution. Eminent Communist writer Xia Yan, for example, was sent in 1947 by future premier Zhou Enlai (周恩來)[11] to strengthen the Party's influence in the region. He made contact with the overseas Chinese community in Southeast Asia, and led United Front efforts to build coalitions with anti-Nationalist elements and to expand propaganda work. Particularly noteworthy were the creation of a stellar cast of film critics in the CCP organ *Huashang Daily* (華商報), who took turns promoting the Communist viewpoints, and the formation between 1947 and 1948 of several small studios, most notably the Great Brightness (大光明) and Southern Masses (南群). They produced a number of low-budget political dramas, with the 1930s Shanghai left-wing realist style, to drum up support for the destruction of the old order. The Communists also built a network of fronts, such as "study groups," among émigré filmmakers, endeavoring to position themselves in Yung Hwa and other major studios to take control of their productions (see below). As Mao's forces swept across China in 1949, Xia Yan (夏衍), then serving as head of the local Party branch, hosted a public reception in honor of the Communist victory. Some pro-Communist groups tried to follow suit. And the Great Brightness launched an adaptation of *Marriage of Xiao Erhei* (小二黑結婚), a popular novel about peasant liberation in the Communist base area. All these activities notably challenged the British colony's legitimacy in the face of Mao's victory.[12]

In fact, the Communist forces could have seized the colony as they were sweeping through the south and seized the city of Guangzhou.[13] It did not happen. The consensus among scholars is that the CCP leaders were likely worried about the possibility of provoking US military intervention at a time when they needed to concentrate on consolidating the victory by finishing off Chiang's remnant forces on the island refuge (which continued to blockade China's eastern coasts).[14] As the Cold War rivalry heightened, keeping Hong Kong under British control also had the perceived benefits of driving a wedge between the United States and Great Britain regarding their policies on Asia. With London's large commercial interests in the region and desire to keep Hong Kong, and Washington's effort to undermine Mao's revolution, the allies failed to agree even on whether they should recognize the People's Republic. Beijing might have gotten wind of this by way of Moscow. It tried to exploit the differences for China's own benefit.[15] This tactical approach led to the formulation of the national policy toward the British colony that was to last until the 1990s: "making full use of Hong Kong in the interests of long-term planning." A recently available CCP document, "A Fifty-Days Rectification Meeting Transcript" (五十天整風會議紀錄), from a high-level meeting held in Beijing in mid-1959 aiming to reemphasize the Party's pragmatic policy, revealed that the main purpose of keeping Hong Kong under British rule was to take advantage of its "free port" in the war against the United States. It would enable Beijing a "window" to collect intelligence on the capitalist world and build a large "patriotic" United Front and propaganda network to counter American containment efforts in the region.[16] As a result of the US-led trade embargo plus, also, according to former colonial official Leo Goodstadt, the worsening Sino-Soviet economic relations after 1957—Hong Kong became ever more important as China's trade and "international finance center" that provided its national economy with much-needed foreign exchange earnings.[17] This pragmatic use of colonial Hong Kong, as noted above, was in effect continuous with the Communist civil war strategy. It was no surprise that there were frustration with and constant opposition within the Party to the gap between the anti-imperialist rhetoric and what Premier Zhou Enlai kept instructing his aides of the party's policy: "to preserve the status quo of Hong Kong" in the East-West struggle. [18] In fact, anticolonial confrontation erupted every now and then in Hong Kong (most notably in 1952–1953, 1957–1958, and the 1967 riots) during the Cold War.[19]

It had always required a modicum of realism and diplomatic skills to deal with its giant neighbor as the colony was reliant on the mainland. "As a community and as a trade center it is a portion of China from which it is separated by political barriers," the colonial government declared in 1935. "It shares in the strength or weakness of its neighbor's conditions and institutions."[20] But now it was a Communist military power dedicated to fomenting world revolution that posed a fundamental—even existential—challenge to the colony's legitimacy. The great uncertainty of if and when—and how— the Communists would cross the border to seize hold of it led *Far Eastern Economic Review* journalist Richard Hughes to call Hong Kong, grievously, a "borrowed place living on borrowed time."[21]

To perpetuate its rule, the British colony had always made itself useful to whoever the rulers were on the mainland. Its importance lay in its laissez-faire business-friendly environment: low taxes, free trade, minimal state intervention, and no currency restrictions.[22] As the United States tried to isolate China in the Cold War contest, then, Hong Kong became its "bridge-head with the rest of the world and most convenient springboard for export dumping forays into Southeast Asia."[23] According to US diplomat Syd Goldsmith, Beijing owned more than three hundred businesses and banks in the colony—including film studios, bookstores, and nine newspapers—that pushed Chinese products and services to the world and supplied essentials (e.g., food and water) to local markets. As a result, along with remittances from overseas Chinese, British Hong Kong provided at least half of China's foreign currency reserve before the 1990s.[24] Moreover, it was an open secret that the trade embargoes during the Cold War created opportunities for many to get rich by smuggling strategic goods—such as rubber, steel, petroleum, tires, and engines for aircrafts—into the mainland. "This was quite simple since there was only a small, symbolic fence marking the China–Hong Kong border," one smuggler recalled later, "so it was easy to get back and forth."[25]

In a highly politicized situation of Sino-American conflicts and extended Chinese civil war, as scholars and many contemporary observers have noted, the colonial government was careful not to provoke Beijing.[26] However, as Governor Alexander Grantham (1947–1957) proclaimed, "The government was master in its own house." It tolerated no threats to its authority and legitimacy.[27] Endeavoring to keep a distance from London's policies, which often had differing calculations of the "China factor" in Cold War geopolitics,[28] Hong Kong maintained neutrality in the superpower conflicts. "We have no intention of allowing Hong Kong to be used as a base for hostile activities against China," Governor Robert Black (1958–1964) explained his way of managing political conflicts, which was continuous with his predecessor. "Subversive activities from whatever sources are absolutely put down whenever they are found and the Hong Kong Police exercise complete impartiality in action against any persons attempting to create disorder. The basis of our administration is the rule of law, before which all parties are equal."[29] With its efficient antisubversive Police Special Branch, and support of the British foreign intelligence service, the colonial government kept a close eye on any potential political trouble. Included among these troubles were US intelligence work and covert support of Taiwan's sabotage and military action against the mainland, and the huge intelligence and propaganda networks that the Communists and Nationalists had built—and their secret contest for control of trade unions, schools, sports, and mass media. In addition, the exodus from China after 1949, with more than a million refugees entering the city in 1950 alone, exacerbated the disastrous effects of the US trade embargo on the colony's economy, making overpopulation, housing shortages, and glaring social inequities a humanitarian crisis. "The hanging gardens and golden roofs of terraced villas on The Peak," a longtime journalist noted, "overlook the diseased scabs of squatters' huts corroding distant hillsides . . . which succumb so often to typhoon and fire or collapse from old age."[30]

The colonial government worried that the social discontents would be easily exploited by Communist or Nationalist agitators or American special agents (see chapter 2 and the Epilogue).[31] As the Communist forces were sweeping across Manchuria in 1948, Governor Grantham's administration had begun to place particularly CCP activities under increasing surveillance for fear of destabilizing the colony. Communist leader and writer Xia Yan, for example, complained that he was followed by Police Special Branch agents, who also monitored the Communist-backed newspaper *Huashang bao*, which placed in its payroll editors and correspondants doubled as intelligence officers and political organizers. Since then, a slew of laws and regulations were introduced to criminalize political activities. For example, the Emergency Regulations Ordinance (although the colony never declared an emergency, like that of Malaya) and Deportation of Aliens Ordinance (1950) gave the government authority to arrest and expel "troublemakers" without trial. Throughout the chaotic fifties, as a result, hundreds of Nationalist and Communist activists were deported. The Societies Ordinance (1949) and Representation of Foreign Powers Ordinance (1949) required government registration of all local groups (ten people or more), which could be rejected for reasons of affiliation with any foreign country. The first victims were thirty-eight leftist cultural groups that were forced to close down after taking part in a Communist victory celebration event in 1949.[32]

The colonial government was vigilant against ideological advocacy from all sides for fear of inciting political troubles. The Control of Publication and Consolidation Ordinance (1951) and Sedition Ordinance (1950) in particular placed newspapers and magazines under the strict control of the government. For cinema, popular across generations and literacy levels, the Grantham administration had tried to ban all Communist films, as in other British colonies in Southeast Asia. Discouraged by the Colonial Office, it promulgated instead in 1950 a "Directive for Film Censors," which penalized "pure political propaganda," defining as "one dedicated to a particular political system and which seeks to convey an impression of that system's superiority over all others to the complete exclusion of all others."[33] Indeed, the aforesaid revolutionary film by the Great Brightness, *The Marriage of Xiao Erhei*, was allowed to go public after one-fifth of it was cut. The studio moved to China shortly afterward.[34] At the same time, some studios were banned from getting film stocks from Japan or Germany (in place of American ones) because the government suspected they were Communist fronts trying to ship them to the mainland. In fact, Cantonese film producer Yung Kuo

Yew and famed director Mok Hon Shih 莫康時, who was chairman of the pro-Beijing South China Film Industry Workers Union (see below), hired a British lawyer to appeal to the Department of Labor and Department of Commerce and Industry against the ban. They argued that "many people in the industry" would be out of work if there were no alternative filmstocks from Japan.[35]

In 1953, the colonial government introduced the more elaborate and stringent Film Censorship Regulations. They required that all movies—from features to documentary shorts—be sent to the Censors Board for screening permission. The board adamantly forbade violence, political propaganda, and racial "bias." For example, it would ban "anything which is liable to provoke feelings of racial or national hostility . . . anti-foreign slogans, misleading comparisons between different political systems," and "anything which incites any section of the community to attempt to overthrow by force the rule of law and order or the established government." The pro-Beijing film establishment has to this day accused the censors of anti-Communist bias, which forbade even the appearance of images of Mao's face or the PRC flag. Washington had also protested, on the other hand, to London that not just Hollywood movies but also official United States Information Service (USIS) films were banned in Hong Kong, violating the principle of reciprocity in their relations.[36] According to the Tokyo-based trade journal *Far East Film News*, 660 films were reviewed by the censors in 1959–1960. Out of 183 US films, 9 were banned, while one of 16 PRC films failed to pass, and 4 of 57 Japanese films and 5 of 57 British films were banned. The one film from Taiwan was approved for release.[37] Film historian Jing Jing Chang argues that the Film Censorship Regulation was part of the colonial government's effort to foment an "apolitical society" amid Cold War hostilities.[38] Indeed, along with other laws and ordinances enacted since 1948, film censorship policies aimed to uphold the colonial authority and legitimacy by striving to depoliticize and deescalate the Cold War rivalry between the Communists, Nationalists, and Americans. This created, ironically, what can be called a space of a "Cold War gray zone"—where friends and enemies coexisted side by side as they fought with each other, as we can see, to win the hearts and minds of Chinese audiences in the region—that was "rigidly confined by the colonial legal frame."[39] British Hong Kong became their cinematic battleground because of, as noted above, its longstanding industrial apparatus, concentration of film talents from Shanghai, and the tradition that, as *Wall Street Journal* correspondent Guy Searls observed, "Asian film buyers watched Hong Kong box office returns before ordering [the film] for their own countries."[40]

It's Like an Army's Flank

Building on their civil war works, the Communists were in a strong position to engage in cinematic warfare. While some filmmakers found work in China, many émigré actors and directors who stayed behind had joined "study groups" to address Mao's works and keep abreast of the political development on the mainland. In January 1950, a large number of the study group members, including big stars Li Li-hua (李麗華) and Tao Jin (陶金), took part in a delegation organized by Communist leader Sima Wensen (司馬文森) to entertain the troops in Guangzhou. They met with senior officials and used their influence to drum up support for the new order.[41]

After returning to Hong Kong from China, the Communists secretly organized fundraising events in support of the Korean War and stepped up efforts to control a major studio. At the time, there were fierce battles between the Nationalists (often in tandem with US efforts) and Communists for control of key KMT-owned organizations in the British colony, such as the Bank of China and the China Civic Aviation Corporation.[42] A chief Communist target was Yung Hwa, which they had started to "infiltrate" before 1950. Although never owned by the Nationalists, the pro–Chiang Yung Hwa studio was a prime target because of its top-of-the-line production facilities.[43] It had been in financial woes, as discussed above, since 1949, unable to pay salaries. Pro-Communist employees took advantage of the situation to produce several films with strong antifeudal messages. Refusing to allow his company to "fall to communism," Li required all film projects to be approved by him before going into production. The conflicts led to a strike in late 1951 demanding back pay and better working conditions. Quickly, the colonial government stepped in, invoking the Emergency Regulations Ordinance to deport eight suspected ringleaders, all key players in the pro-Communist film community, including Sima Wensen, writer Shen Ji (沈寂), actors Liu Qiong (劉瓊) and Shu Shi (舒適), to the PRC. They received a hero's welcome as they arrived in Guangzhou in recognition of their "anti-imperialist patriotism."[44]

On the other hand, T. S. Lee was praised by the pro-Taiwan press as a hero of "anti-Communist loyalty," and received a loan from the Nationalist regime to restructure its corporate debt and resume production. However, just at this juncture the Grantham Administration took back the studio's leased land, which was possibly a political move aiming to dial down the Communist-Nationalist tension. Burdened with added relocation costs, Yung Hwa closed down in 1956 and its studio facilities passed to its major creditor, Singapore-based entertainment group the Cathay Organization, which went on to found the Motion Pictures and General Investment (MP&GI) and took the lead in modernizing Mandarin film production (see below).

Despite the setback, the Communist filmmakers made headway in building an interlocking network of production and distribution companies from 1950 to 1953 that targeted the overseas Chinese markets in the region. They included, most prominently, Great Wall Movie Enterprise (長城影業) and Phoenix Film Corporation (鳳凰影業), both focused on Mandarin production; Cantonese studios United Film Corporation (Sun Luan [新聯影業]); and a myriad of subsidiaries created mainly for co-production purposes. There was also the Southern Film Corporation (南方影業), a secret subsidiary of the Beijing-based China Film Distribution Corporation. Originally founded in Shanghai in the 1940s to distribute Soviet films with branch offices in Kuala Lumpur, Singapore, and Saigon, the Southern became after 1949 the sole agent for Hong Kong pro-Communist studios to the mainland market, and official distributor of PRC motion pictures to the world, including supplying feature films and newsreels to Chinese consulates and overseas Chinese organizations in India, Egypt, the United States, Canada, and many African and Latin American countries. Starting in the second half of the 1950s, the Southern also secretly ran a theater circuit that, following the classic Hollywood business model, brought all the pro-Communist studios into a vertically integrated system, striving to gain a competitive edge. Camouflaging as entertainment enterprises with private capital or overseas Chinese investment, the pro-Communist film groups—today known collectively as the "Chang-Feng-Xin" triumvirate (長鳳新)—were characteristically what historians call state-private networks that hid from the public their role in China's cultural Cold War.[45]

Some untapped sources regarding the Great Wall bring to light the workings of the pro-Beijing film studios. Great Wall was founded by S. K. Chang and Yuan Yangan (袁仰安), a former Shanghai lawyer and magazine publisher in 1949. The two friends quickly found themselves deep in the red after launching a series of expansive pictures. Their partnership fell apart when Yuan, likely because of his relationship with Fei Yimin (費彝

民)—eminent publisher of the Communist organ in Hong Kong, *Ta Kung Pao* (大公報)—brought in Lv Jiankang (呂建康), a shipping tycoon with strong Beijing connections. According to a secret CCP document, the "Red Capitalist's" investment and emphasis on strengthening production capacity "reduced people's bias against [Communist control]."[46] And Chang was swept out of Great Wall, as it increasingly turned left, cooperating with Beijing's cultural policies. The new management let go a few superstars, notably Li Lihua, who then "defected" across the ideological border (see below), and in their place recruited new talent among young émigrés. Carefully groomed, several of them—such as Moon Hsia (夏夢), Fu Qi (傅奇), and Shi Hui (石慧), became favorite stars to Chinese audiences. Working with such veteran directors as Li Pingqian (李萍倩) and Zhu Shilin (朱石麟), who fled to the British colony to escape the accusations of collaboration with the enemy during World War II, they contributed to the "success of Great Wall," as a *China Mail* correspondent remarked, in the Mandarin cinema of the 1950s, "popular among intellectuals and Cantonese-speakers who understood Mandarin" in Hong Kong as well as in Vietnam, Thailand, Indonesia, Borneo, Singapore, Malaya, Philippine, and Borneo.[47]

Beijing provided financial support to its Hong Kong studios in the form of guaranteed purchase. According to archival sources, the Southern arranged a bank loan of HK$60,000 (ten thousand US dollars) to Great Wall on top of a guaranteed minimum of HK$200,000 for each film purchased by PRC.[48] Another source, however, pointed out that the studio received every year preproduction fees for four pictures to sell to China: ranging from HK$200,000 (A-class) to HK$160,000 (B-class) and HK$120,000 (C-class).[49] Given that the average cost of a black-and-white Mandarin film in this period was around HK$200,000, the subsidies were modest, but they provided a stable source of revenue and support.[50] And stability was of paramount importance to the Mandarin filmmaking industry in the first half of the 1950s, a period characterized by a challenging business environment thanks to the geopolitical turmoil and economic uncertainty in the region (see chapter 3). This enabled the Beijing-backed studios, in effect, to maintain an identity of moral idealism and careful craftsmanship carefully orchestrated by the studio leadership, in contrast to the allegedly egotistic and materialistic lifestyle of the majority of filmmakers in the capitalist colony. Indeed, instead of partying and hobnobbing with the rich, they organized "wholesome, collective" activities such as picnics, hiking, basketball games, and various trips to China (including, for some of them, meeting with political elites).[51] Most important for the rank-and-file workers, moreover, was the five-hundred-strong South China Film Industry Workers Union, which was formed in 1949 to promote communal solidarity. Under the colonial government's surveillance, through most of the fifties, the Union generally avoided political activities and was devoted instead to providing welfare and assistance for the poor and destitute among its members, such as maternity subsidies and unemployment support. [52] Again, although this financial assistance was small, they meant a lot to those in the lower rung of the film industry. American and Taiwan agents frequently blamed the union benefits as the prime reason for "defection" of pro-Nationalist studio rank-and-file employees to Chang-Feng-Xin groups.

Like all Communist-controlled local media and cultural organizations, Great Wall and Phoenix were under direct control of the CCP Hong Kong and Macao Work Committee, which was housed inside the Xinhua News Agency–HK, China's quasi-official representative in Hong Kong. The committee implemented policies and instructions from the State Council Foreign Affairs Staff Office in Beijing, headed by Zhou Enlai and Foreign Minister Chen Yi. Coordinated with various government ministries and bureaus, Liao Chengzhi (廖承志), Zhou's lieutenant responsible for overseas Chinese and United Front works, was charged with overseeing Hong Kong affairs. Born in Japan to a revolutionary family, he had been involved in covert intelligence and resistance work in the British colony during WWII. Consistent with Zhou's and Chen's pragmatic policy regarding Hong Kong, Liao was known for his emphasis on the difference in purposes as well as approaches of propaganda between the British colony and the mainland. "Hong Kong cinema is part of the motherland's [Socialist revolutionary] cinema," he explained. "To use a military analogy, it is like an army's flank that serves different purposes and requires differing tactics." Since PRC-made films were banned in many parts of the world, the main difference, therefore, was that in British Hong Kong, with its free port and international trade networks, films would be "made for the 12 million overseas Chinese," The purpose was to win their support in the CCP struggles against the Nationalist claim as China's sole legitimate government, he emphasized, and American containment along strategic points in China's periphery, stretching from the southern and eastern coastline to the western provinces and Southeast Asia. Indeed, in order to protect the revolution, Mao gave strategic emphasis to expand influences with its Southeast Asian neighbors. Starting from 1950, as is well-known, Beijing established relations with Sukarno's Indonesia (which boasted 2.5 million ethnic Chinese) and provided training and military aid to Ho Chi Minh's Viet Minh guerrillas in the anti-French war.[53]

Just as with Zhou's emphasis on "maintaining Hong Kong's status quo," therefore, Liao emphasized appealing to the overseas Chinese audiences' patriotic sentiment and their ethnic ties to the homeland, and instilling socialist messages, if ever possible, only gingerly and covertly, in order to avoid confrontations with political censorship in Hong Kong and elsewhere. He emphatically referred to them as "patriotic" studios.[54] There was, nonetheless, bitter ideological opposition to this moderate approach within the party. PRC Film Bureau chief Chen Huangmei (陳荒煤), for example, felt the heat to defend the $1 million subsidies to the patriotic studios for purchase of eighty films from them during 1954 to 1961, and only thirty-five of them were shown to the public because of their lack of revolutionary content. "Their work is not something that we can take over at the moment," he explained to a meeting of film workers. "It's not easy to [make films] under colonial rule. . . . If they ever stop production, overseas Chinese would only watch American imperialist movies. . . . Their mission is to send propaganda overseas. Comrade Chen Yi said Hong Kong can make any film as long as it does not oppose people and Communism. We therefore cannot judge them by our standards."[55]

With Mao's blessing, Zhou and Liao convened the 1958 "Rectification Meeting," as noted earlier, which was specifically to criticize the CCP Hong Kong and Macao Work Committee and other cultural officials for their mistake of imposing revolutionary anti-imperialist standards on patriotic media. This deviated from the propaganda strategy adopted in 1953, after a direct confrontation with the colonial government that led to massive arrest as well as a Sino-British diplomatic disaster over the suspension of *Ta Kung Pao* on sedition charges.[56] The strategy called for recognition of the colonial status quo and trying to make use of its free port and crossroads location to push propaganda and United Front work overseas. Instead of challenging the colonial authority, the committee should strive for a "long-term existence" and adopt a "gray disguise" for all its propaganda activities.[57] Indeed, back in 1954, the Ministry of Culture Film Bureau had brought forth three documents to provide instructions and guidance to the pro-Beijing "patriotic" film community—"Reference Materials for Hong Kong Film Personnel" (香港電影節人物參考資料), "Reference Materials for Hong Kong Cinema and Film Circle" (香港電影與電影界情況參考資料), and "Reference Materials for Hong Kong Film Production Companies" (香港電

影製片公司情況參考資料). The documents found fault in their tendency toward overpoliticization and urged them to keep a low profile, to tone down their rhetoric, to refrain from forcing ideology on others, and above all, to avoid head-on clashes with the colonial government.[58]

In order to maintain a long-term position in Hong Kong, "patriotic" films had to accommodate to the colonial surveillance and censorship and the capitalist logic of the entertainment business. They needed to be commercialized and entertainmentized. If propaganda was soft power, Communists had to learn how to put a soft touch to their propaganda. "We think that in a way unpolitical," Liao Yiyuan (廖一原), who headed all three patriotic studios, told the Rectification meeting, "was actually political, just as not to follow the American way was tantamount to opposing the US."[59] In their effort to stay away from subversive themes and to inject more entertainment values to their production, but without succumbing to vulgarity and profanity, as Liao Chengzhi repeatedly warned, the pro-Communist studios championed a wholesome, lighthearted, and uplifting aesthetic, with careful plotting and a didactic and pedagogical impulse that they called "guiding people to do good" (導人向善).[60]

This new propaganda strategy marked a clear departure from the earlier social realist films. For example, Great Wall announced after turning left in 1950, "We now enter a new stage of development. We'll follow the cultural and education policy set forth in New Democracy and the Common Program [China's interim constitution], to produce movies that people need." This overt pro-Communist stance drew the ire of the colonial government, which was forced to cancel two long-announced debuts, one of which, *Joy of Liberation* (翻身了), supposedly tells the story of peasants' and workers' overthrow of local oppression with Communist guidance.[61] Similarly disappearing was the anticolonial theme of "returning to the homeland," which highlighted the exploitation and alienation of colonial capitalism, in implied contrast to the social harmony of New China. A prominent example was Zhu Shilin's popular social drama *The Wall In-Between* (一板之隔, 1952), which brings to focus poverty, the housing crisis, and social inequality in postwar Hong Kong. Living in tiny rooms divided only by a paper-thin wall, and burdened by economic distress, two male petty urbanites, an office clerk and a school teacher played grippingly and intensely by Shanghai actor Han Fei (韓非),and Li Qing (李清), fight ceaselessly over petty conflicts (see Figure 1.1). A new neighbor, a female teacher of the pro-Beijing patriotic school (Jiang Hua, 江樺), helps them realize their shared victimhood under colonial

Figure 1.1 Frustrated with their works and cramped living condition, the two petty urbanites fight ceaselessly over trivial things.

exploitation. They should join together, instead, to stand up against colonial capitalism. The film comes to a close as the two neighbors take down the wall between them, while the schoolteacher returns to the homeland for a better life (see Figure 1.2). Its message did not escape its viewers. A Singapore fan told a newspaper, "This movie is so dear and heartwarming to us in Southeast Asia, especially Southeast Asian overseas Chinese intellectuals. Hong Kong today is not that different from here. . . . Our real enemies are the [colonial] overlords."[62] Troubled by the threatening antagonism, according to Indonesian-born Sun Luen manager Huang Yi, besides the draconian film censorship, colonial government placed moles and undercover agents in all three pro-Communist studios to increase surveillance in the early 1950s and throughout the Cold War period.[63]

After 1953, pro-Communist production increasingly took on an entertaining and what a US intelligence report, written by an unidentified local newspaper editor doubled as (probably freelance) spy sarcastically called a "pinkish" look.[64] Like other film companies, it placed emphasis on star appeals and diversified its products in terms of content and style, striving to engage with popular genres in order to stay close to the changing tastes of local and regional audiences. As exemplified by such movies as Li Pingqian's *Three Loves* (三戀, 1956), Hu Xiaofeng (胡小峰)'s *Those Bewitching Eyes* (眼兒媚, 1958), Zhu Shilin's *The Way of a Husband and a Wife* (夫妻情), 1958), Li Pingqian's *Miss Fragrant* (香噴噴小姐, 1958), Luo Junxiong (羅君雄)'s

Figure 1.2 The "Patriotic" schoolteacher brings her male neighbors together in understanding their shared victimhood under colonial rule before she "returns to the homeland" for a fulfilling life.

Fantasy of Youth (青春幻想曲, 1959), Zhu Shilin's *A Well-to-Do Family* (金屋夢) and Ren Yizhi (任意之) and Chen Jingbo (陳靜波)'s *Sweet as Honey* (甜甜蜜蜜), Phoenix and Great Wall were giving focus to family dramas, love stories, romantic comedies, and screwball comedies. They were always carefully crafted stories centered on coincidences and plot twists, witty dialogues, and farcical situations revolving around family relations or conjugal conflicts and romantic battles. Also, in striking parallel to the middle-class, middle-brow orientations of MP&GI productions, which contained evident Hollywood influences, their films often depicted a world of urban, middle-class affluence and well-to-do protagonists that contrasts sharply with the working class or petty urbanites milieu in most leftist films from the first three years of the 1950s. The 1959 screwball comedy *Sweet as Honey*, for example, tells the story of a newly married couple who live in a spacious apartment filled with modern furniture and amenities. The husband (played by Fu Qi) has a tendency to lie to his wife (Moon Hsia) in order to please her (see Figure 1.3). His cousin and high school sweetheart visits Hong Kong from Singapore in search of her husband. To avoid jealousy, he lies that the woman is a coworker's girlfriend. One lie leads to another, involving also his quarrelsome parents-in-law, and all the "well-intentioned" deceits and deceptions build up to a climactic scene of farcical brawl at the Singapore visitor's hotel room (see Figure 1.4).

Figure 1.3 The newly married couple in *Sweet as Honey* return to their modern apartment from their honeymoon trip.

Figure 1.4 All the husband's lies and deceptions build up to an absolute farce in the climactic scene.

True to their "Guide people to do good" mantra, Great Wall and Phoenix entertainment films always included light satire on capitalist hypocrisy or human follies and provided audiences with a comforting optimism that all conflicts could be solved, in one way or another, by time-honored Chinese precepts such as honor, decency, and filial piety. The brawl scene that concludes *Sweet as Honey*, for example, affirms the common virtues of honesty and trust in conjugal relations. With these lighthearted, feel-good movies, in addition to attractive stars, the Communists enjoyed a loyal fan base in Hong Kong and, as a demonstration of their United Front business flexibility, reached Southeast Asian audiences through non-Communist distribution giants, the Cathay Organization and the Shaw Brothers (see chapter 4).

The Southern also changed its distribution strategy around the same time. After many missteps and flops, it launched Sang Hu (桑弧)'s *Liang Shanbo yu Zhu Yingtai* (梁山伯與祝英台, 1954), a lavishly made, culturally rich, and romantically themed Shaoxing opera film shot in color. As scholar Xu Lanjun points out, the film was part of Zhou Enlai's "cultural diplomacy" effort to present "a peaceful China" to the bipolarized world. After the premier showed *Liang-Zhu* at the Geneva Conference, the Southern brought the color film to overseas markets with the aim of showing the Chinese diaspora "the achievements of newly established PRC in preserving cultural heritage."[65] Clearly they were trying to mobilize their patriotic support against their Nationalist rival in claiming political legitimacy. Starring Shaoxing opera legend Yuan Xuefen (袁雪芬) and displaying elaborately drawn sets and costumes, the film was an instant sensation, shattering box-office records in Hong Kong, with more than half a million people watching it during two months of nonstop screening. Working with the Shaw Brothers and Cathay, the Southern sent it to Singapore, Malaya, as well as the Indonesia, Philippines, and Thailand, with huge success. "Red China's soft-peddling of propaganda," American journalist Guy Searls noted, "would make their influences far and wide among overseas Chinese in the region."[66] Indeed, two blockbuster films followed suit: the black-and-white Huangmei opera *Marriage of a Heavenly Princess* (天仙配) in 1956 and Cantonese opera *Searching a School* (搜書院) in 1957. The latter, the first Chinese film in Eastman color, brought the cinematic sensation in Chinese communities across the region to a "climax," as Southern executive Xu Dunle (許敦樂) puts it. In Hong Kong alone, one-third of its roughly two million people were said to have watched it.[67]

US and Taiwan journalists and intelligence and psychological warfare officials sounded alarms of this "unprecedented movie sensation" and the popularity of Great Wall and Phoenix "pinkies." "Red China is de-communizing its movies," an American correspondent declared, "[It will start] an intensified propagandistic war between the US and Communist China for the sympathy of some 14 million overseas Chinese scattered throughout Asia."[68] It was therefore no coincidence that the US government slapped a sanction on the pro-Communist film community around this time. Fourteen Hong Kong and Macao businessmen, firms, and theaters were listed as "designated nationals," prohibited from purchase of American film products and showing films in the US market. They included the Southern, Great Wall, Phoenix, Chung Lien, Lee Theater, and "Red" tycoons Ho Yin (He Xian) and Wong Kwan Cheng (Huang Kuancheng), both said to be secretly supporting Communist efforts to acquire theaters (see above) and aiming to show both pro-Communist and Hollywood films in order to conceal its political identity.[69] In Taiwan, at the same time, government documents revealed that the Nationalists were troubled by the "emotional attachments to the Communist regime on the mainland" that these movies evoked in overseas Chinese audiences. They pressured the US State Department to diplomatically intervene in Thailand, resulting in the prohibition in 1958 by the Sarit Thanarat regime of media imported from the PRC, while strategizing on how to strengthen Taiwan film propaganda to meet the Communist challenge.[70]

The Battlefront Is Overseas, in the Oversea Chinese Areas

After his total defeat on the mainland, Chiang Kai-shek set up his exiled government on the island of Taiwan and resumed the presidency in 1950. The conflicts in the Korean Peninsula made it, once again, a key force in the US anti-Communist alliance system in Cold War Asia, and American aid poured in that strengthened the Nationalist rule. Vowing to "fight back to the mainland, restore the lost land" (反攻大陸，收復失土) from the island fortress, the "last bastion of freedom," the generalissimo purged several top military commanders and launched a series of changes to the party and state machinery, pulling it under his authoritarian control. More than two million mainlanders fled to the island in the years immediately after 1949. Constantly vigilant against Communist infiltration, Chiang's government tightened the martial law that it had imposed on the Taiwanese since 1947. Accusations of "pro-communism" brought disasters. Taiwan became a virtual police state. It also pushed forward a "vast programme of educational and cultural enlightenment," which included adoption of Mandarin as a language of Chinese nationhood, to "de-Japanize" the Taiwanese and turn them into citizens of Chiang's "bastion of national revival."[71] As part of these efforts, the Nationalist state privileged and encouraged Mandarin films in an effort to repress Taiwanese-language production.[72]

As the United States recognized the Republic of China (ROC) on Taiwan as the sole government of China, the Nationalist regime buttressed its legitimacy by (re)claiming to be the custodian of Chinese culture and tradition in opposition to the rival regime across the Taiwan Strait as "bandits" and "traitors," selling out to the Soviets, the "Red Imperialists." It was Chiang's mission to take back the Communist mainland. This legitimacy narrative gave shape to the Nationalist propaganda drive and cultural Cold War policy in the 1950s. As David Der-wei Wang points out, there were "striking similarities in Nationalist and Communist ways of administering literary" and artistic activities.[73] Learning from past mistakes, one writer went as far as blaming the blockbuster film *The Spring River Flows East* (一江春水向東流, 1947) for the fall of the Nanjing regime. Chiang strived to turn literature and cinema (which he called "dianhua jiaoyu" [電化教育] or audiovisual education, that in theory include also radio broadcast), into a potent weapon of consolidating Nationalist control. In his "Supplementary Treatise on Education and Recreation to Sun Yat-sen's Principle of People's Livelihood" (民生主義育樂兩篇補述) of 1953, Chiang called for literature and arts "for the sake of war" (戰鬥文藝), and "state control of cinema" that gave special attention to "the film contents." All three major film studios at the time were, indeed, state-owned, and between 1954 and 1960, a slew of film censorship rules and regulations were enacted trying to ban movies containing and promoting "venomous ideas of Communism" and "views of Soviet Bloc countries."[74]

Films also became a weapon for the Nationalist government in its effort to win over Chinese in Southeast Asia and the world. Overseas Chinese had played an important role in the Nationalist history since the days of the anti-Manchu revolution, and their support was now deemed more instrumental than ever in legitimizing (and financing) Chiang's anti-Communist crusade. Chiang Ching-kuo (蔣經國), Chiang's elder son, who was in charge of national security intelligence and army political warfare, placed increasing emphasis on psychological warfare, beyond the overt, "black" propaganda (such as loudspeaker broadcasts from the offshore islands and air dropping of leaflets to the mainland), to fight the Communists. Living twelve of his formative years in the Soviet Union, he was familiar with the Leninist model.[75] "Psywar is the most potent weapon against the enemy," he told a meeting of political work officers. "We should all build within ourselves a fortress of faith [in our leader]. . . . The strongest drive for an anti-Communist, anti-terrorist campaign will be when people refuse to see any longer the demolition of our traditional culture and ethics by the Communists."[76] Backed up by his father's "Supplementary Treatise," he started new initiatives along the American cultural warfare strategy that sought to fashion cinema (along with literature, music, and stage drama) into a vehicle of anti-Communist mobilization.

The Taiwan cinema industry was, however, underdeveloped in production technology and lacking Mandarin-speaking actors. Since Hong Kong had a large concentration of émigré film talents and an established media business infrastructure, it became a natural site for Taiwan to use as a launching pad for its propaganda and cultural warfare. In contrast to the Communist strategy, the Nationalist government took on an approach that can be characterized as mainly defensive and countervailing. It did not build its own network of production facilities in the British colony. Instead, it weaponized Taiwan's film market to draw film studios into its orbit. Allegiance to the authority and legitimacy of "free China" became the sine qua non of access to the largest Chinese film market outside the mainland. Its control was indirect and mostly on the basis of economic interests. To counter the Communist influences in the film world, moreover, the Nationalists incited defection in an effort to erode the enemy's morale while striving to strengthen the boundary between the two opposing camps.

According to Sha Rongfeng (沙榮峰), cofounder of Taiwan's largest private film company, Union Motion Picture Co. (聯邦影業), which had started as a distribution company promoting Mandarin-language content and developed extensive and mostly secret ties with the Nationalist propaganda agencies, KMT agents began in 1953 to initiate secret contacts with leaders of the non-Communist émigré film community.[77] The timing was right. After the PRC closed its film market to the capitalist world, the few studios that did not turn left were in a state of turmoil. The business condition for Mandarin films in most part of Southeast Asia, which was in the throes of decolonization and great power rivalry—especially Vietnam, Indonesia, and the Philippine—had been volatile since 1952–1953.[78] On top of this, production costs greatly increased thanks to exorbitant salaries of big stars, notably Li Li-hua, who were key to sales in overseas markets. Struggling to stay afloat in this difficult environment and not sure what the future held, some studio heads began to turn their attention to Taiwan, with its huge number of Mandarin-speaking refugees from the mainland. The questions were: Would the Nationalist regime be able to survive on the island and make good its claim of returning to the mainland? What would be its policy toward the Hong Kong film industry?

In October 1953, about eighteen anti-Communist studio chiefs and actors—including T. Y. Lee, Wang Yuanlong (王元龍), and S. K. Chang, who just restarted his old studio, New China (新華影業), which was founded in 1934 and dominated the industry in wartime Shanghai—took a good-will tour of Taiwan. They returned to Hong Kong a week later allegedly to organize another delegation to celebrate the presidential inauguration of Chiang Kai-shek. Thus started Taiwan's involvement in Hong Kong's film propaganda warfare. In May 1954, as the ROC government was preparing to sign a mutual defense treaty with Washington, a well-publicized delegation of sixty-four top Chinese-language cinema celebrities from Hong Kong visited the island, and their ten-day visit included meeting with Chiang and entertaining the troops on the offshore islands of Matsu and Quemoy. The minute they got off the plane, the celebrities extolled Chiang's undisputed leadership of Chinese people around the globe. Fashionably dressed and smiling, the stars drew enormous crowds of mainlanders everywhere they went on the island, and their various activities became a media sensation in Chinese diasporic communities across the world. The purpose of the visit was made all too clear by the superstar Li Li-hua when she told the solders in Quemoy, just six miles off the mainland, "We come with our warm hearts to link with yours as one." While pointing a rifle symbolically across to the mainland, she enthused, "Let's fight back to our homeland!"[79] Chiang Kai-shek was said to be deeply impressed by the success of the delegation's publicity stunt, allegedly masterminded by Chiang Ching-kuo. As he wrote in his diary on June 16, 1954, "Dianhua jiaoyu was indeed an important instrument of propaganda" and agreed to "quickly move ahead" with the political warfare plan.[80]

The pro-Nationalist patriotic slogans these celebrities called upon appeared to have been transposed from the War of Resistance against Japan propaganda, with a new Cold War twist. They sought to project the unity of all Chinese people around the world behind Chiang Kai-shek, the "national hero," ensconced in the temporary capital of Taiwan, just like he had led the anti-Japanese war from Chongqing to defeat the foreign invasion of Soviet Communism and its "puppet regime" in Beijing. This historical analogy was, in effect, part of an interconnected discourse trying to explain away Mao's seizure of the mainland as a temporary setback in the Nationalist march toward "national restoration and national construction" (復國建國) under Chiang. In fact, in a little-known Taiwan-financed Hong Kong–produced film, *Bloody War* (血戰, 1959), for example, the opening voiceover explains, "All of us . . . need to adopt the spirit of kangzhan (war of resistance), fighting to the finish . . . and restore the mainland." This cinematic use of anti-Japanese theme was rare, however, because of the Nationalist effort to avoid provoking Japan, its major "free Asia" ally (until the 1970s when Japan recognized the PRC).[81]

Another part of the discourse was the anti-Manchu revolution, as articulated in one of the first overtly pro-Nationalist films produced in Hong Kong. Produced by New China and directed by nine veteran and young directors, including Bu Wanchang (卜萬蒼), Evan Yang (aka Yi Wen [易文]), and Chang himself, *The Sacrifice* (碧血黃花) was made to show the unity of the Hong Kong émigré film community in support of the Chiang regime. Didactic and loaded with one-dimensional characterization, it tells the famous story of the "72 Martyrs" or the "Guangzhou Uprising" of April 1911, which was considered in official historiography as paving the way for the Wuchang Uprising that brought down the Qing dynasty. The story was chosen probably because of its Southeast Asian connection as well: the event was planned by Sun Yat-sen (孫中山) in British Malaya with support from the overseas Chinese community. Poorly coordinated, however, it failed disastrously in the face of brutal Qing army suppression. All the young revolutionaries were killed, except Huang Xing (黃興), a top leader of the anti-Manchu movement, who escaped, proclaiming for the audience that "those who survive are destined to bring to completion the arduous task in hand." The parallel with Chiang's escape to Taiwan and claim to retake China was all too clear. Indeed, the film closes with a carefully edited newsreel showing the Nationalist military parade in celebration of Chiang's second term of presidency. The reelected president honored *The Sacrifice* with a special award during the 1954 delegation visit. The film, however, achieved limited market presence outside Taiwan (see Figure 1.5).

Starting in 1953, with support of US cultural warfare officials, Nationalists engineered a series of high-profile defection campaigns to undercut the Communist influence. The first target was famous actress Li Li-hua, who embodied the political ambiguity of the émigré filmmaker struggling to survive the quandary of the Cold War in Hong Kong. Li entered the film world in a young age in Japanese-controlled Shanghai. After the war, with a long shadow of "traitorous filmmaker" looming over her life, and recently

Figure 1.5 *Sacrifice* displayed ROC's military might with the parade celebrating the reelection of Chiang Kai-shek.

divorced, she escaped to Hong Kong with her mother and daughter. She worked for studios of various political backgrounds and quickly became the highest-paid actress in the British colony. Gradually, she became radicalized, swept up in the patriotic fervor and involved in Communist-sponsored activities. She brought her star power to such leftist movies as Great Brightness's antifeudal drama *Family Treasure* (詩禮傳家, 1950) and Great Wall's social commentary film *The Awful Truth* (說謊世界, 1950), and she took active part in "study groups."[82] In 1950, Li joined the Communist-organized delegation to entertain Mao's troops in Guangzhou. When she returned to Hong Kong, according to Liao Yiyuan, the colonial Police Special Branch placed her under surveillance. At the same time, her contract with the reorganized Great Wall expired.[83] Nationalist agents took advantage of Li's fear and desperation to made her an offer she could not reject. In 1953, she signed up with the pro-Taiwan Shaw Father and Son studio and, as her confidante Chia Lee-Ni (賈麗妮) recalled many years later, was promised an American green card, so that she could "leave behind all the political troubles" (see Figure 1.6).[84]

Cold War turmoil continued to engulf her through the 1950s, however. As noted above, Li went with the 1954 delegation to entertain the Nationalist troops in Taiwan and had an audience with Chiang. Around the same time, her memoir narrating her conversion was published in *World Today* (今日世

Figure 1.6 Li Li-hua reunited with former Asia Foundation officer J. Ivy, who helped sponsor her immigration visa to the United States, in New York in 1972.
Courtesy of Jia NiLee

界), gray propaganda camouflaged as a glossy news-and-culture magazine published by the USIS Hong Kong that reached a large Chinese audience in the region. At the heart of it was a binary Cold War narrative highlighting her bad experiences in Communist film activities and her new life of freedom and professional happiness now. From now on, she vowed, she would apply herself to "make the best pictures for the sake of the audiences in Free China and overseas Chinese communities."[85] Two years later, she went around the United States visiting Chinatowns to drum up support for the Nationalist cause while preparing for her role in Frank Borzaga's *China Doll* (1958). It was a World War II drama produced by Hollywood legend John Wayne that featured her, a poor refugee turned submissive wife, meek and quiet (because of her lack of English proficiency), uncharacteristic of her established film personae, as something like a symbol of China's sufferings under foreign invasion in a cliché-ridden intercultural romance with an American Air Force pilot (played by Victor Mature). Sympathy for Chiang's China was evident (see Figure 1.7).

Li's defection sparked a round of Nationalist media frenzy, which declared that 1953 was the "year of Red fading" (褪紅年), marking the beginning of

Figure 1.7 Li Li-hua on an US tour to rally overseas Chinese communities to the cause of "Free China."

Yue Qing, *Wanzhi qianhong Li Li-hua*

the "decline of Communist influences" in the quest for the sympathies of the Chinese people. [86] The Communist film establishment in Hong Kong, on the other hand, was in crisis mode, and its ripples reached Beijing. Xia Yan, who was in charge of Hong Kong affairs during the civil war and now PRC deputy cultural minister, for one likened Li's desertion to the loss of Zhang Ailing (張愛玲), bringing to light the "Party's failure to live up to its United Front policy" of recruiting and retaining talents of different backgrounds. The Cultural Ministry Film Bureau (文化部電影局), as discussed earlier, instructed Hong Kong in 1954 to give emphasis to "the work of unity."[87] The defected star, for her part, received numerous physical threats and was subjected to all sorts of verbal abuse by Beijing sympathizers on her tours to promote "free China" in the United States and Southeast Asia.

A central part of the Nationalist plan since 1953 had been to enforce clear-cut division and contain the Communist influences in the ideological battle. When members of the first Taiwan delegation returned to Hong Kong, they began pushing to create an organization unifying the non-Communist film community. After several years of negotiation over the Societies Ordinance with the colonial administration, in 1957 the Hong Kong and Kowloon Free Filmmakers General Association (港九電影戲劇事業自由工會, hereafter HKFFGA) was established to covertly coordinate what it called efforts to "stem the Communist Bandits Cold War offense." It formally buttressed the binary division in the Hong Kong film industry that lasted until at least the early 1980s: pro-Taiwan "free Chinese" cinema versus pro-Communist "patriotic" cinema. Among its major functions was to serve as a political gatekeeper for films imported to Taiwan. It scrutinized the contents as well as the political backgrounds of cast and crew members of all films for the island market. With assistance from Taiwan's quasi-official Union Motion Picture Co., HKFFGA mediated disputes and facilitated movement of people between the two cities. Moreover, it kept Taiwan abreast of Hong Kong's developments and allowed access to Nationalist intelligence and propaganda agents to infiltrate and incite defection in the émigré community. Also a major function of HKFFGA was its leading role in the annual competition with the pro-Communist film community over National Day commemorations: namely, October 1 for the PRC and October 10 for the ROC. The rivalry was fierce, bitter, and sometimes violent in the 1950s, as the legitimacy of the two rival regimes was at stake for their supporters. The two camps competed in numbers of participants, sizes of celebration programs, and prominence of flags displayed, all of which became in effect a political ritual reinforcing the Cold War division.[88]

Most of the pro-Taiwan studios, chief among them New China, were small businesses dependent on quick returns on their production. Despite the official promise of support in market access, they were frustrated by poor Nationalist policy coordination, draconian censorship, and fluctuating foreign exchange rates. They called for government subsidies and tax reduction in recognition of their loyalty. At the same time, however, Taiwan's propaganda officials were annoyed by what in their view was the "free Chinese" cinema's lack of commitment to the ideological battle. They claimed that while colonial censorship and market demands discouraged focusing on anti-Communist themes in their films, it was questionable why "Hong Kong producers [were] so reluctant to publicize scenes and life of the island citadel of Free China." Instead, they did location shooting in Japan or Thailand. Actually, under S. K. Chang and his wife, Tong Yujuan (童月娟), who headed HKFFGA for almost a decade, New China made several musical films in rural Taiwan, such as *Fair Maidens among the Melons* (採西瓜的姑娘, 1956) and *The Nightingale of Alishan* (阿里山之鶯, 1957) , and it shot films in Tokyo in an attempt to learn color film techniques. The truth was more likely that the Nationalists were upset that, despite the "free Chinese" cinema's demands for more funding and better market access, Communist opera dramas and "pinkies," as discussed above, continued to hold sway in Hong Kong and Southeast Asia's overseas Chinese audiences.[89]

The situation began to gradually change after the creation of MP&GI (國際電影懋業) in 1956. As noted above, it was the production arm of the Cathay Organization (國泰機構), a corporate entertainment group founded by Chinese-Malayan billionaire entrepreneur Dato Loke Wen Tho. Aspired to "bring cultivated leisure to every person in all corners of Southeast Asia," he had built a large and luxurious theater circuit in Singapore-Malaya, and acquired some of the biggest names in the film industry to turn MP&GI into a leading film studio in mid–twentieth century Hong Kong.[90] Its stylish, sleekly made musical films and urban romances—bringing audiences' attention to men and women trying to grapple with Asia's rapid modernization—made a splash in the region. Recent materials reveal that the studio was sympathetic to Chiang's government. MP&GI executives frequently traveled to Taiwan to recruit young talent and meet with cultural officials about production plans and market access. The Nationalists pressed for showing the audiences their economic and social achievements.[91]

The 1959 film *Air Hostess* (空中小姐) did just that. The idea of the project came from female lead Grace Chang (Ge Lan [葛蘭])'s close friend Chia LeeNi, both of them recent mainland émigrés. Close to graduation from New Asia College (see chapter 2), Chia found a job in early 1957 as an air stewardess, a new profession in Asia at the time, in Taiwan-based Civic Air Transport (founded in 1946 by the World War II "Flying Tigers" commander Claire Chennault). Chia wrote numerous letters to Chang detailing all sorts of unusual training she went through in Taiwan. When director Evans Yang heard about it on the set, he decided to launch a project about air hostesses. With Loke's passion for travel (he was the first Asian chairman of Malayan Airlines), the Singapore office quickly approved it, and in summer 1957, the crew went to Taiwan for a month, prepping to make *Air Hostess*, presumably in consultation with Nationalist officials, and scouting locations[92] (see Figure 1.8).

On the surface, it looks like another popular MP&GI entertaining urban romance, with glamorous stars, songs, and American dances (swing,

Figure 1.8 Grace Chang met with *Air Hostess* friend Chia LeeNi in Taiwan while prepping for the shooting of *Air Hostess*.
Courtesy of Jia NiLee

cha-cha, and calypso) and all characters fashionably dressed, running in and out of chic places. A careful reading of it, however, reveals themes of Cold War rivalry. Shot in Eastman color, it tells the story of a young woman, Lin Kepin's search for identity and independence in a rapidly modernizing society. Played by young star Grace Chang, her job as a flight attendant allows the film to bring the audiences to view Asia as a modern, flourishing region of interconnected urban centers of capitalist prosperity and cultural change. As the film follows the movement of the character across borders, with montages of Singapore's Raffles' Landing Site, the Cathay Building, and

從香港飛來的班機已經到達

Figure 1.9 Arriving in Taipei, *Air Hostess* brings the audience's attention to Asia's flourishing, interconnected pro-capitalist bloc.

Bangkok's majestic temples, pro-US Asian nations are linked together into an integrated and flourishing "free Asia." At the heart of the free Asia narrative is a long scene celebrating the modernity and natural beauty of Nationalist Taiwan: its airport and Presidential Office Building, the luxurious Grand Hotel (Taipei's tallest building at the time and Madame Chiang's pet project), and a mise-en-scène of tourist attractions, including Wulai Falls and Ali Mountain (see Figure 1.9).

Inside the Grand Hotel, the flight attendant entertains her colleagues—pilots, air stewardess, and local staff—with a riveting folk tune (one that remains popular today in the Sinophone world), "Song of Taiwan" (台灣小調), written by director Evan Yang, a migrant from Shanghai and member of the 1954 delegation to Taiwan, to express her love of the "Treasure Island." She sings, "I love my fellow Taiwan compatriots / All the harbors are so strategic / The most forward outpost in the Pacific Ocean / Taiwan is called a Treasure Island / Laughter and joy everywhere in the countryside / Every family is well fed / What makes us so proud is that / People stick together like glue / We are all of the same mind" (see Figure 1.10).[93]

Pro-Communist critics blasted the film as a Cold War "propaganda tool" of the US-Chiang "clique." The lines about Taiwan's strategic importance in the US containment strategy and the successful US-sponsored land reform program in opposition to Mao's disastrous Great Leap Forward on the mainland most antagonized them.[94] This led a KMT newspaper editor to highlight the

Figure 1.10 Lin Keping sings "Song of Taiwan" to an enthusiastic crowd inside the Grand Hotel.

cinematic role of Hong Kong cinema in the cultural Cold War. "In our war against the Communists, military warfare happens only intermittently," he noted, "but political warfare is fought with ferocity almost every day. The battlefront is in overseas, in the oversea Chinese areas. Although most of the films that [promote 'Free China'] were not produced in Taiwan, but were in Hong Kong . . . they touched the hearts of overseas Chinese around the world all the same."[95] In fact, the success of *Air Hostess* and other MP&GI films encouraged small studios to boost production, according to Tong Yuejuan, that helped expand the Nationalist influences in the film propaganda war. But MP&GI's success also posed a threat to its business rival, the Singapore-based non-Communist exhibition giant Shaw Organization (邵氏機構), whose production studio, Shaw Father & Son, was in decline. This led Run Run Shaw (邵逸夫), the future entertainment business legend, to move to British Hong Kong to revitalize the family's production business and thereby inaugurated what insiders called the "age of Cathay-Shaw rivalry." It transformed the colony's Cold War media ecosystem with emphasis on big capital, new technology, enhanced entertainment values, and modern management systems, which contributed to the fall of the Communist cinema in the 1960s (see chapters 4 and 5).

A Key Base for Information Programs

In the Cold War crossroads of mid–twentieth century Hong Kong, the United States had waged a covert propaganda and psychological war against

Communist China, sometimes in tandem with the Nationalists' plans, and other times on its own. As the principal listening post to China and the regional communication hub, the US Consulate General in the British colony was "one of the very largest American posts in the world at that time, larger than most embassies." Inside the building on Garden Road were large numbers of China watchers and local national assistants, who worked in such agencies as the Political Section, Economic Section, Consular Section, the secretive CIA, and the United States Information Services (USIS). Central to the propaganda warfare in the region, USIS boasted a senior public affairs officer and information, press, and cultural officer. It was an overseas post of the USIA (United States Information Agency), which was founded in 1953 with the objective of being what the British Foreign Office described as "a weapon of political warfare in the struggles against Soviet Communism." Under the Eisenhower administration the cultural propaganda activities the agency implemented, unlike the brazenly anticommunist propagandistic approach under Truman, had largely expanded and become increasingly reliant on covert and gray tactics that placed emphasis on the superior way of American life.[96]

As Mao's revolutionary stature rose steadily in the decolonizing world beginning with the Korean War, Washington was obsessed with combating what policymakers called the "domino effect" of communism in its periphery; especially in resource-rich Southeast Asia, many of the region's countries were in the throes of anticolonial struggles. It was also a potential vast market and raw materials supplier for Japan, the key US partner in its Communist containment strategy.[97] The USIS, along with the CIA, in Hong Kong had for its main purpose combating China's efforts to mobilize patriotic loyalty from the overseas Chinese in support of their revolutionary cause in the region. The goal was to win over hearts and minds, to persuade them that "it lies in their own interests to take action consistent with the national objective of the United States," in the words of Eisenhower's psychological warfare advisory committee.[98] This was clearly spelled out in the USIS "Country Plan" of June 1953.

In striking similarity with the Communist and Nationalist regimes, it called for understanding China in terms of culture, so it included in this framework the Chinese diaspora living in foreign lands. It also privileged Mandarin, the official language on both sides of the Taiwan Strait, as the "common language," the language of Chineseness that defined the cultural China. To speak Mandarin was culturally superior to speaking any other regional dialects. It amounted to speaking "Chinese." It became the lingua franca of Asia's cultural Cold War in Hong Kong, as noted earlier, and Mandarin-speaking émigrés figured most prominently in the cultural battlefield. In fact, as Syd Goldsmith recalled, for all "the proud [Mandarin-speaking] China watchers, Cantonese was nothing more than a local dialect in a backwater colony." The same prejudice was indeed prevalent in the region's "White Chinese" community (such as the way that mainlander refugees regarding Taiwan Hokkien).[99] The Country Plan went on to lay out three propaganda objectives: To "give hope and encouragement to anti-Communist elements" in Hong Kong and elsewhere, to induce "Chinese in Southeast Asia to support US and Free World policies and actions," and to increase "anti-Communist sentiment and action" in the British colony. In order to achieve these objectives, it urged efforts to "increase the output of pro–'Free World' and anti-Communist publications and motion pictures," and aim propaganda campaigns to specific "target groups" that included intellectuals, businesspeople, students, laborers, and refugees.[100]

Indeed, USIS had published many pamphlets, distributed leaflets to each "target group," and planted news articles. Based on what former USIA official Wilson Dizard called "books as weapons," Hong Kong had a well-designed and easily accessible American library stocked with thousands of books, magazines, and USIS documentary films as "primary sources of American ideas."[101] And the agency published the monthly *World Today* (originally *Jinri Meiguo* [今日美國] or *USA Today*), which, as discussed above, mixed news propaganda with celebrity news and cultural reviews, and a translation series of mainly American literature consisting mainly of classics by white men to promote the American Way. Boasting a large group of leading émigré authors, including Eileen Chang, Stephen Soong, and Dong Qiao, thanks to their high writing fees and the Chinese editorial staff's extensive networks in the émigré community, both were hugely influential among students and professionals in the Sinophone world.[102]

In Hong Kong, for example, a 1953 USIS-sponsored reading habits survey conducted among all the target groups found that the most-read magazine in the 22-to-30 age group was *World Today*.[103] Besides running the Voice of America, moreover, the USIS was active in the film world. "We did a fair amount of work supporting filmmakers who were producing anti-communist pictures in Hong Kong and Chinese-language pictures in Southeast Asia." As information officer Richard McCartney recalled the agency, "We were very much involved in the Chinese motion picture industry."[104] The USIS played an active role in Nationalist efforts to poach from pro-Beijing "patriotic" studios. For example, it provided logistics and financial support to pro-Taiwan production, assisting Hollywood studios' location shooting in Hong Kong and celebrity tours to the region, as well as facilitating personnel exchange between Hong Kong, Taiwan, and Southeast Asia. Thus, the British colony was valuable to the United States as "a key base for information programs with respect to Communist China and the Far East in general," CIA chief Allen Dulles told a National Security Council meeting in 1960. "Hong Kong was particularly useful as a listening post and as a publishing center for anti-communist [propaganda]."[105]

Actually, Allen Dulles's comments were made as the White House assessed the role of British Hong Kong in the US Cold War policy in Asia in the immediate aftermath of the second Taiwan Strait crisis, in which the PRC shelled the offshore islands of Quemoy and Kinmen, and decided whether Washington needed to intervene militarily if the Communists decided to invade the colony. Throughout the early Cold War, American officials often ran into conflicts with the colonial government that sometimes became sources of tension in the already complicated Anglo-American "special relationship," as the two Western powers differed in opinions regarding the Cold War in Asia.[106] Unlike Washington, London sought to avoid being drawn into new conflicts with Mao's China, which it believe could retaliate by taking over Hong Kong. In an effort to maintain alleged neutrality in the US-China conflicts, shy of becoming in the eyes of Beijing "an anti-Communist base," as discussed earlier, the colonial government was vigilant in monitoring US and Nationalist political warfare activities. CIA agent James Lilley, for one, complained that despite the Anglo-American partnership, the Hong Kong Police Special Branch "put the CIA on a tight rope," especially in the 1950s, forbidding it from conspiring with Nationalist paramilitary groups to mount attacks on China's fringes, recruiting young refugees to gather intelligence and incite unrest on the mainland, or infiltrating Communist organizations in the colony.[107] Governor Grantham, on the other hand, complained in a later interview that the American intelligence agency had been "extremely ham handed," and his administration "had to take a very strong line to stop them" from unnecessarily involving the colony in confrontation with China.[108]

The colonial government was also annoyed by the aggressive USIS propaganda strategy. As Johannes Lombardo's archival research reveals, the colonial government complained to the US Consulate in the early 1950s about the anti-Communist pamphlets and leaflets that USIS agents distributed to schools and labor unions as the colony was experiencing a wave of strikes, and the heavily political reading materials at the American library. It also censored USIS documentaries and short films the same way as it did with PRC or Soviet Union official movies in the name of political neutrality. American officials in Hong Kong were frustrated by the "increasingly uncooperative attitude" of the British ally,[109] leading to the protest of the US State Department to Whitehall in 1956, as noted above, over the "diplomatic reciprocity" of their "special relationship." The diplomatic crisis was averted when the colonial administration agreed to exempt American official films from censorship. All this happened while the pro-Communist press attacked the collusion of British colonialism with American imperialism and Nationalist reactionaries were trying to secretly subvert China.[110]

Along with the American Consulate, there were other US NGOs deeply involved in covert activities along China's periphery designed to destabilize Mao's revolution and enmeshed in British Hong Kong's cultural Cold War. A particularly active one was the Asia Foundation (TAF), an element of what author Frances Saunders calls the "CIA's designated Cold War venture capitalists."[111] Camouflaged as a nonprofit foundation, TAF was in effect created and funded (at least the 1970s) by the CIA in 1951, "a propaganda machine and a front for covert activities" including psychological warfare and intelligence gathering. Originally called the Committee for a Free Asia (CFA), it aimed, in part, to penetrate the "Bamboo Curtain" with propaganda warfare that included running Radio Free Asia, to "encourage subversion of the Communist Government," without "bearing US label."[112] In an effort to give a public impression of non-partisan open-mindedness, after complaints by "Asians who objected to the notion that they needed to be freed," the NGO changed its name to TAF in 1953 but remained a clandestine CIA-funded anti-Communist cultural warfare front. After its reorganization, TAF discontinued the radio broadcast program, which seemingly diverged from Secretary of State Dean Acheson's approach of avoiding direct confrontation with Beijing, and gave increased emphasis to the CFA's original objective to attract overseas Chinese especially in Southeast Asia. In order to accommodate to the region's increasing anticolonial nationalist aspirations after World War II, the organization emphasized supporting projects and initiatives started by "local groups comprised of selected Asian leaders." In Hong Kong, it focused on the cultural and educational fields, aiming at arousing support among the USIS-defined "target groups" of students and intellectuals (see chapter 2).[113]

TAF chose Hong Kong as its base to reach overseas Chinese because of its strategic location as the region's crossroads and concentration of émigré artists and intellectuals. The colony also did not have all the restrictions and bureaucratic inertia as in Chiang's Taiwan under martial law.[114] In the first half of the 1950s especially, TAF gave covert assistance to many émigré groups. US dollars that it made available for intellectual refugees and exiles, along with those from other US government agencies and private foundations (notably the Ford and Rockefeller Foundations), were pejoratively termed by the locals as "greenback culture" (綠背文化). The term conjured up complicity with American cultural imperialism that still provokes bitter controversy. These American dollars, however, as eminent writer and editor Dai Tian pointed out, that made possible the enormous numbers of literary and popular magazines and media outlets that made mid–twentieth century Hong Kong such a dynamic and heterogenous cultural marketplace and battleground.[115] Most of these émigré ventures were small and to disappear after one or two years, except arguably the Union Press and Asia Press. They were by far TAF's largest investments in the region's ideological contest, and they form the subjects of the following chapters (2 and 3).

The Union Press (UP) (友聯出版社) was formed in 1951 or earlier by a group of young intellectual refugees and exiles on the fringe of the Third Force movement, which opposed the one-party regimes on both sides of the Taiwan Strait. Homesick and idealistic, they used TAF support to try to realize their dream of creating a new culture that would transform China when they returned. Combining an anti-Communist crusade with a mix of cultural nationalism and liberal values, the UP group quickly expanded into a transnational enterprise, with a research institute and several magazines catering to readers of different age groups that had branch offices in Macao, Malaya, Singapore, Indonesia, and Thailand. The most influential of its publications, *Chinese Student Weekly* (中國學生週報), continued to shape the hearts and minds of readers until the 1960s. Around the same time, Southeast Asia–born Chang Kuo-sin (張國興), a former Associated Press wartime correspondent in China, created the Asia Press (亞洲出版社) with TAF secret financial support. It aimed to mount what he called a "three-dimensional psychological warfare" against Chinese communism, with a publishing house, a news agency, and a movie studio, Asia Pictures (亞洲電影). The studio called for taking on the Beijing-backed Great Wall with bigger, more entertaining movies in combating Communist domination in the film industry. Unlike TAF's emphasis on winning the overseas Chinese markets in Southeast Asia, Chang tried to use American resources to transform the media environment and push his studio onto the world stage. The complex entanglement of film and media production, their contents, and their distribution in changing political contexts constituted the agents of the cultural Cold War in British Hong Kong. We now turn to the Union Press's *Chinese Student Weekly* and Asia Press's China Pictures.

2

Third Force in Exile

Chinese Student Weekly and the Cultural Cold War, 1952–1960

This trend today indicates that the Chinese socio-political life, Chinese culture, and the Chinese habits of heart have all lost [their] force of solidarity. It scattered around with blowing winds. The [flower and fruits of the Chinese Nation] have to survive in other people's gardens, [trying to] evade the burning sun under other trees. They are forced to the corners just to absorb nutrients, to share soil and water with others. This is nothing but an astonishing tragedy of the Chinese people.

Tang Junyi

Southbound émigré intellectuals didn't see Hong Kong as their home, and they didn't like Hong Kong either. But the seeds they planted here remain here

Lo Wai-Luen

The role of culture in the Cold War has attracted wide attention in the last two decades. This focus on the cultural Cold War is inspired by the increasing awareness that just as important as military campaigns and high-table diplomacy were the covert acts of propaganda war that often went hand in hand with intelligence collection and cultural and academic exchanges in efforts to combat the enemies across the geopolitical-ideological divide. Just as C. D. Jackson, chief adviser to President Eisenhower on psychological warfare, told his colleagues, "[Culture] is no longer a sissy word. . . . The tangible, visible and audible expression of national idealism is culture."[1]

This cultural dynamic of the Cold War played out with as much secrecy and antagonism between the opposing forces in Asia as in Europe. As

Hong Kong Media and Asia's Cold War. Po-Shek Fu, Oxford University Press. © Oxford University Press 2023.
DOI: 10.1093/oso/9780190073763.003.0002

William Colby, the former CIA director, remembered his experiences, "The great challenges to secret intelligence gathering were . . . in Berlin, Vienna and Hong Kong."[2] However, in comparison to the blossoming scholarship on the cultural Cold War in Europe and the United States thanks to the widespread declassification of archives, our knowledge of the battle for minds in Hong Kong or, more broadly, in China or other Asian countries remains constrained by the more limited availability of research materials.

As discussed in the previous chapter, Hong Kong was a small outpost of the declining British empire marginal to superpower geopolitics. It was, however, a strategic crossroads in the war for hearts and wills in Asia. In recent years, the cultural Cold War in Hong Kong, along with those in South Korea and Taiwan, has begun to attract scholarly attention. Notably among these new works are historians Grace Chou's and Zhang Yang's works on the secret US involvement in the establishment of the Chinese University of Hong Kong, Shuang Shen's exploration of the regional network of Asia Foundation–sponsored student publications and Xiaojue Wang's systematic study of textual and cultural practices in Chinese-language literature across the 1949 divide.[3]

Drawn from the Asia Foundation Collection at Stanford's Hoover Institution Archive and oral history, including multiple interviews of *Chinese Student Weekly* (中國學生週報; *CSW*) editors in *Xianggang wenhua zhongsheng dao*, edited by Lo Wai-luen and Hung Chi Kam, this chapter is an archive-based reconstruction of the ambivalent role of *CSW* in the battle between China and the United States for ideological primacy in the Sinophone communities. As the flagship publication of the Asia Foundation–sponsored émigré cultural enterprise, the Union Press (UP), a third-force group opposing both Chinese regimes across the Taiwan Strait, *CSW* combined ideological crusading with cultural news, literary works, and organized outreach activities, calling for building a free, "democratic China" while promoting a transnational community of imagined "Chineseness." It began in July 1952, quickly expanding to overseas Chinese communities in Southeast Asia and many parts of the globe over the next few years. Until its close in 1974, *CSW* was arguably the most influential youth magazine in the Sinophone world.

Covert American funding, however, has made *CSW* the object of an ongoing dispute with regard to the Cold War politics of Chinese-language cultural production. On the one hand, detractors have criticized it for serving the interests of American imperialism. On the other, many *CSW* activists emphasized that they had little knowledge about the weekly's ties with the

Asia Foundation. They also argued that the American money came with "no strings attached," that they did not serve anyone's interests other than their own.[4] Archival materials and systematic readings of *CSW* give us some perspective on the relationship between the two sides that is far more intricate and nuanced than binary oppositions would have us believe. They allow us to gain insight into the ways liberal émigré intellectuals grappled with Cold War antagonism and also provide us an opportunity to explore from ground up the extent and nature of American Cold War intervention in Asia, and the related question of whether the émigré group has agency of their own in the propaganda warfare. The clandestine US involvement in *CSW*'s cross-regional and transnational expansion of influences also sheds important light on the ways in which global ideological confrontations intertwined and overlapped with local historical imperatives in shaping Hong Kong's development into the regional hub of Chinese-language cultural production.

The Politics of the Third-Force Movement

Situated right across from the southern province of Guangdong, Hong Kong had long been the key gateway to China trade. Under British rule, with its prosperous entrepot economy and espousal of rule of law, it had since the turn of the twentieth century been an important refuge for Chinese people to flee poverty or political suppression. Sun Yat-sen, "Father of the Chinese Revolution," for example, launched military campaigns during his exile against the Qing government that were linked to the 1911 Revolution. Similarly, many Communist leaders and anti–Chiang Kai-shek militarists since the 1920s fled there. Most of those who came had no intention staying permanently, however. After making some money or when political winds changed in China, they would return home.

This situation shifted in 1949. The swift Communist conquest and the ensuing political campaigns drove more than a million Chinese to seek refuge in the colony. Thus, at the time Hong Kong was retaken by the British after the Japanese surrender in 1945, its population was estimated at around six hundred thousand, by early 1951, it rose to over two million. This time, few chose to return, after the colonial government began setting up a boundary in 1950 along the Shenzhen River in an effort to put a brake on the inflow of refugees.[5] As the then-governor Alexander Grantham later remarked: the "picture is changing since China went Communist, as few Chinese in Hong Kong now intend to return to the country of their birth. They are becoming permanent residents."[6] With a huge number of refugees pouring in, the colony experienced all manners of shortages, especially jobs and housing. Most of the refugees had lost everything fleeing for their lives, ending up living on the streets, in rooftop slums, or in "lean-to shacks of muds and sticks" on hillsides vulnerable to fires and flooding (as immortalized in Richard Quine's 1960 Cold War romance *The World of Suzie Wong*). Massive unemployment forced them to scrounge for any jobs they could possibly find. Many well-educated exiles had to take up such risky and demeaning work as breaking stones with a tiny hammer and selling them as building materials, or for women, making matchboxes at home or becoming prostitutes for a pittance. The enormous humanitarian crisis was made worse by the colonial government's refusal to provide large-scale relief. Hong Kong was turned into a Manichean world of vast inequality and human sufferings: "Rich Chinese, Europeans, and Americans in Hongkong lived well," an American journalist wrote in 1952; "Poor Chinese lived hardly better than animals."[7]

Among these refugees were many "White Chinese" political figures, young professionals, and liberal intellectuals exiled from areas north of Guangdong, especially Shanghai. Living in poverty in squatter shantytowns of Diamond Hills or Rennie's Mill in Kowloon, where there were so many refugees that they could get by speaking only their respective dialects or Mandarin, they were bitter and anguished with the loss of their home to Communist takeover, frustrated with the only humiliating work they could find, and alienated from what they perceived as the exotic, inferior Cantonese-speaking cultural environment, where people had little concern for all the sufferings just across the border. "Living in the margin of the Mainland's margin, most people here in Diamond Hill share in common a deep sense of attachment to the homeland." A refugee author alluded to the fourth-century division of China in describing the exilic condition: "All these people love their motherland, treasure their freedom, and they refuse to become slaves to the new communist country. They have the pioneer spirit characteristic of Chinese people: They endure hardships and overcome adversity. They remind us of the story of the people migrating southward from the Central Plains during the period of the 'Sixteen Kingdoms of the Five Barbarians,' who had turned the Jiangnan area [Yangtze River Delta] into a paradise."[8] Alienated and longing to return home, justifying their exiles as a painful preparatory for restoring peace and national strength with their return, many of these émigré intellectuals became centrally involved in the development of the third-force movement that, in retrospect, marked the onset of US cultural intervention in postwar Hong Kong.

The third force had its origin in China during the 1920s, attracting international attention during World War II and the ensuing Nationalist-Communist civil war when Washington, to prevent Soviet threat, tried to push Chiang Kai-shek to pursue political reform and made peace with Mao's forces.[9] The movement enjoyed particular influence among Western-trained intellectuals and professionals in major cities, especially Shanghai and Beijing. Organized in small third parties—most prominent among them the Democratic League, the Chinese Youth Party, and Chinese Democratic Socialist Party—they sought to chart a middle course between the Nationalists and Communists in building a united, "democratic China" that respected human rights, individual freedom, and economic justice. However, the third-force liberals were "more inclined to fractious debate than to joint action."[10] Without an armed force, they were also ineffective in the face of naked power. By the time of the Nationalist defeat in 1949, some of their leading figures stayed on to join the Communist United Front government, while others, if they did not feel welcome in Taiwan—notably Carsun Chang (張君勱), who helped draft the 1946 Constitution, and former National Central University president Gu Mengyu (顧孟餘), fled to Hong Kong.[11]

Around this time, the Truman administration made public in August 1949 the *China White Papers* in an effort to counteract especially the Republican attacks over the American failure to bolster the Chiang Kai-shek regime that led to the "loss of China." The White Paper argued, in essence, that despite enormous American assistance over the years, nothing could be done to save Chiang's corrupt and inept regime. The most contentious part of the document was Secretary of State Dean Acheson's "Letter of Transmittal," which, echoing March's NSC-48 policy guideline from the National Security Council (NSC), advocated encouraging internal forces within China to undermine Communist influences. It claimed that communism was alien to Chinese culture. Beijing had in fact "foresworn their Chinese heritage" by "publicly announc[ing] their subservience to a foreign power, [the] Soviet Union." Possibly with the Chinese third force in mind, Acheson continued, "the profound civilization and the democratic individualism of China will reassert themselves and she will throw off the foreign yoke." This logic reflected as it did Truman's belief that the Chinese people would eventually rise up to subvert Mao's rule.[12]

The *White Papers* sent a shock wave to the émigré community in Hong Kong as well. The Chiang Kai-shek regime would be doomed without American aid: who would then lead the people to defeat the Communists and take back home? To many émigré intellectuals in particular, the optimism in the document about the vitality of "democratic individualism in China" that would lead to the subversion of Communist rule indicated Washington's support of the third-party liberals' struggle to chart a future course for China between the Communists and the incorrigible Nationalists. Gossips and rumors abounded about US funds to further its China policy pouring into Hong Kong especially around the time when Ambassador-at-Large Philip Jessup visited in January 1950. Indeed, American refugee relief aids (including, most notably, Aid Refugee Chinese Intellectuals) and secret funding for political and psychological warfare ventures surged. US greenbacks were widely sought after by many refugees. Trying to survive skyrocketing unemployment, they formed groups of varying sizes claiming to be affiliated with anti-Communist networks on the mainland or trying to sell alleged "reliable intelligence" (most of these were actually "carefully crafted fakes" drawn from rumors and local newspapers) to American officials, who were "hungry" for information on the other side of the Bamboo Curtain in return for financial aid.[13]

Most prominent among the US covert ventures were the ramped-up efforts led by the US Consulate General Political Section (headed by Ralph Clough in 1950–1954), and the newly created Hong Kong CIA station under chief Fred Schultheis, to support prominent exiled political and cultural figures with third-force orientations and encouraged pro-liberal views in local media, which outlasted, as a result, many third-force organizations and publications that sprang up in the early 1950s. As historian Qian Mu (錢穆) confided to his diary shortly after he escaped China, "I met my old friend Zhang Junmai again in Hong Kong. . . . He wanted to gather together the China Democratic Socialist Party and the China Youth parties and other people exiled in Hong Kong and found a new party, and he encouraged me to join. . . . Later on in Hong Kong I heard that the formation of a Third Party was being planned and that the United States was giving it monetary support. I was asked many times to participate in their meetings, but I never dared to attend."[14]

What Qian referred to was likely the US-christened Steering Committee, which consisted of twenty-five prominent third-force figures, including Zhang Junmai, Gu Mengyu, former Guangdong commander General Zhang Fakui (張發奎), and ex-Communist leader Zhang Guotao (張國燾) (who defected after losing a leadership battle with Mao in 1938). Its alleged purpose was to unify all the groups to fight for the creation of a "democratic China." Among its activities were launching several publications, attacking authoritarian regimes on both sides of the Taiwan Strait, and using CIA- and Supreme Commander of the Allied Powers-sponsored training facilities in Okinawa and Saipan Island to conduct a series of abortive anti-Communist insurgency activities that included airdropping Chinese refugees into the mainland. Lacking a broad mass base, the committee failed to act together and was instead paralyzed by incessant factional fighting and political opportunism. In 1952 it reorganized under a more militant name as the League of Struggle for Chinese Freedom and Democracy, but remained hopelessly ineffective. When the United States gradually reversed its policy after the outbreak of the Korean War to resume support of the Chiang Kai-shek regime, which claimed sole leadership of the Chinese people's struggle against communism, the third-force movement came to a halt, as signified by the league's demise in 1954. Also contributing to the movement's quick decline was the colonial government's suppression thanks to political pressures from the governments on both sides of the Taiwan Strait. For example, committee founder Gu Mengyu fled to Japan (and later, Zhang Guotao to Canada) after being repeatedly harassed and threatened with deportation by the Hong Kong Police Special Branch, which was in charge of counterintelligence, for his leadership role.[15]

There was a third-force group that outlasted the political wing, and, in retrospect, had a continuing and shaping influence on the émigré intellectual community, especially on the UP and *CSW*. It was the magazine *Freedom Frontline* (自由戰線) and its parent organization, Freedom Press (自由出版社). Founded in late 1949 by some second-generation Youth Party leaders, most notably the Columbia University–trained political scientist Xie Chengpin (謝澄平), who had served as a mid-level Nationalist official before fleeing the mainland, to voice dissent against the one-party dictatorship of the two ruling parties. The magazine was close to bankruptcy when Philip Jessup (who was said to have taught Xie at Columbia) visited Hong Kong. According to the group's lore, Xie tried to meet with Jessup but ended up talking to the US Consulate Political Section and USIS officers about the future of the exiled third-force movement, and, not long after, got secret funding to expand his cultural enterprise.[16] Aside from resuscitating *Freedom Frontline*, the Freedom Press now launched three newspapers, a "Freedom Book Series" (which had released over 200 titles by 1954), a printing press, and a research center collecting materials on Communist China. Xie also supported a few small splinter cultural groups, including in their ranks the future UP group.[17] In 1951, hostile to its attacks and competition for American money, Chiang Kai-shek sent two emissaries to keep tab on the third-force activities. The emissaries observed, "Xie Chengping publishes *Freedom Frontline*. . . . His pay checks have sustained many famous scholars and young students in dire needs, and they cost him no less than $60,000 a month. All the money comes from American intelligence officials in exchange for information about the Communists (all of which are cullied from newspapers and personal interviews [with refugees])."[18]

Marginally related to the league, Xie's Freedom Press still played a significant role in making known to the public the ideas and development of the third-force movement in exile.[19] The press projected aspirational faith in the coming of a China taking pride in, as its rallying cry went, "political democracy, economic justice, and cultural freedom" (later to become the UP's motto).[20] Through *Democracy Frontline*, it urged readers to press on fighting against one-party tyrannical rules on both sides of the Taiwan Strait. Third force liberals should "embrace a fighting outlook of life," an author declared, "in an effort to establish a free and democratic new China."[21] Perhaps the most important legacy of Freedom Press was Xie's insight that the third-force movement, with all its major figures in their forties or fifties, could not sustain its antiauthoritarian struggle without winning and energizing the younger generation. He thus made efforts to involve young émigré intellectuals—including several UP founders—in his cultural endeavors and used his US State Department funds to subsidize their activities and publications. However, his alleged high-handed manner and proneness to suspicion, and especially his inability to develop new communication strategies and the language and style of cultural engagement to cross the generational divide, failed to win over the very people to whom he wanted to "pass the mantle" of third-force struggle. Still, its effort to win support of the youths lived on and, as discussed later, found echoes in the UP and its *CSW* as it emerged as a key cultural intervention in Cold War Hong Kong.

Colonial Neutrality and Communist Influences

Hong Kong provided refugees fleeing the Communist rule a safe haven, but it was a haven rift of anxiety and uncertainty. How long could the city continue under British rule? When would Mao's forces cross Shenzhen River to take over the colony? As discussed in chapter 1, no conclusive documentary evidence explains why the Communists stopped short of marching into Hong Kong in 1949, when they had swept over the southern city of Guangzhou, other than the prevalent interpretations on the basis of British intelligence sources or individual memoirs—namely, Beijing's fear of provoking a full-fledged war with the Western powers or its strategic effort to drive a wedge between Washington and London. Similarly, it has become a truism now that China had pursued a policy of "long-term planning and full utilization" regarding Hong Kong until the 1997 handover. However, for ideological and political reasons, this policy had not been communicated beyond the party hierarchy.

The ambivalence of Communist policies and decisions had created a prevalent sense of uncertainty in the British colony. As a US press officer told an interviewer many years later, "The feeling was that the Chinese might invade at any time. In the 1950s, no one in Hong Kong was really sure how long the territory would survive as an independent entity. Some thought it might last until the 1960s. Others were even more pessimistic."[22]

One of the major figures in shaping the governance and policy of Hong Kong in this precarious time was Sir Alexander Grantham, the governor from 1947 to 1957. Tall and authoritative in appearance and a veteran of colonial affairs, like many colonial officials and British taipans (big business leaders), he saw Hong Kong unique in the British Empire: it was "China's irredenta" that could "never be independent."[23] On this premise, he believed governing Hong Kong was primarily a matter of cooperating with whichever government in China—Communist or not. This put him occasionally at odds with London, which tended to make policy decisions in consideration of British national interests and global geopolitics, especially with regard to its special relations with the United States. For Grantham, managing China, in particular under the strong, anti-imperialist Communist government, involved a skillful and careful "balancing act" of "avoiding unnecessary provocation of the Chinese" while standing firm on the legitimacy of British rule—as he called it, the true "master in its own house."[24] Similar to many of his predecessors at precarious moments of the colony's history, he endeavored to pursue a policy of neutrality in relation to the global Cold War and the cross-Strait conflicts. It meant in practice keeping Hong Kong if ever possible open and equally accessible to all contending powers, but at the same time—through a legal and extralegal regime of censorship, surveillances, counterintelligence, and deportation, refusing to allow any of them to take advantage of the colony's "vulnerable position" and rock the boat of British rule.[25] As a longtime observer put it figuratively, throughout the 1950s, the colonial government had tried to play the self-appointed role comparable to an "umpire," trying to enforce strict rules to all the players in an especially rough-and-tumble game.[26]

As the Cold War intensified in the region, especially after the onset of the Korean War and the subsequent US-led global trade embargoes against China, the role of Hong Kong only increased in importance. It became, to use Hong Kong–based *Far Eastern Economic Review* correspondent Richard Hughes's phrase, "China's only rewarding bridgehead with the rest of the world and China's most convenient springboard for export dumping forays into Southeast Asia."[27] As noted in the previous chapter, the sprawling retail business and trading network Beijing controlled there, according to a US Consulate General estimate, made an average of at least around five hundred million dollars annually.[28] Along with remission from overseas Chinese communities, Beijing acquired almost half of its foreign currency reserve from Hong Kong.[29] It was easy to see why it tolerated a British colony along its southern border.

But it was another thing if the colony became a bridgehead for anti-Communist influences. With its strategic location and free port, Hong Kong had been a playground for agents and double agents since at least the Second World War. The Cold War upped the ante of its covert actions. Premier Zhou Enlai was known "as adept at espionage as diplomacy," with long experience creating covert cells and planting moles in the Nationalist government. During the civil war, the Communists used Hong Kong as a hub of intelligence gathering and other surreptitious works. [30] It was thus no surprise that, after 1949, Beijing had built a huge spectrum of government organizations, secret party cells, and front companies that made up an enormous intelligence and propaganda apparatus in the colony. They included the China Travel Service (Office of Overseas Chinese); the so-called Five Red newspapers (including *Ta Kung Pao* (大公報) and *Wen Wei Po* [文匯報]), and the New China News Agency (新華社), which housed the local Party leadership and the Public Security Bureau and State Security Bureau agents. They clandestinely collected information; engaged in other activity, including putting under surveillance various "hostile elements," particularly US government personnel and the Nationalist intelligence agency; and infiltrated into the higher echelons of the Hong Kong government as well as business and cultural circles.

According to *New York Times* journalist Christopher Rand, it was an open secret that Chinese agents worked undercover around the US Consulate General on Garden Road to monitor its activities and contacts with the émigré community. A Chinese staff member of the USIS–Hong Kong who had been working for the US Consulate since World War II, Richard Lee, revealed that the Communists used his family on the mainland as "hostages," to force him to "spy on" the US propaganda activities.[31] Another liberal figure affiliated with US cultural diplomacy deplored that all such measures "have [done is], succeeded in instilling fear into the mind" of many people.[32]

The Communists' intelligence and infiltration prowess was amply illustrated by the Kashmir Princess incident. Beijing had gotten wind of a Nationalist plot to bomb the flight that Zhou Enlai was scheduled to take to the Afro-Asian conference in Bandung, which was to be best remembered for its declaration of mutual respect and peaceful coexistence among poor and rich countries, and tipped off the Hong Kong police. Before the police took action, the plot succeeded and killed everyone on board except Zhou, whose travel plans had changed. Beijing used the incident to its advantage by blasting London for allowing the colony to become a base of anti-Communist sabotage. This led to a massive crackdown and deportation of underground Nationalist agents, and a reorganization of the colonial police force that, paradoxically, resulted in the discovery that a Scotland Yard–trained Chinese officer, Zeng Zhaoke (曾昭科), was a Communist mole. He quickly escaped to safety across the border.[33]

American Intervention

Hong Kong was similarly important, though in a different way, to the US Cold War policymakers. As diplomat Syd Goldsmith recounted, "We valued Hong Kong for its trade and as a port of call for our warships taking a break from the Vietnam conflict, but the highest value of the colony to the US was as a base for spying on China."[34] In fact, while the United States was the British colony's key export market and foreign investment, Washington saw it as the principal listening post to Communist China. Tiny as it was, as discussed in the previous chapter, the US Consulate General there was "bigger than 90% of [US consulates and] embassies around the world."[35] To satisfy Washington's hunger for information about Communist infiltration in Asia, it became the center of what was to become a catchphrase in the Cold

War: "China watching." The consulate was swarmed with "China watchers"—
especially in the Political Section, Economic Section, and the United States
Information Service (USIS), which was responsible for US cultural diplomacy in the region—whose job, as an American officer described it, was "like
an ornithologist at the edge of woods looking into China from outside."[36]
Their regular work involved, for example, tracking down and poring over
information ranging from overt (Chinese press), semi-overt (e.g., interviews
with refugees and "interceptions of Chinese military communications"), and
covert (e.g., CIA counterespionage on and penetration of local Communist
organizations) sources;[37] overseeing translation of them into English; and
sending them to Washington as well as major Western news media outlets
and university libraries.

Hong Kong also played a central role in the US propaganda campaign
in Asia. As "U.S. Policy on Hong Kong" (NSC 5717) revealed in 1957, "The
USIS office in Hong Kong has in recent years placed major emphasis on the
production of news periodicals, books, movies, radio scripts, and other anti-
Communist materials directed at the Overseas Chinese [in Southeast Asia]."[38]
At an NSC meeting in June 1960 discussing if the United States should send
in military forces in the event of Communist-inspired civil disturbances that
put the colony in peril, CIA chief Allen Dulles described the colony as "a key
base for information programs with respect to Communist China and the
Far East in general. Hong Kong was particularly useful as a listening post and
as a publishing center for anti-communist books, periodicals, pamphlets,
etc."[39]

Indeed, in its struggle to counter the expansion of Communist influences
in the region, the State Department and a host of what Frances Saunders
provocatively calls the "CIA's designated Cold War venture capitalists"—
most notably the Ford and Rockefeller Foundations and the Asia
Foundation, which we discuss in detail later, had spawned a huge array of
cultural and information programs in the colony to sell democracy and the
American Way to overseas Chinese communities. They included, among
other endeavors, the publication by USIS of a highly respected translated
book series (mainly American literary classics and nonfiction works with
an clearly anti-Communist slant), and *World Today* (今日世界), a gor-
geously printed, Chinese-language lifestyle magazine that was said to have
a remarkable circulation of over 120,000, both of which paid their authors
well above the standard rates and thereby brought many émigré cultural
heavyweights to their ranks (notably Eileen Chang [張愛玲], Stephen

Soong, and George Kao [高克毅]), and both of which catered to readers across the region.

US officials in Hong Kong also sponsored various gray and black propaganda efforts, such as clandestine funding for the already-mentioned Freedom Press and widely popular pocket-sized "50-cent novels" with anti-Communist messages, and planting of works propounding American viewpoints in mass media as objective sources originating from Asians themselves. For example, as the colonial authority found out after months of investigations in the early 1950s, the widespread story of Beijing's involvement in Asian drug trafficking turned out to be merely results of well-placed American propaganda.

In addition, the US Consulate General also housed a well-appointed USIS library that, aside from US-published books and magazines, offered regular English classes, exhibits, and film screenings, and lectures on applying to US colleges). The physical comfort of the library study areas and the rich collection of American reading materials made the library a home away from home for many émigré intellectuals. "I went to the USIS Library every day during unemployment," as young economist Cheng Chu-yuen [鄭竹園] recalled his early exile in Hong Kong. "Every day after eating something I spent ten cents riding the lower deck tram (upper deck cost twenty cents) to the Library on Garden Road in the Central. I read all the different American magazines and newspapers there until lunchtime. After eating at some open-air food stalls (*da pai dang*) in the neighborhood, I went back to read more before going back to [my leaning cramped room in the Western District]."[40] As USIS information officer Charles Cross (1951–1954) described, all these various cultural enterprises constituted "American Cold War weapons" against Chinese communism in the fight for ideological supremacy.[41] Among these US-funded anti-Communist weapons, in the words of two activists in the émigré cultural circle, the longest-lasting and most "dynamic and innovative" one, the one that represented "the most conspicuous newly emerged power in the Third Force movement," was the UP (亞洲出版社) and its flagship journal, *CSW*.[42]

The Asia Foundation and Émigré Hong Kong

In an October 1951 memorandum to the Committee for a Free Asia (CFA) head office in San Francisco, J. Ivy, the Hong Kong field representative,

wrote in excitement that he had met several key members of a Chinese refugee student group who, unlike the students he knew at the colonial Hong
Kong University, were "whole-heartedly concerned with student movements
and with anti-Communist programs." So impressed by their idealism and
the "democratic and freedom principles they believe in," he recommended
giving "full support" to their proposed activities. As revealed in recently
declassified materials, the CFA was a CIA front organization incorporated
in March 1951 as a nonprofit foundation largely along similar lines of the
National Committee for a Free Europe. Camouflaged as a private organization, it aimed to launch propaganda and psychological warfare across
the other side of the Bamboo Curtain and other Communist-leaning Asian
countries in ways that official US psychological warfare agencies like USIS
could not do. Around the time the Ivy memo arrived in San Francisco, as
discussed in the previous chapter, the organization gave increasing strategic
priority to mobilize support of the "Overseas Chinese" in combating communism in the region. Recognizing the nationalist surge in the decolonizing
territories, it tried to soften its Cold War crusader image by emphasizing
"Asian coloration," meaning to "decentralize" daily responsibilities in local
regions by identifying, nurturing, and providing financial and technical assistance to "local groups comprised of selected Asian leaders."[43]

In August 1953 Robert Blum became president of the CFA, and the organization changed its name to the Asia Foundation (hereafter TAF) shortly
afterward. Blum had played an instrumental role in the US intelligence community before joining TAF. According to recent exposure, after the war he
served as Secretary of Defense James Forrestal's assistant and helped coordinate NSC policies on covert propaganda activities and paramilitary action.
In the early 1950s he served as the special technical and economic mission
chief to Indochina, helping with the US military buildup in Vietnam, and
later worked on the Jackson Committee and coordinated with CIA director
Allen Dulles on information and psychological warfare, especially about the
"possibility of bringing in private enterprise—the super foundation idea."[44]

TAF had an obviously more neutral tone. As a key element of the
camouflaged propaganda and psychological warfare machinery in Asia's
cultural Cold War, with its headquarters in San Francisco, TAF had altogether thirteen branch offices across many countries in "free Asia," which
included Burma, India, Japan, Taiwan, and South Vietnam. Each of the
local offices was supposedly headed by a white American representative,
most of whom had prior work experiences in journalism, foreign service,

or intelligence and psychological warfare, and the support of a bilingual staff.[45] Under Blum, TAF intensified what amounted to a localization strategy of "Asian coloration" in the war of ideological dominance. TAF prioritized its Hong Kong program in the fields of culture and education, aiming to attract overseas Chinese in Southeast Asia, with particular emphasis on mobilizing the "younger generation, who tomorrow will wield the large share of political and ideological influence in their respective countries."[46]

TAF supposedly provided small grants as seed money to groups of local coloration whose objectives aligned with US Cold War interests, with the intention of helping them become self-sustaining. "To make private American support available to individuals and groups in Asia," its Articles of Incorporation declared, "who are working for the attainment of peace, independence, personal liberty, and social progress."[47] Actually, TAF was discreet and prudent in its Cold War investment. It tried to use its power of the purse as leverage to shape its sponsored groups' general direction and administrative matters by carefully monitoring uses of funds and requiring application renewal every three to six months and separate requests for different programs and activities. Most of the requests had to go through the local office, usually in consultation with other officers in the region, before being sent to San Francisco for approval.

During the Truman and Eisenhower administrations, Washington perceived Southeast Asia as the hot spot in its confrontation with communism in Asia. After the Communist victory in China, the anticolonial nationalist insurgencies in, for example, Burma, Vietnam, Malaya, and Indonesia caused US leaders alarm that, as an NSC document explained in 1949, "If Southeast Asia is also swept by Communists, we shall have suffered a major political rout the repercussions of which will be felt throughout the rest of the world."[48] Moreover, with its potential market of about 170 million consumers and rich resources (such as rice, tin, and rubber), Southeast Asia was important to Japan's postwar revival. Reflecting this strategic emphasis, TAF emphasized Hong Kong as a regional hub where "talents of the refugee intellectuals" could be employed to win the hearts and minds of "the Chinese population of Southeast Asia," aiming to "neutralize them and keep them from yielding to Commies." The centrality of the colony in the cultural warfare, a TAF internal memo emphasized, laid precisely in the "recognized fact that Hong Kong has considerable talents and that its leaders . . . can exert influence on their compatriots overseas."[49]

In the early Cold War, TAF secretly funded a wide array of émigré cultural, educational, and media organizations and activities in the colony with various interregional and transnational claims. They included, most prominently,

- New Asia College;
- the Pan Asia News Agency (which allegedly provided "non-Communist news" to overseas Chinese communities around the world);
- the Mencius Education Institute (among its popular programs were a well-stocked library and a youth hostel for overseas students and exchange faculty from Southeast Asia);
- a "Special Overseas Chinese Scholarship" that supported Southeast Asian students to study at New Asia;
- journalist Chang Kuo-sin's high-profile Asia Press (see chapter 3);
- Yale-trained dramatist Yao Ke's (姚克) "Hong Kong Players" project that sent drama troupes to perform in Southeast Asian urban centers; and
- various travel grants to pay for émigré cultural leaders' lecture trips and exchange visits to different parts of the region.

The Cold War as a "Total Struggle"

Texas Lieutenant Colonel J. Ivy (retired) was Hong Kong representative in the 1950s. He joined TAF in 1952 after working for three years in Taiwan for the China Relief Mission. Traveled widely in Asia and known for his deep interests in Chinese culture and close relationships with émigré intellectuals, Ivy moved to the British colony and helped give shape to the Hong Kong activities of US senator Walter Judd's influential Aid Refugee Chinese Intellectual program. The refugee student group that he was enthusiastic about was the Youth Union for Democratic China (民主中國青年大同盟; YUDC).

In the October meeting with YUDC leaders, Ivy asked them to write him a letter explaining their history and suggest areas in which they could "mutually cooperate." In this lengthy letter, the Youth Union's leaders described the YUDC as part of the third-force movement in exile. Framed in Cold War Manichean rhetoric, the letter claimed that YUDC started as a student organization in wartime Chongqing, boasting thousands of members scattered over various university campuses across China. It set out to "create influence besides Kuomintang and the Communists . . . a democratic course for an ideal

China with political democracy, economic justice and cultural freedom." This objective was, in fact, almost a verbatim reiteration of the Freedom Press's democratic mission cited earlier. After the Communist victory in 1949, the letter continued, like other Chinese third-force groups, the YUDC moved to Hong Kong. Its aim was to "strengthen overseas activities," while "the majority of its members" were said to be engaging in anti-Communist "military and cultural activities" on the mainland. It is evident that many details of this narrative were doubtful and perhaps even self-serving. Clearly, though, these young émigré intellectuals, echoing the refugee author's agonizing sense of patriotic duty cited earlier, saw fighting for an "ideal China" their life's cause during exile in overseas communities, which fit into TAF's Asian coloration agenda.[50]

According to historian Yu Ying-shih (余英時), who was briefly involved with the group, it had around twenty active members, and about ten of them played leading roles, and their ages ranged somewhere between twenty-four and thirty-two.[51] Archival materials reveal that, with the sole exception of a former junior Nationalist army officer, Anderson Sze Kong-ngai (史剛毅, aka Shi Chengzhi [史誠之]), most key YUDC members were recent graduates of elite Chinese universities and were only remotely active in politics before moving to Hong Kong. Arguably the most famous among these émigré intellectuals was Qiu Ran (邱然, aka Maria Yen Yun or Yan Guilai [燕歸來]) because of her influential book *University Life under Red Banners* (紅旗下的大學生活). The sole woman activist whom we know of in the YUDC or the third-force movement, she had a degree in philosophy from Peking University and was widely admired for her intelligence and total dedication to the cause.

Other leading YUDC members included William Hsu Tung-pien (徐東濱), conscientious and well-rounded, who had worked as translator for the US Air Force in Chongqing before graduating in Western languages from Peking University; John Paul Yu Tak-foon (余德寬), an enterprising graduate of Beijing's Fu Jen Catholic University; and the charismatic Jefferson Chen See-ming (陳思明, aka Chen Weicang and Chen Zhuosheng [陳濯生]) was a political science major at Nanjing's Central University. Forced into exile to an alien place, living in poverty in Diamond Hills, these young idealists found comfort in each other's company and survived on various odd jobs and Jefferson Chen's income as a staffer at his father-in-law, Ding Tingbiao's 丁庭標, newspaper, a right-hand man of Xie Chengping. This personal connection likely linked the young émigrés to the Free Press.[52]

The Cold War was "a total struggle" as William Hsu, who attended the meeting with Ivy, explained the YUDC vision in a letter to TAF, which was "above all a struggle of culture, a struggle of ways of living." However, he pointed out with alarm that Washington and the "free world have neglected cultural warfare," resulting in the "flood of Communist propaganda in Hong Kong." While pro-Beijing bookstores were lined with books and magazines "attractively designed" and "surprisingly cheap," only detective stories or pornographic books could be found in the few noncommunist ones. To win this "cultural battlefield" of unequal forces, the YUDC, like a "lone platoon," therefore, needed reinforcement of "hundreds of regiments and divisions."[53] It was for this "cultural warfare," Hsu urged, that US-China "cooperation" was in dire need.[54]

Maria Yen, another attendee of the meeting, brought up specific suggestions to Ivy in a May 4, 1952, letter. She pled support for young Chinese refugees who were committed like no others with "a strong will to fight" in the effort to build a "democratic China," and yet, unlike their older counterparts, were eligible for such American aid such as the Aid Refugee Chinese Intellectuals. They were poor and frustrated. She proposed, therefore, two new YUDC initiatives. The first was to set up something like a free mobile library to make reading materials available to young refugees who could not continue their studies. The second idea was to publish a "student weekly" to inspire and give voices to the young generation.[55]

The young émigré group had published four books, including Anderson Sze's *The Military Development of Communist China* and Maria Yen's *University Life under Red Banners,* as William Hsu recalled later, and they thought it was time to "launch a publication solely for students."[56] As they were just beginning to envisage the project, Maria Yen was vague as to the weekly's possible format or editorial policy, except proposing that student volunteers be involved in editing and distribution, especially refugee students from New Asia College.

UP, *CSW*, and New Asia College

The proposed connection between the YUDC and the venerable émigré institution of higher education in Hong Kong became a moment of significance in Asia's cultural Cold War. The small third-force splinter group

THIRD FORCE IN EXILE   57

gained what sociologist Pierre Bourdieu calls "cultural capital"—knowledge that was considered socially valuable and respectable—by associating with the intellectual powerhouse and, even more important, acquired from its students a lifeblood of new talent, ideas, and skills.[57] This enabled the young group to succeed where the originally well-funded Free Press failed in extending the dream of remaking China in and for the generations to come.

New Asia College was founded against all odds in 1949 by a group of intellectual exiles, including New Confucian philosopher Tang Junyi (唐君毅), German-trained economist Zhang Pijie (張丕介), and most prominently, historian Qian Mu. Known for its staunch antiauthoritarianism, expansive vision of liberal humanism, and fervent commitment to the preservation of Chinese Confucian culture, the college had become a symbol of cultural nationalism and intellectual autonomy, a beacon of hope to many young refugees trying to continue their disrupted education. Started with about forty students in a small, rundown apartment building on Kwelin Street in the poor neighborhood of Shum Shui Po, in space that served as classrooms, the student dormitory, and faculty living quarters, the college constantly struggled to survive against financial pressures and with poor facilities. Despite the cramped learning environment, New Asia was energized by an atmosphere of intellectual dedication and nationalist sentiment and its students had a deep sense of belonging. The college's "doors were always opened for the students who wanted to learn [in disregard of their backgrounds]," one graduate remembered many years later. "All the scholars were friendly and students loved to go to their residences to discuss and seek their views on national or global matters. . . Students knew that the school was in financial difficulties and offered help such as cleaning the classroom, or doing free-lance writing jobs or working so that they could contribute their income to the school for the improvement of facilities."[58]

New Asia began to receive financial support in early 1950s from Taiwan and then various US cultural and educational foundations, most importantly TAF, the Ford Foundation, and Yale in China. The college gradually upgraded and expanded to a small campus on Farm Road in Kowloon City, and in the mid-1960s was incorporated into the newly established Chinese University of Hong Kong—also partly funded by TAF.[59] The YUDC had formed close ties to New Asia College because of the young intellectuals' admiration of the eminent scholars, and because of Marian Yen's connection to Qian Mu, a friend of her father's, Qiu Chun (邱椿), a well-known Youth Party liberal opposition figure and John Dewey–trained education professor. He decided to remain on the mainland after the Communist victory in 1949, according to Yu Ying-shih, but "encouraged his daughter to struggle for freedom and democracy" in exile.[60]

How did the YUDC and TAF meet? According to Ho Chen-yah (何振亞), who became involved in the YUDC shortly after moving to Hong Kong, He Yijun (何義君), Jefferson Chen's former political science adviser at Central University and a consultant to the US Consulate in pre-1949 Guangzhou, helped arrange the meeting. However, in another interview, Shanghai-born Robert Hsi (奚會暲), a New Asia College graduate well known for his magnetic personality, dedication to the cause, and management skills, who had likely taken part in the meeting with Ivy, claimed that C. S. Kwei (桂中樞) introduced the young refugees to Ivy.[61] He Yijun was one of the third-force leaders and well connected with the US diplomatic establishment. Kwei, on the other hand, was a prominent liberal cultural figure in pre-1949 Shanghai, editor of the colony's top English-language newspaper, *Hong Kong Standard*, and part-time TAF consultant after he moved to Hong Kong after the Communist takeover. Kwei was also a good friend of Maria Yen's father. Either He or Kwei, or perhaps both, could have played certain roles in arranging for both sides to meet.

Ivy also consulted with the colony's US cultural diplomatic corps. Consulate General Political Section chief Ralph Clough, especially, who had been closely following the exiled third-force movement since its inception and knew the players well, gave a thumbs-up to the YUDC, which he called a "Third Force group." USIS officials working on the émigré community were also enthusiastic about the group.[62] USIS had earlier connections with the young émigré group, and as we can see, USIS continued to support the YUDC's various ventures through the early Cold War. In the early 1950s, for example, when the US authorities defunded the Third Force Group military training facilities in Okinawa, they tried to send all the people there to Taiwan. This group included one Ivy YUDC member, Manchuria-born Hu Yue (胡越, aka 司馬長風), and the émigré group pled with USIS for intervention because it would put the "writer, confirmed democrat" at risk in the hands of the Nationalists.[63]

On June 2, 1952, Ivy forwarded Yen's letter to the headquarters for support for the YUDC: a moderate five hundred dollars apiece for the mobile library and the publication of a student weekly. In the meantime, Ivy arranged to have YUDC activist Robert Hsi and other New Asia students join a weekly Voice of America broadcast to the mainland audience (hosted by USIS staff member Raymond Chow [鄒文懷], who later went on to become a Hong Kong film legend, see Chapter 4). Over time, Ivy became friend to many New Asia College students. He hosted parties for them, helped them apply for graduate studies in the United States, and filed applications for student visas (See Figure 2.1).

It was no surprise that Ivy recommended to the San Francisco office Zhang Pijie, provost of New Asia College, to advise, assist, and "give general guidance" to the YUDC. This effectively gave official endorsement to a cross-generational collaboration between the two émigré organizations in the years to come.[64] This proposed connection between the YUDC and the venerable émigré institution of learning in Hong Kong became a moment of significance in Asia's cultural Cold War. Sharing a deep-seated nostalgia of the homeland now under Communist conquest and belief in Chinese cultural values in a world spilt into two ideological camps, New Asia alumnus and *CSW* female editor Gu Mei (古梅) reflected, "*CSW* and UP had close relationship with New Asia, because their ideals were quite similar and various New Asia scholars held the UP intellectuals in high esteem."[65]

Figure 2.1 J. Ivy (*right*) hosting a picnic for New Asia College students circa 1956.

Courtesy of Jia NiLee

"We Are All Children of the Yellow Emperor"

As a local youth group with proven anti-Communist credentials and of unmistakable Asian coloration closely tied to a prominent émigré cultural institution, approval of the YUDC request from San Francisco came in just one day, June 3, 1952.[66]

On July 25, 1952, about a month after TAF began to secretly provide funding, *Chinese Students Weekly* (*CSW*) began publication from the UP. The UP was a new name for the YUDC, meaning "literally Friends and Allies or Friends United," referring to the group of founders sticking together against all adversity. The new name carried a markedly less apocalyptic Cold War overtone.[67] This change of name went hand in hand with efforts to make *CSW* a covert vehicle of what can be called Cold War enlightenment, endeavoring to inspire, guide, educate, and connect Chinese students scattered across the region and around the globe into an unified and transformative force to remake China into a strong, modern member of the free world.

Over the next two decades the UP built a transnational cultural enterprise, with branch offices and distribution networks spanning across East and Southeast Asia. It owned a printing press, published several longstanding multibook series on literature and social science (such as Contemporary Intellectual Trends and World Scholarship), and a widely influential *UP Loose-Leaf Reader* (友聯活頁文選) aimed at high school students that consisted of selected texts from Chinese classics with clearly and lively written notes. It was launched in 1954 in an effort to counter the Communist move (especially the Chung Hwa Book Company [中華書局]) into history and literature textbooks catering to overseas Chinese readers.[68] At the center of the UP's Cold War enlightenment were several magazines that targeted readers of different age groups and education levels. They included *University Life* (大學生活) for college students; the popular *Children's Paradise* (兒童樂園), which aimed to "influence the minds of primary school students"; *China Weekly* (祖國), for well-educated readers; and what came to become the UP's flagship publication, *CSW*.[69]

The UP also had a research arm, the Union Research Institute (友聯研究所; URI), which engaged closely with the US cultural diplomatic community. Most important, it housed what in the eyes of US China watchers was "widely considered the most extensive collection" of source materials on Mao's revolution, especially clippings from little-known regional newspapers that the young émigré intellectuals had begun to collect since they had

moved to Hong Kong. Although it was never mentioned in the official communications between TAF and the group in early 1952, the importance of
this collection was obvious to the American intelligence community in Hong
Kong and must have been one of the considerations in their favor. URI also
provided translation services for the US Consulate General, published a
series of research monographs, and translated documents on China's current
developments catering mainly to the China-watcher community. For financial support, moreover, the USIS arranged to have some of its publications
printed and distributed by the UP, and had a "blanket guarantee agreement"
to buy six hundred copies of each of the URI monograph.[70] Until China
opened up to the world in the 1980s, URI was a mecca for researchers about
China from around the non-Communist world.

   CSW debuted on July 25, 1952, getting off to an unpromising start. Among
its three founding editors—Jefferson Chen, William Hsu, and John Paul Yu—
only Yu had some editorial experience from working for one of Freedom
Press's publications. Produced out of one of the editors' rough shanties in
Diamond Hill, its format was austere and primitive: a cheap newsprint sheet
folded into four pages the size of a tabloid, with brief news and short essays
clumsily arranged, and monotonous in black-and-white except the white six-
Chinese-character logo in a simple green rectangle on the top of the front
page. Next to it, set prominently, was the date according to the Republic of
China *mingguo* (民國) calendar, not the commonly used Gregorian calendar, which Mao's new government had adopted. The materiality of *CSW*
was hardly attractive to anyone (See Figure 2.2). In the first several months
of 1952 its circulation was less than one thousand. Only with experiences,
better finances, and addition of young editors over time did *CSW* take on
a clean, creative, and highly readable style that became a trademark to its
readers.

   As German historian Jessica Gienow-Hecht points out, "The Cold War
shaped a new way of transferring and selling ideas, values, productions,
and reproductions. . . . It shaped existing debates and developments more
than it inspired new trends. . . . The Cold War did not trigger this debate, but
it did shape its evolution and affect its outcome."[71] This seemed to happen
in Hong Kong as well. Indeed, aiming to appeal to the largest numbers of
students—secondary school students—across the pan-Chinese world,
which was made possible largely by US financial and logistics support, as
editor John Paul Yu characterized it, *CSW* was the new tool and avenue
available to émigré intellectuals to connect and enlighten a new generation

Figure 2.2 *Chinese Student Weekly*, n.1, July 25, 1952.
Courtesy of Union Press

transnationally.[72] The Cold War enlightenment they promoted became enmeshed and reconfigured in longstanding debates surrounding the relationship between tradition and the modern, the meanings of Chineseness, and the role of third-force intellectuals in times of national (and international) crisis.

In an unsigned editorial, the *CSW* editors cast themselves as the liberal conscience of China, called for a cultural enlightenment to pave the way for China's leap "into a modern nation-state" in a world of superpower conflicts. Actually, there was nothing new in the language of this enlightenment: democratic representation, human dignity, and respect for rights.[73] It attested only to the UP intellectuals' linkage to the liberal tradition of twentieth-century China. They eulogized the May Fourth enlightenment of "Mr. Science and Mr. Democracy," especially its "patriotic resistance" to one-party authoritarian rule, and celebration of youths as agents of reimagining China's future. At the same time, painfully nostalgic of the homeland now under communism, the UP's intellectuals parted ways from the New Cultural iconoclasts who called for trashing Confucian classics. "As Chinese culture is facing devastation today," the editors explained elsewhere, "it is of great importance to pay homage to Confucius." They found answers instead in the conspiratorial language of the Cold War. It was not what writer Lu Xun memorably called the "cannibalistic" feudal tradition, but rather the way "some politicians" (read: the Communists), who manipulated and coopted the enlightenment agenda, were to be blamed for China's crisis today.[74]

It was the 1911 Revolution, not the May Fourth movement, which was celebrated by Mao's government for galvanizing revolutionary anti-imperialist fervor leading to the founding of the CCP, that *CSW* editors cast as the progenitor of China's enlightenment. It brought down the Qing dynasty and two millennia of imperial autocracy, and thereby set off China's struggle to become a modern nation-state. By setting up a republican state that emphasized rights, equality, and democratic citizenship, Sun Yat-sen was lionized as the pioneer of imagining a "democratic China." Many of the republican ideals were, however, betrayed by his successors. Just like Sun, who started the revolution living in exile overseas, they strove to raise consciousness among the young generation to bring out the unfulfilled promises. The *mingguo CSW* honored was, as a matter of fact, emblematic of the republican dream of political modernization the young émigré aspired to realize at a time of Cold War conflicts.

The page design and layout of *CSW* gave eye-catching expression to the content of its Cold War enlightenment. In its first few years especially, its editors always placed news stories about higher education and campus life in China and the United States side by side on the front page. In seemingly matter-of-fact comments that highlighted the crushing of personal liberty and freedom of expression on one side of the Bamboo Curtain and with news stories fed by TAF on the other, the prevalence in the West of academic freedom, intellectual opportunities, and racial tolerance was obvious.[75] In particular, *CSW* took pride in telling the readers about the achievements of Chinese people in the United States, most notably Nobel Prize–winning physicists Chen Ning Yang (楊振寧) and T. D. Lee (李政道), and allegedly increasing influences of Chinese culture on US college campuses (e.g., "Stanford University Creates Scholarship for Foreign Students" to promote cross-cultural understanding, New York City created a "China Day," and "Chinese Students Overturns American Racist Prejudice with Outstanding Academic Performance" at Newberry College).

This admixture of democratic ideal and nationalist pride in Chinese ethnoculture resonated with their mentor Qian Mu's unswerving belief in showing the continuous vitality of Chinese culture to the contemporary world. In his influential *CSW* essay "To All the Chinese Youths in Exile," Qian acknowledged the need for Western ideas of science, technology, and democracy in China's national renewal. However, he deplored the prevailing pessimism and iconoclasm among Chinese people toward their ethnic heritage due to China's uncertain future and its weaknesses in the face of Western domination. Even as it had "turned Red," he argued, China and Confucian tradition continued to inspire hope and remained at the center of global affairs. It was because China's long, continuous civilization had created in it an innate power, an indomitable "China's force" (中國的力量), that enabled it to defeat the Japanese invaders despite military weakness during World War II. Thus, in obvious reference to Dean Acheson's *White Paper* discussions of whether Mao would become a "Chinese Tito" or how long would communism survive in China, Qian proclaimed, all this Cold War geopolitics could be grasped only in the larger context of China's own culture. All the Chinese people, inside or outside China, should steadfastly embrace their Chineseness, taking up the "sacred responsibility" of preserving and promoting China's culture, its indomitable force, in opposition to the Communist ravaging of China and its traditional values.[76]

In a similar vein, Tang Junyi, well known for his rewriting of Confucianism in response to modernity, also helped set the cultural nationalistic tone of *CSW*. In his widely cited essay published in the UP's *China Weekly*, "Flowers and Fruits Scattered of the Chinese People," Tang articulated the exilic experiences of his generation as a result of the Communist conquest metaphorically as flowers and fruits scattered in different corners of the world. Rootless, and losing faith in China's cultural tradition, he abhorred, they became ashamed of their cultural heritage and turned, unreflectively, to Western—especially American—ideas and values as the logical course of human development—capitalist modernization. This was a symptom of the century-long crisis of Chineseness. For him, living in exile in the British colony was like existing in what scholar Thomas Frolich calls a "no-place": culturally isolated and spiritually lost. It was, indeed, China's historical culture and humanitarian values that defined who was Chinese, sustained their well-being, and what contributions they would make to the bipolarized world: "The biggest problem of people in the free world is, precisely, shallowness. . . . People in the free world should not emphasize only progression, [as] progression has its precondition in conservatism." The free world would be stronger in combating Communism if Chinese people could embrace and uphold their cultural tradition before "they start talking about creating a new culture."[77]

This espousal of Chinese cultural nationalism defined *CSW*'s efforts to build bridges linking all its readers among co-ethnics around the free world.

It was a transnational and interregional imagined community with an ethnically defined membership on the basis of "black hair, black eyes, yellow skin," and similar fate. "Although we never met in person, through *CSW* we have communicated our feelings with one another," the editors declared enthusiastically. "[We] are all Children of the Yellow Emperor and share the same hope—-to preserve Chinese culture and rejuvenate Chinese nation." In the Cold War context, it was at the same time a platform for mobilizing support against communism. As the editorial went on, "*CSW* will never limit itself to geographical boundaries. We hope every Chinese student living in the free world can join in solidarity, both spiritually and in our sense of purpose. . . . When we join together with confidence, we won't feel lonely in our fight for freedom and democracy."[78]

The Most Popular Student Publication in Hong Kong

The atmosphere of Hong Kong was tense when *CSW* was developing into a Cold War enlightenment force. As discussed earlier, the situation fire with rumors, surveillance, and threats from different camps. Between the strong, virulently nationalistic neighbor and the superpower having special relationships with London, the colonial government endeavored to keep in check the United States' anti-Communist campaign in Asia. Likely aware of the CIA being behind the organization, the colonial government was wary of TAF intervention in the cultural and educational spheres and concerned that using the territory as a transregional hub linking Southeast Asian Chinese communities would upset Beijing. To avoid political fallout, TAF tried to maintain a good working relationship with the colonial authority. TAF required all the local groups it financed to abide by British rules and regulations. The Hong Kong office also needed to regularly update the governor's political adviser and the Hong Kong Police Special Branch (responsible for counterintelligence) about its programs and plans. In 1954, for example, Ivy accompanied the visiting officer, J. Stewart to meet with Chief P. G. Dalton about hosting the upcoming regional conference in Hong Kong by TAF president Robert Blum. Dalton was said to make no objection but reminded both that TAF activities "would be tolerated" only to the extent that TAF continued to "[be] careful to clear matters with the Government." In order to express goodwill, moreover, the head office played host to Governor Grantham in the Bay Area during his 1954 trip to the United

States to plead for military support for the colony should the Communists attack.[79]

As a young émigré organization affiliated with the exiled third-force movement, the UP could easily be targeted by the colonial government as suspected "politically minded outsiders" conspiring to politicize and organize the large number of troubled teenagers in the face of the colony's mounting social problems. The UP group could also risk a confrontation with the Communist sympathizers. In fact, within the "White Chinese" community, as a New Asia College student recalled many years later, her former Nationalist official father forbade her from becoming too friendly with people associated with the UP for fear of "getting involved in politics and be in trouble with the authority."[80] This explained in part the particular canniness and discretion with which TAF tried to shepherd the launching of CSW and, it will be seen, the efforts of CSW to avoid provoking suspicion and harassment by the colonial government through the Cold War.

This approach was evidenced in the thorough review of the CSW at the San Francisco headquarters just five days after its debut. A P. C. Liu of the "Chinese Relations Section" sang praises to J. Stewart, a former media personage in charge of Asian affairs, about its undeniably "hard core" anticommunism beneath its "quiet, reasoned" style. This would allow, he emphasized, its messages to get through government censorship and "penetrate to the Chinese student groups" in Hong Kong and around Southeast Asia. Two weeks later, the TAF "Editorial Department's" Chinese staff did another review of it and agreed that, with its discreet anti-Communist discourse, it was "the best of its kinds" in the pan-Chinese world. The staff members went on to recommend, as gray and black Cold War propaganda, planting more American materials in CSW and, conversely, picking up writings from it to publish in all TAF-published and -distributed student magazines in the United States.[81]

Most important, both sides pledged to make every effort possible to keep the funding secret. "Only the editor-in-chief knows of TAF's assistance." They agreed that "outsiders [should] not become aware of the source of financial assistance to the CSW."[82] Even as most of the projects TAF sponsored in the British colony were covert, Ivy found it necessary to write to San Francisco to further justify his caution in regard to the weekly. The secrecy was particularly important because of the tension it would provoke and the disappointment it would create in readers who expected no political intervention behind it. "In order to protect the students here, our direct interest in this publication should not be known." He explained the mutual agreement to his supervisor. "Students who purchase *CSW* do so because it expresses free, independent thoughts on the part of students. If it was generally known that it is a subsidized publication, their interests would immediately dwindle."[83] Nevertheless, to be discussed later, the secret backing and maneuvering gave rise only to rumors and bitter controversy that lingered for years to come about the UP's Cold War role and relationship with American interests.

According to their agreements in November 1952, TAF increased its monthly subsidy to *CSW* from HK$7,500 to HK$8,000 with the intention of making it into "a more effective instrument for supporting the ideals and principles of the Free World." Started with a meager distribution of fewer than one thousand copies, the weekly's circulation increased dramatically in barely a year to around twelve thousand copies and expanded from four to sixteen pages, and then rose to more than twenty thousand copies in 1957, while most magazines sold about three thousand to five thousand copies per issue at the time, including the UP's *China Weekly* and *University Life*.

Meeting the needs especially of young émigré readers was the foremost reason for *CSW*'s popularity. Neatly organized into different sections consistent with the theme of Cold War enlightenment, its pages were filled with information and news stories written in simple, lively language on such subjects as science and new technology, Chinese historical figures and artistic and cultural traditions, discussions of free world and communism, and learning English and Western cultures. Writings from high school students sharing their emotions, people describing family life or experiences adapting to life in displacement, and a series on adolescent guidance and counseling under the general title of *Letters to Big Brothers* (大孩子信箱). These stories made the weekly what a reader later respectfully called a "mentor," a "lighthouse" to many young people.[84]

An editor also attributed the huge jump in sales to a new approach employing student volunteers to sell the periodical at their respective schools and the creation of the press's own Union Press Distribution Company to sell directly to bookstores.[85] This was true, yet he left out two other important reasons. The first was *CSW*'s low price: HK$.20. In the crowded postwar marketplace of ideas, making the weekly affordable to lower-income readers was paramount to expand its reach—and the TAF subsidy made this pricing strategy possible. In fact, TAF decided to make an exception of its seed funding policy early on because it thought, given its emphasis on wide circulation without succumbing to commercial orientation, *CSW* would never be "a potentially self-sufficient enterprise."[86]

The second was the great success of its various organized extracurricular activities, which, as Ivy proudly told a TAF colleague in Malaya, "multiplied the effects and influences of the publication many fold."[87] Indeed, for the first time in Hong Kong's media history, *CSW* created what it called "correspondents" (通訊員) from its devoted readers, who were recruited and mentored to write or provide details about their respective schools, and to distribute the weekly to their fellow students. These correspondents in due course formed close-knit communities by joining various culturally themed clubs held at the *CSW* office—such as a stamp club, theatre troupe, sports events, writers' club, music club, and summer camps. At a time of poor living and housing conditions, and the limited availability of entertainment and social and cultural activities for youth in 1950s Hong Kong, these clubs were a big draw to young readers—especially those who had recently migrated from China. Many of them went on to form close relations with the editorial staff and to increasingly identify with the weekly. Rapidly increasing in numbers, these correspondents helped make *CSW* a powerful force in ceaselessly pushing new boundaries to build an ever wider readership.[88]

Indeed, in 1954 *CSW* extended its ideological warfare to the neighboring Portuguese colony of Macao by setting up a bookstore and a branch office called Home of Students (學生之家).[89] In 1957 *CSW* boasted of a total circulation of about thirty thousand copies, forty-five thousand including also Southeast Asia; other UP magazines except *Children Paradise* sold about three thousand copies per issue).[90] With more than twelve hundred correspondents and an expanding array of organized activities, most prominent among them were a series of regular region-wide essay contests, on such topics as "Why I Study Chinese" and "What Is Scientific Knowledge?" (both of which were said to have attracted more than five thousand participants); cultural trips, which included a tour of the US Navy antisubmarine carrier USS *Kearsarge* while on shore leave in Hong Kong; and "photographic exhibitions" of postsecondary education opportunities in "Free China" and the United States, which aimed to compete with Communist promotion of further study in Chinese colleges on the mainland that had attracted many students from the region through the 1950s (See Figure 2.3).

No wonder *CSW* became TAF's poster child in Asia's cultural Cold War. In San Francisco's strategic view, *CSW* was an important part of "Free World strengths in Asia." The budget allocated for its program expansion increased

Figure 2.3 *CSW* correspondents visiting US warship USS *Kearsarge*.
The Asia Foundation Collection, Box P-57, Hoover Institution Library and Archives, Stanford University

continually through the 1950s. [91] "It was the most popular student publication in Hong Kong." Ivy told Singapore representative Patrick Judge, with almost paternal pride, that CSW was "the most successful publication in Hong Kong for which we are responsible for bringing it to being."[92]

The rapid surge of *CSW*'s influence drew antagonism from the pro-Beijing cultural establishment. In 1956, veteran Communist and pro-Beijing "Patriotic" Pui Kiu Middle School principal, Ng Hong-mun (吳康民), launched *Youth Paradise* (青年樂園), aiming to counter *CSW*'s influence on secondary school students.[93] Camouflaged as an unpolitical culture and information magazine, according to the memory of longtime Communist student activist Leung Mo-han (梁慕嫻), it was a product of a key underground Communist youth organization in Hong Kong aiming to extend its influence to prestigious colonial secondary schools.[94] Trying to confuse the readers, *Youth Paradise* looked like a *CSW* clone—from its front-page header in green color to its content and layout design that also emphasized short, simple essays covering science, literature and other seemingly ideologically innocent subjects. It also gave personal advice and guidance to teens and sold for a very low price. Some students, such as Clementi Secondary School student and future eminent scholar of Hong Kong literature Lo Wai-luen (盧瑋鑾 aka 小思), perhaps unclear of their political differences, made it a habit of buying both magazines at the same time.[95] And, just like *CSW*, *Youth Paradise* organized an array of extracurricular activities for its contributors and readers. It spawned a large network of so-called paper carriers (送報員), fueled by a strong spirit of collectivism and social service. The most dedicated ones among them became sympathetic to Mao's revolution. The two magazines competed furiously for market share and cultural influence, with *CSW* steadfastly holding a competitive advantage in circulation as well as numbers of club activities. (*Youth Paradise* was banned by the colonial administration during the 1967 riots when its true color was exposed.)[96]

Reflecting its important role in the cultural Cold War, for example, more than five thousand people were said to have attended *CSW*'s fifth anniversary reception in 1957. Among the attendees were senior New Asia College faculty members, editors of the Taiwan-backed press, leading figures of the third-force movement and other TAF-sponsored cultural groups, and students from Southeast Asia. Also prominent among the guests were a number of young actors from the newly established MP&GI who gave best wishes on behalf of the entire crew of *Air Hostess* (see chapter 1) who were filming on location in Taiwan at the time. In fact, mostly recent émigrés from Shanghai, people of non-Communist cultural organizations closely interacted with each other by virtue of school networks, social circles, family relations, and political outlooks (See Figure 2.4).

The anniversary celebration reached its climax with the costume play *Flower in Blood* (碧血花), produced jointly by the *CSW* Drama Club and New Asia College students. It was a blockbuster drama set in wartime Shanghai that reconfigured the anti-Manchu theme into a nationalist metaphor, rallying support for patriotic resistance against Japan. As discussed previously, propaganda officials were trying to make anti-Japanese subjects into a Cold War metaphor for anticommunism as part of the Nationalist legitimacy discourse that gained increasing currency in overseas Chinese media. At the *CSW* anniversary reception, *Flower in Blood* brought the audience to their feet repeatedly, vowing to "fight back to the homeland" in opposition to Stalin's "Red Imperialism."[97]

Figure 2.4 (*Right to left*) Robert Hsi in discussion with playwright Yao Ke and MP&GI actress and scriptwriter Qin Yu and editor Gu Mei at a *CSW* reception party.
Courtesy of Robert Hsi

A Pretty Inspiring Example

Archival materials reveal that as early as July 1952, the UP founders agreed with TAF that CSW's mission was to have "a good circulation . . . built in Southeast Asia."[98] Once the UP and *CSW* took up the challenge, with their personal connections in the overseas Chinese communities in Southeast Asia, they moved forward with zeal and organizational ingenuity.

In February 1954, with new TAF funding providing for transregional activities, *CSW* started extending what many of its overseas Chinese readers came to view as the "bridge from hearts to hearts" across the region.[99] In Southeast Asia at this time, as CIA field officer James Lilley, who was deployed in Asia, recalled later, "Chinese and American clandestine forces were facing off in places [in Southeast Asia] such as Philippines and Indonesia." From the US policymakers' strategic assessment, "the Chinese Communists were trying to turn local populations against their former Western colonial overlords" and destabilize the region to their advantages. He explained, "The PRC's chief instrument was the overseas Chinese populations."[100] It was thus no coincidence that TAF saw as one of its key missions to mobilize overseas Chinese students to combat communism.

The first target was, indeed, Sukarno's Indonesia. *CSW* set up its first Southeast Asian branch office in Jakarta. The quick success in sales of its Indonesian edition that emphasized content localization came to shape its general editorial policy for the region. On the premise that "ideals of freedom can be most effectively strengthened when they are related to local conditions," TAF agreed with the young editors' localized strategy of devoting half of the Southeast Asian edition to local subjects in any one of the decolonizing nations, written by local authors, and the other half from the "general edition" shipped there from Hong Kong.[101] Following the Indonesian success, *CSW* expanded in short order into Malaya, Burma, and Thailand with the same localization strategy. To meet the needs of rapid expansion, *CSW* brought editors and activists from Hong Kong to staff the editorial offices and organize various social and cultural activities for local students. The campaign was most successful in the newly formed Federation of Malaya, where *CSW* staff had extensive personal relationships with the Strait-born English- and Baba Malay-speaking or newly migrated Mandarin-speaking upper echelon in the Chinese community.

Its activities in British Malaya were illustrative of the nature of *CSW* involvement in the region's propaganda and psychological warfare against communism. In December 1955 UP founder John Paul Yu made a scouting trip to Malaya-Singapore. In a series of letters to his comrades as well as TAF in Hong Kong, he brought up some observations that revealed the group's third-force outlook and view of their role in Cold War Southeast Asia. First, he sounded an alarm that Malaya was in danger of quickly "turning Red"; against the background of the surge of Chin Ping's Communist insurgency, he said, while the government and most of the Chinese professionals and community leaders he had met were "decidedly anti-Communist," the majority of young people in general, and Chinese school students in particular, were sympathetic to communism. If Malaya fell, like domino effects, one nation after another in the region would be in danger of Communist control, he warned. Fortunately, he argued, *CSW* could play a significant role in winning over Malaya's overseas Chinese community to the "free world" cause because they trusted the CSW intellectuals as "saviors." "The people here have a special respect for people from Hong Kong," he proudly declared. "They think everything from Hong Kong is good." So it was *CSW*'s responsibility to connect to the young readers, mobilizing their support for the Malayan war against Communist insurgency.[102]

Although written like personal communication, Paul Yu's information-rich letters could easily be seen by TAF as intelligence documents describing the Cold War situation in Southeast Asia for its planning. His correspondence was tendentiously one-sided. While he explained in detail the threats that the Communist influences on Chinese Malay posed, he was silent on British colonial repression, the poverty experienced by low-income Chinese migrants, and especially all the counterinsurgency violence and restrictions imposed on the Chinese in rural areas (including the "New Village"). But in an important way the letters deviated from the United States' Asia policy, which reflected Yu's third-force convictions. Yu also made clear his opposition to the Nationalist dictatorship, with its extensive propaganda and business apparatus in Southeast Asian Chinese communities, even as it ran counter to the US military partnership with Taiwan, the "unsinkable aircraft carrier" in the Pacific. He accused Nationalist officials in Malaya of being corrupt and out of touch with the young generation, and he admonished all his colleagues to stay away from the Nationalist-backed organizations when they arrived. After further discussions with some Malayan Chinese community leaders and recent migrants from China, who had similar third-force leanings, Yu shared his optimism with his UP colleagues back home that "the independence of Malaya seems inevitable." As long as it would not become "a second Indonesia," with a strong Communist movement contesting for postcolonial state power, he went on with excitement, "Malaya may become a strong member of the free world and a main base for the revival of China!" Along with Hong Kong, then, Singapore and Kuala Lumpur would serve as the springboard for the UP's Cold War enlightenment.[103]

The Malayan-Singaporean edition of *CSW* started in 1956 in Singapore, and the editorial office moved to Kuala Lumpur two years later. With the alleged purpose of giving local authors a voice for the "nourishments and benefits of the youths," *CSW* further reinforced its localized strategy by renaming itself in 1957 *Student Weekly* (學生週報), without the "Chinese" qualifier, Undergirding this new local edition, at least until the 1960s, was the same discourse of Cold War enlightenment. Along with all the local stories, Robert Hsi explained in an interview, "We [continued to] promulgate to overseas Chinese students the ideals of freedom and democracy and the preservation of Chinese cultural values." He was one of the UP's inner circle, including John Paul Yu, Maria Yen, and Jefferson Chen, as well as such recent New Asia College graduates as Wang Jianwu (王健武) and Gu Mei, who moved to Southeast Asia to join the Malay campaign against communism.[104]

Student Weekly aimed principally at students of Chinese secondary schools, which were a major site of ideological contest and ethnic tension that the Malayan government conceived as a breeding ground for Communist influences.[105] Similar to the Hong Kong model, its price was set artificially low (Strait dollars: ten cents) so that low-income students could supposedly afford it. And just as in Hong Kong—as well as in Indonesia and Burma—the weekly had "correspondents" recruited from devoted readers who were organized and who participated in extracurricular activities that aimed to develop group identity. TAF-funded student activity centers sprang up in various parts of the federation, and UP leaders and *CSW* activists visited them on a regular basis to give lectures and guidance. There were also summer camps every year at Cameron Highlands, a popular resort destination for colonial officials, to bring together selected "correspondents" across British Malaya for sports events, cultural activities, and seminars on Chinese values and anti-Communist nationalist themes.[106] (See Figure 2.5)

Moreover, the UP supported Chinese Communist leaders, notably those affiliated with the Malayan Chinese Association, an organization purportedly

Figure 2.5   Robert Hsi leading a Chinese Malayan students' music group at the *CSW* summer camp in Cameron Highland, a famous resort area about ninety miles from the capital city of Kuala Lumpur, which was developed by the British in the 1940s as a hill station.
Courtesy of Robert Hsi

representing Malay's Chinese population, attempting to provide a bridge between the Malay-biased government and the many alienated Chinese people. For example, as these leaders were mostly English-educated *baba* Chinese, they needed help in translation when they visited "New Villages," where many poor rural Chinese suspected of pro-Communist sympathy were settled in response to the "Malayan Emergency," or when they tried to better understand Chinese school curriculum and the politics of Chinese-speaking students. With the Malay Chinese community leaders' support, it did not take long that the UP began to publish Chinese-language middle school textbooks. In Hong Kong, as we discussed, the colonial power allowed publication of only supplementary materials (*UP Loose-Leaf Readers*) to avoid compromising its neutrality in the eyes of Beijing.

Amid the chaos of the British counterinsurgency, as Gu Mei and Robert Hsi later recalled, pro-Communist students were organized to harass *CSW* readers, disrupt the distribution network, and sabotage its organized activities. Moreover, UP activists like them were at risk when they traveled through "Communist territories," where guerrilla fighters often exchanged fire with the colonial forces, and at the many government checkpoints in between for suspicion of political activities during their routine visits to schools and student activity centers.[107] Despite these challenges, in 1957 *CSW* reached combined sales of twenty-two thousand copies each month for its Indonesian, Burmese, and Malayan editions, and it boasted of more than 1,606 correspondents and seventeen branch offices–student activity centers, which together had "organized four hundred meetings with total attendance of 16,000!"[108] For its "important services" in educating Chinese school students in opposition to communism, UP's textbook publishing and printing businesses quickly expanded into a large and profitable enterprise that became a key source of funding for its Hong Kong office in the latter part of the 1960s and early 1970s (see chapter 5).

San Francisco was elated with the success and asked the Hong Kong representative to make all efforts to "continue to encourage the UP and the *CSW* to expand their programs in as many areas as possible in Southeast Asia."[109] Asia chief Stewart in particular was proud of the young émigrés' assiduous transregional work. "The extreme gravity of what we are facing [in Southeast Asia has] no quick solution," he wrote Ivy in 1958. "What you are doing, however, with the *CSW* certainly indicates the nature of the solution and provides a pretty inspiring example. . . . The Weekly and yourself are to be congratulated for the excellent work." In the same year, TAF upgraded the weekly from a local (Hong Kong) to a "regional Chinese program" in the propaganda and psychological war against Mao's revolution.[110]

"If the Chinese Had the Opportunity to Go to Hungary . . ."

For all its vehement promotion of individual rights and creating a "democratic China" proud of its cultural tradition, *CSW* was aloof from actual politics. It was strikingly silent about social problems in the colonial and postcolonial societies of the region. In Hong Kong, *CSW* inflexibly veered readers from involving themselves in local political activity but instead advised them to focus on schoolwork and "learning more about ideas of freedom and democracy" in preparation for changing China in the future. *CSW* warned them, in particular, to stay away from print media and political activities associated with Communist causes or figures. Or, for example, when Chinese school students protested against the new Malayan educational policy in 1957 that in their view was to "marginalize" the Chinese language as a medium of instruction in a supposedly multiracial nation, *Student Weekly* urged students "not to take action on their own," but rather to leave the conflict for government officials to resolve and seek in the meantime other ways to continue to preserve and promote Chinese culture.[111]

The aloofness of the UP and *CSW* to local politics, and especially the unequivocal aversion to student involvement in collective action, was likely a result of fear and misgivings that, like the portrayal of the failure of the May Fourth enlightenment project, youthful idealism would easily play into the hands of the Communist political machinery. The Cold War struggle for ideological supremacy only amplified this fear. In addition to it was the menace of the colonial power's surveillance and draconian censorship (and TAF's requirement of its strict adherence to government regulations in all funded activities[112]). All these limitations contributed to their strategic focus on enlightening the young generation with cultural-national and antiauthoritarian consciousness in an ideologically divided world.[113]

Perhaps more fundamental was the UP intellectuals' obsession with the homeland right across the Shum Chun River. They longed to return there. New Asia College philosopher Tang Junyi, their mentor, revealed in the 1970s that when radicalization and local consciousness swept across the British colony's college campuses, he and other émigré intellectuals turned a blind eye to the colonial condition of Hong Kong and all the accompanying problems, because they saw themselves as exiles in diaspora, staying there as long as China remained under Communist rule. "We remained determinedly Chinese while living here," he explained. "I can say that, we and the Hong Kong government had nothing to do with each other in those days. What we cared about were changes in China, nothing about Hong Kong."[114] This sentiment of what Hong Kong scholar once called "a patriotism of the émigré"—which was "not connected to the tangible reality" of the colonial and postcolonial world[115]—prevailed in all UP publications, including notably *CSW*. Indeed, not until the 1960s did Mandarin, not the local Cantonese, become the recognized language used at the UP meetings or at *CSW* or *University Life* editorial offices.

The popularity of *CSW* created tension with other non-Communist émigré groups vying for greenback assistance, which generated rumors and vicious gossip aimed especially at Maria Yen, because of her gender. For example, several refugees wrote to USIS chief Arthur Hummel in 1954 to accuse the UP of being a "political organization . . . to help the Communist regime of China by undermining the Nationalist Government."[116] But the most intense competitor was Asia Press, another major beneficiary of TAF assistance. Founded in 1953 by former Associated Press journalist, Chang Kuo-sin (張國興), the organization ran a film studio, a news agency, a publishing house, and a monthly general-interest magazine modeled after Henry Luce's *LIFE, Asia Pictorial* (亞洲畫報), all with eye-catching news photographs that pointed to the affluence and good life of the free world (see chapter 3). The young UP intellectuals, who prided themselves for their self-sacrificial élan (low pay and long working hours) and puritanical lifestyle, saw Chang as a "megalomaniac," wasteful of ideological warfare resources for self-aggrandizement. For Chang, however, the UP staff, and especially their influential student weekly, were ungrateful upstarts who needed to learn their place in the anti-Communist cultural order. What most enraged him was their third-force attacks of the one-party Nationalist rule in the Cold War fortress, as most evidenced in John Paul Yu's refusal to meet with pro-Nationalist overseas Chinese organizations in Malaya (as discussed earlier), as did Maria Yen when she attended the US-backed Conference on Cultural Freedom in Asia in Burma. Chang complained this to San Francisco and openly attacked UP leaders in the conference. TAF officials were "unhappy" about the acrimonious relationship between their two largest Chinese organizations in the region, weakening their anti-Communist forces. Some field officers agreed that the UP "over[did] the 'liberalism' atmosphere" in their dissent against Chiang's authoritarian rule, when it was Washington's propaganda goal to cast Taipei as the "underdog steadfastly holding to the [democratic] ideals of the Chinese Republic." But they were also disappointed with Chang Kuo-sin's failure to support the young intellectuals as a "big brother" that he should be. San Francisco urged Ivy to try to resolve the conflicts between Chang Kuo-sin and the UP groups and to bring the young intellectuals into line with the US policy.[117]

Nonetheless, scathing criticism of Taiwan's one-party regime continued to appear in *CSW* until the 1960s, and the UP and Asia Press remained in conflict.[118] At the same time, TAF tried to make the amazing URI collection that the UP intellectuals had been collecting since their move to Hong Kong in 1949 easily accessible to China watchers around the "free world." San Francisco sent scholars and doctoral students periodically from Yale and University of Washington as "consultants" to push for reorganizing the rare materials as well as the URI research monographs series (mostly based on the collection) according to modern "American research technique." TAF also wanted to affiliate the URI with a US-based university. The UP refused to go along with the plan because, the UP said, such an affiliation would identify their collection in the public mind as part of the US intelligence machinery.[119]

These instances of resistance revealed that it was questionable to assume that the émigré intellectuals of the UP and their popular *CSW* lacked agency in the cultural Cold War. The secret greenbacks they received did not seem to bind them subserviently and sycophantly to American strategic interests in the region. In fact, Ivy liked to tell his colleagues, the group enjoyed "complete independence" because of San Francisco's satisfaction with its proven "reliability and dependability."[120] He might have exaggerated the "autonomy" they had, in part because of the trust and friendship he had developed with them over the years. Ivy more than once stepped in to defend the UP when disputes arose between the two sides.

San Francisco often tried to intervene in the émigré intellectuals' organizational and budgeting practices, most notably requiring them to vigilantly follow colonial regulations in all their programs, or demanding that they expand leadership in the UP and its *CSW*, or urging them to better coordinate their cross-regional programs with TAF offices in Southeast Asia.[121] Rarely, however, would San Francisco need to intervene in matters of ideology or editorial content. For one thing, the Hong Kong office did not have enough manpower to look through each of its many magazines each month. More importantly, Ivy and other staff members had trust in the émigré intellectuals' commitment to the global anti-Communist crusade. In fact, to use William Hsu's metaphor, from his 1951 letter to Ivy, the UP émigrés were a "lone battalion" of willing cultural Cold Warriors who saw it their lives' cause in exile to maintain their deep sense of Chineseness and keep up their hope to return to a free, democratic China. Opposition to Mao's revolution, so to speak, went down to their bones. "Lone battalion" was a reference to the heroic act of patriotic resistance by the 1st Battalion of the 524th Regiment to Japanese invasion in October–November 1937. For Hsu and his comrades, echoing ironically the Nationalist reconfiguration of the anti-Japanese war metaphor, the "reinforcement" by TAF by means of financial assistance and logistical support in transregional expansion was a continuity of US-China "cooperation" from World War II in the new context of the global Cold War.

During the Hungarian Revolution of 1956, while expanding *CSW* works in Malaya-Singapore, Maria Yen expressed her outrage at the Soviet destruction of Hungary's traditions and aspiration for freedom. In a militant tone, she wrote of her generation's disillusionment with communism and her frustration with so many young people in Malaya and other parts of decolonizing and postcolonial Asia who were fighting for its realization. "If Chinese had the opportunity to go to Hungary to assist you in resisting the brutal power," she declared, "I would rush to volunteer."[122] This depth and intensity of anti-Soviet wrath powered the UP émigré intellectuals to fight the cultural Cold War. To them, cooperating with the United States did not mean giving up their third-force conviction and aspiration to carve out a democratic China between the authoritarian one-party rules on both sides of the Taiwan Strait, even if it meant openly opposing the American Cold War realpolitik in Asia. This dream of delivering China from cultural destruction and authoritarianism by means of Cold War enlightenment also powered the émigré intellectuals, in the words of editor Woo Bing Man (well known under his penname, Hu Juren [胡菊人]), to build *CSW* into a transregional, multigenerational community in the Sinophone world. Resorting to images of trees, fruits, and flowers that echoed Tang Junyi's evocative essay on the crisis of Chineseness, Woo Bing Man wrote with a poetic touch, "It has grown into an evergreen tree of deep, lush green, and its branches and leaves extending to every corner of the free world, creating a paradise for all its readers to share with each other their agonies and hopes."[123]

3

American Cinematic Intervention

Asia Pictures and the Asia Foundation

Fiction merits the rank of General in the anti-Communist force in
Asia today. At the present he is a Marine Corps–type General.

Robert Sheeks[1]

The Third Asian Film Festival was held in Hong Kong in 1956. Governor
Alexander Grantham opened it by highlighting the colony's cinematic
achievement. It "ranked fourth in the world in the number of films produced
annually," he proclaimed "with pride," citing that over three hundred films
were made each year and most of them were for export. A festival organizer
followed by referring to Hong Kong as "Asia's biggest film exporters."[2] The
governor's remarks must have come as a surprise to local representatives, especially because the Mandarin film industry of the day was immersed in a
state of economic crisis, struggling with ongoing market shrinkage. The governor evidently knew little of the details beyond the possibly inflated export
figures, since his government was reputed to be the least financially involved
in mass entertainment business in Asia, and he had little personal interest in
what was soon to become the "Hollywood of the East." There was, indeed, no
mention of it in his wide-ranging memoir, *Via Port. [See note 1]*

It was Governor Grantham's suggestion to reflect the festival's many
East Asian members that caused the three-year-old festival to change from
its original name, the Southeast Asian Film Festival. Recent research has
brought to light the secret role of the Asia Foundation (TAF) in trying to turn
the festival into a political weapon promoting the US Cold War agenda.[3] It is
oversimplistic, however, to place undue emphasis on the politicization of the
annual festival, as there had always been a strong countervailing force among
its member states that prioritized commercial and technological imperatives.

Hong Kong Media and Asia's Cold War. Po-Shek Fu, Oxford University Press. © Oxford University Press 2023.
DOI: 10.1093/oso/9780190073763.003.0003

Indeed, in the wake of the Third Asian Film Festival, TAF began to reassess its future connections to the festival, and especially its covert interventions in Hong Kong's émigré film industry through financing a minor studio, Asia Pictures.

Asia Pictures was founded in 1952 by Chang Kuo-sin (張國興) as part of a TAF-sponsored cultural enterprise that included magazine publication and news services, with a covert agreement to extend US cultural warfare to the struggling Mandarin film business. Chang was a longtime journalist widely known among the British colony's foreign expatriates as the "China authority." His film endeavor was, however, brief and futile. Asia Pictures had produced merely nine feature films before it closed down in 1959; all of them, including the acclaimed drama *Long Lane* (長巷, 1956), are now known mainly in academic circles. There has been, understandably, scant attention to Chang and his studio, with the notable exception of Law Kar's and Charles Leary's pioneering works from a Cold War perspective. Actually, although Chang—unlike contemporary film giants such as Sir Run Run Shaw or Dato Loke Wen Tho—had limited resources and came up short in establishing a sustainable organization to leave a strong footprint in Chinese-language cinema, he was a pioneer in trying to modernize and professionalize film-making practices, and especially played a significant role in using greenback aid to politicize and polarize the émigré cinema.

Based on untapped historical sources, including film journalism and memoirs, and the Asia Foundation Collection at Hoover Institution, this chapter builds on earlier research work to reconstruct the brief and futile efforts of Chang's Asia Pictures to crush Communist influences. This from-the-bottom-up reconstruction sheds light on the history of covert US interventions to enlist the support of Hong Kong popular culture to compete with China for the hearts and minds of Chinese diaspora in the region.

We Have No Home Market

In the early 1950s, the influx of refugees from across the Sham Chun River increased Hong Kong's population by more than a million people. Side by side with housing and public health crises and massive poverty, as documented in chapter 2, the population increase spurred demand for consumer goods and entertainment for those who could afford it. There was also an excess of capital brought in by émigré businessmen and former Nationalist officials and military commanders. Speculative investment in gold, commodities, stocks, and foreign exchanges—as well as, especially after the onset of the US-led global trade embargo against China in 1950, risky but get-rich-quick smuggling of goods to the mainland—became popular outlets for idle capital.

The film business enjoyed a boom in investment as box-office receipts soared and new theaters opened around the city. The investments were mostly speculative in nature, however; an intelligence report declared that "independents mushroomed" as a result. In a city of about two and a half million people, between 1950 and 1952 there were a whooping number of about one hundred film companies and similar numbers of distributors![4] While most distributors had no film promotion or marketing experience, only a handful of studios boasted sound stages or other production facilities, or contracted film artists and technicians of their own. Even the best among the studios were small in scale, antiquated in technology, old-fashioned, handicraft-esque in production practices (usually following the longstanding master-apprentice hierarchy and inefficient, nepotic management), and short of working capital that gave them constant cash flow problems and left them lacking an overall business plan or consistent production schedule.[5]

Most of Hong Kong's studios were, indeed, what industry insiders mockingly called "fly-by-night, one-movie companies," which, after obtaining financing on the strength of a marketable story with one or two big stars (such as superstar Li Li-Hua [李麗華] or Zhou Xuan [周璇]), signed up actors and directors and rented equipment along with crew members from one of the studios with shooting or sound stages for about HK$800 each day. In order to save money, they used stock sets and costumes that came mainly with the studios (or, for costume dramas, from local opera troupes), and finish their products in as short a time as possible—usually from one to two weeks. In 1950 and 1951, when demands for Mandarin films were fierce, especially among the mainland transplants in Taiwan, some just made new prints from old Shanghai movies and marketed them as new ones by inserting some new scenes or adding songs here and there, or simply dubbed Cantonese movies in Mandarin. Running like a "racket," as a San Francisco theater owner told an interviewer, these "one-movie companies" flooded the marketplace with hastily made, low-budget pictures—about HK$50,000 to $100,000, a fraction of a Hollywood B-movie. The colony's film industry fell into disrepute almost as quickly as it had begun to experience a boom.[6]

Demand from overseas markets shrunk quickly. The loss of public faith in Hong Kong films added fuel to the rapidly deteriorating business landscape as a result of increasing geopolitical tension, political censorship, fluctuating exchange rates, and various kinds of import restrictions in the region. Producers struggled to find buyers. Also troubling was a transnational challenge that came from the other side of the Pacific. Around this time, Hollywood flooded Asia with big-budget pictures with widescreen technology (principally CinemaScope and VistaVision) and improved Technicolor and Eastmancolor. The new audiovisual offerings, along with the projected images of American wealth and modernity, took audiences in Hong Kong and beyond by storm, exacerbating the already commanding US position in the film market and bringing to stark relief how decrepit and technically backward were the local productions. The hardest hit of this reversal of fortune were expatriate Mandarin productions. Unlike Cantonese movies, which had a steady and sizable local audience, albeit mostly poor and semi-illiterate, Mandari cinema did not have the support of what some industry analysts called a "home market" (家鄉市場). The majority of Mandarin films did not get theatrical release in Hong Kong.[7] "Mandarin film was in doom and gloom," one veteran studio head grumbled at a roundtable discussion, "as the markets are shrinking day by day!"[8] The only way to go forward, as all major industry players came to agree, was to extend transnationally in order to develop "more overseas markets." But could this happen without access to capital investment and modernizing the aging technology and equipment that make possible production of bigger-budget, higher-quality movies to draw audiences back to the theaters?[9]

Struggling to navigate this doom and gloom were four major producers of Mandarin films: Yung Hwa (永華); Shaw and Sons (邵氏父子); the cash-strapped Longma (龍馬), which was to be reorganized into pro-Beijing Phoenix [鳳凰] in 1953, and the pro-Communist "Patriotic" Great Wall. As Yung Hwa continued its downward spiral after the Communist-instigated strike in 1951 (see chapter 1), and as the SFS, with the second Shaw brother, Runde, at the helm, remained stuck in its business focus on quantity over quality and the bottom line—even as it enjoyed an ongoing supply of capital from the family-run distribution and exhibition giant (the Shaw Brothers Organization) in Singapore—Great Wall attracted most public attention. As a Communist-backed enterprise, Great Wall boasted a strong stable of talent (such as directors Li Pingqian [李萍倩] and Yue Feng [岳楓]) and skillful technicians, and emphasized careful attention to production details and bringing poverty and social problems to public consciousness. Between 1950 and 1953, Great Wall produced a string of popular, well-acclaimed dramas, including *A Liars' World* (說謊世界, 1951), *A Night-Time Wife* (禁婚記, 1951), and *Modern Red Chamber Dream* (新紅樓夢, 1952), mostly sympathetic portrayals of ordinary men and women falling prey to violence and social injustices or oppressive patriarchal traditions, whether taking place in Hong Kong or in an indeterminate Chinese city (assumably Shanghai). *A Night-Time Wife* ranked first in the box-office. "Hong Kong movie circles and audiences consider productions of the Great Wall rather 'progressive' if not 'pro-Communist,'" *Far Eastern Economic Review* told its readers. "Most of its productions have been well received by the Chinese public in Hong Kong and overseas Chinese, who are leading a hard life, find these progressive melodramas very entertaining. . . . With comparatively old equipment, the Great Wall is struggling to put out technically perfect pictures."[10] At the same time, according to a US State Department–sponsored survey from 1952, *A Survey of the Reading Habits of the Chinese of Hong Kong*, Great Wall's official fan magazine, *Great Wall Pictorial* (長城畫報), was the most popular of its kind among young and educated readers.[11]

"To Beat the Great Wall"

In this gloomy business landscape, a small film studio sprang up to spearhead a cultural Cold War in Mandarin cinema: The Asia Pictures Limited (亞洲影業, hereafter Asia Pictures), established by veteran journalist Chang Kuo-sin with the objective of "cleansing the Chinese movieland here of Chinese Communist influences."[12] Born in 1916 to a peasant family in Hainan Island, in 1928 Chang went with his father, a migrant laborer, to North Borneo. A gifted student, Chang won a scholarship to return to China to study at the National Southwestern Associated University in 1945. Before graduation, he had served a brief stint as interpreter for the Allied forces in the China-Burma-India Theater. Smart, fluent in English, and well connected with senior Nationalist officials and the diplomatic corps in wartime Chongqing, after graduation he worked as a correspondent for the Central News Agency and then Associated Press covering the Marshall peacekeeping mission and the Nationalist-Communist civil war until he went into exile in 1949, when Mao's government set out to close all foreign news agencies. "I applied for a travel permit. I explained to the authorities that my destination was Hong Kong," he remembered with obvious scorn. "One of the cadres, a Long March veteran, looked at me intently and asked with obvious contempt and animosity: 'Why do you want to go to Hong Kong, we are yet to liberate it?' These loyal dogmatic Chinese Communists! They thought they could liberate Hong Kong or anyplace else. They called it their historical mission."[13]

Shortly after his arrival in Hong Kong in 1949, Chang expanded a series of essays for the United Press into *Eight Months behind the Bamboo Curtain*, a reportage of life under the new regime, that captured wide attention among émigré intellectuals and American China watchers. Staunchly anti-Communist and with a ringside view to the US-Communist conflicts, Chang was to become, inadvertently, a strong voice in the early cultural Cold War. In fact, to use Latin America historian Patrick Iber's phrase, he was one of Asia's highest-profile "anticommunist entrepreneurs." Like entrepreneurs in the business world, anti-Communist entrepreneurs, "some for opportunistic purpose and others married opportunities to convictions," took advantage of the new resources made possible by the US cultural intervention to pursue their plans and goals. They often tried to use the greenback support and anti-Communist agenda for their own purposes.[14] The challenges, in Asia as in other non-Western regions, were how successful they were in institutionalizing their undertakings to serve the political interests and survive beyond US assistance.

On November 26, 1952, as the Korean War was underway, Chang sent a memo through Hong Kong representative J. Ivy to the Asia Foundation (originally named the Committee for Free Asia; see chapter 2). Chang requested financial support for setting up a film production company. He had already received funding from TAF since early 1952 to launch the Asia News Agency—which sent news stories to Chinese-language newspapers in Taiwan and Southeast Asia—and the Asia Press, a publishing house that released until its demise in the early 1960s more than three hundred titles (mostly literature and political economy written by émigré non-Communist authors). Asia Press was code-named "Fiction Enterprise"—and Chang became thereby "Fiction" in TAF internal communications. Adding Asia Pictures, combining print and visual media based in British Hong Kong, he urged, would create "a tri-dimensional battle for men's minds" against Communist influences in Asia.[15] On January 8, 1952, he followed with yet another memo, "Motion Picture Project," laying out in more specific detail his grand vision for the film enterprise.

In less than a month, TAF approved it "in principle" because of the importance of Hong Kong as a Chinese-language film production hub in Asia. San Francisco allowed Chang to draw funds from his publishing house account to start the "motion picture project" immediately. "We have high hopes for motion picture work in Hong Kong," J. Stewart, who was in charge of Asian affairs, explained. "If we intend to make an impact on the people of Asia, and more particularly on the overseas Chinese in Southeast Asia, we must pay close attention to films and do all we can to strengthen production of entertaining feature movies of non-Communist and potentially anti-Communist nature."[16] The TAF decision, as a matter of fact, reflected the Truman administration's NSC-48 (1949) directive, "The Position of the United States with Respect to Asia," which, as Kevin Peraino described, championed "extending the concept of containment to China's periphery" and robust support of anticommunism in Southeast Asia. The subsequent State Department USIS plan of 1952 called for stepping up "anti-communist propaganda" targeting overseas Chinese in the region. In fact, the prevailing belief among US psychological warfare officials in the early Cold War was that overseas Chinese were mostly of low literacy and culture levels, which made them particularly receptive to the power of motion pictures and other visual instruments. However, USIS efforts to support film production with a local cast and crew in Singapore and Malaya, for example, had failed to excite the viewing public. Where else would be better than British Hong Kong to produce good-quality films to capture a loyal audience?[17] Chang's request for funding of the motion picture project came at the right time.

Chang requested an initial capitalization of HK$ one million, or at least HK$500,000, an enormous amount of working capital for the émigré film industry at the time. He justified it by claiming, with obvious exaggeration, that Great Wall had received HK$ five million in aid from Beijing that allowed it to produce "the best" films and thereby "has done and is still doing lots of harms to us" in the propaganda war. The claim was clearly overstated. Chang probably thought TAF would be sold on competing with Great Wall. Chang also requested generous funding for publishing an official magazine, *Asia Pictorial* (亞洲畫報), because Great Wall had its *Great Wall Pictorial*— which was "the best-selling one in town and in the Far East"—to bring news of non-Communist cinema to ethnic Chinese communities around the globe, especially Southeast Asia. The objective of Asia Pictures was thus, with greenback support, nothing short of seizing "control over the movieland" from the Communists: "To beat the Great Wall," Chang proclaimed as if he was leading a combat mission. "This is going to be our war cry![18]

He went on to lay out in "Motion Picture Project" his production strategy for winning "men's minds": First, to make as many quality films as possible, because every successful film that came out from Asia Pictures would mean one resounding defeat for the Communists. A constant flow of products, more importantly, would "encourage defection" of talent from pro-Communist studios. Hence, in the first year, he vowed to produce a total of six projects, starting immediately with three. Second, he intended to stay away from "direct attack" of the enemy, but rather to convey the "crusade against Communism" subtly, in "an artistic and entertaining way," so as not to run afoul of colonial censorship or to alienate the emigre audience, which was allegedly "extremely wary of open propaganda." Obviously having in mind the popularity of historical subjects in the patriotic media in Shanghai under Japanese occupation, he proposed making all three new features costume dramas "themed on . . . revolts for freedom." Third and especially important was identifying the studio in the public's mind as a "purely commercial enterprise," independent of any political interests. Hence, its Cold War ideological agenda and connection to TAF had to be kept secret.[19] Grand as it sounded, the proposition was long in making a political statement but short in explaining the business plan. Assuming that Asia Pictures (just as Chang envisioned *Asia Pictorial*) targeted overseas Chinese, especially in the region, the plan said practically nothing about who and where its targeted audiences were and how to market its products to them. The memo also said nothing about whether the new company had the manpower and proper equipment or technological capacities to produce three ambitious films all at once. Politically ambitious as he was, this approach betrayed Chang's lack of film business experiences to navigate the complex and volatile Cold War media environment.

Since it was TAF's first active involvement in the film business in Asia and would involve a huge capital investment, San Francisco took great care in deliberation, bringing together its senior staff and film experts to weigh in on the feasibility and future direction of Asia Pictures. These discussions revealed how the organization assessed the strategic role of the British colony in containing Communist aggression in Asia's cinematic Cold War. Recall that TAF saw Hong Kong as the crossroads between the forces of capitalism and socialism, a production hub linking the universal values of American democracy with the regional battlefield of campaigns for ethnic Chinese sympathies and support. Following this logic, Charles Tanner, TAF's Hollywood liaison, among other senior officers, was enthusiastic about the project. He was frustrated by the failure of the US State Department to provide much-needed film production support for Asian film industries, despite Washington's advocacy of using "audio visual means" to mobilize overseas Chinese against Communist influences, and by the Motion Picture Association of America's lack of interest in collaborating with TAF in making popular anti-Communist pictures for Asian markets. "There is obviously a need for movie production in Hong Kong for non-Communist Chinese," Tanner counseled. "Films made in Hong Kong could and should be distributed to the overseas Chinese as well as in Hong Kong. As has been said many times, the motion pictures is one of the most important media that can be used in Asia."[20] TAF should, therefore, take the leading role in the field. Tanner also agreed with Chang that Asia Pictures, at least at the beginning, aimed to produce the best entertainment, not just overly political propaganda for the audiences, because only if "pro-democratic films [became] more entertaining, thereby bigger at the box office, eventually it's hoped, entertaining enough and big enough in the theater to drive out the commie products."[21] The foundation also sought an opinion from the well-connected San Francisco Grandview Theater owner, the "Chinese Movie Man" S. C. Chang, who, after complaining about the depressing business environment and "shady-fly-by-night producers" in the British colony, expressed optimism that émigré Mandarin filmmakers took "considerably more pride" in their work (in comparison to the "dialect people") and were "better received" in Southeast Asia.[22]

At the same time, the Hong Kong representative submitted an eight-page intelligence survey of the film industry from an unnamed insider, which gives us a detailed perspective of Mandarin cinema at the time. It emphasized that Great Wall after "turning left" let go all of its top talent (especially actress Li Li-Hua) in order to cut overhead expenses and targeted its products to Southeast Asian audiences. It continued to enjoy the largest fan base in the region. With shrinking overseas markets after the golden age of 1950–1952—especially in Indonesia and the Philippines, and the limited, uncertain market access to Taiwan—the expatriate filmmakers were "in doldrums." The viewing public "lost confidence" in their products. In fact, although Hong Kong had more than fifty theater screens, all gave the "best billings on scheduling" to Western and local Cantonese pictures. Completed Mandarin films almost never got "specific dates of showing," and as a result, some were dubbed into Cantonese to get played in theaters. It was thus imperative for non-Communist producers, the report urged, to improve their production values and win back market share, if they wanted to survive and compete with the Communist studios.[23]

In August 1953, San Francisco agreed to allocate a total of $120,000 (roughly the HK$ one million that Chang requested) to support the new venture, which it intended to develop into a "self-sustained business" in two years. This was a huge amount in comparison to the mostly modest subsidies TAF gave to Asian cultural production projects such as *Chinese Student Weekly* and the Union Research Institute or most South Korean print media and film studios. The foundation expressed "high hopes" that this huge injection of capital, as J. Stewart proclaimed, would put out "the best Chinese motion pictures in Asia" and win the war for the hearts and minds of the forty million overseas Chinese.[24] To achieve its political goal, TAF constantly emphasized the crucial business imperative: to send the product to as many theaters across the region as possible. "Distribution is the key to the entire project," TAF repeatedly admonished Chang and his employees in Hong Kong, Japan, and Southeast Asia.[25] TAF also tried to ensure "ideological and financial control" over the expansive cultural war project, as Tokyo representative Delmer Brown explained, by incorporating Asia Pictures as a limited company "with a trustee agreement" that allowed Chang to hold 2,998 of its 3,000 shares in trust for TAF. Chang was the owner of the enterprise only in name, in other word. And unlike with San Francisco's alleged localized, arm's-length approach to its Asia projects, Chang was required to receive approval for each of his projects—from selection of scripts and production planning to completion—before public release.[26] These institutional arrangements created ongoing tension between the foundation and Chang, who, because of his own anti-Communist credentials in Asia and entrepreneurial aspirations, saw himself at least as the equal "partner" in the cultural Cold War enterprise.[27]

"General in the Anti-Communist Force in Asia"

TAF officers in Asia shared high hopes for Asia Pictures to turn a new page in the chapter on Hong Kong's cinematic war, especially since *Asia Pictorial* quickly caught up with its rival, *Great Wall Pictorial*, with a claimed circulation of around sixteen thousand copies each month. However, in about a year, the foundation started to doubt Chang's promise to "beat the Great Wall." He had barely completed only two projects (instead of six as promised), namely *Tradition* (傳統) and *Heroine* (楊娥), and both of them were way over budget and scrambling to schedule limited theatrical releases only in Hong Kong and Taiwan. At the same time, however, while the Shanghai-made Yue opera film *Butterfly Lovers* (梁山伯與祝英台; see chapter 1) dominated the 1954 box office in Hong Kong, with almost half a million viewers, and Singapore and Malaya, Great Wall's family drama *Children Grew Up* (大兒女經), a mediocre sequel to its 1953 top-grossing picture *Raising Children* (兒女經) easily beat *Yang E* in the top-five Mandarin films box-office chart.[28]

What also irked the foundation leadership, as the Korean War moved into a new phase of peace talks, was Chang's refusal to follow its suggestion to make a political drama about Chinese Korean War POWs' rejection of communism on grounds that overtly anti-Communist content would fail to pass censorship in most Asian countries, especially in British Hong Kong—thereby thwarting the studio's future development. Agreeing that the debate about repatriation would be an important propaganda coup nonetheless, he proposed instead to have Asia Press publish a translated book on the armistice and POW controversy, and explore the possibility of making a documentary film—which for unknown reasons did not seem to materialize.[29]

Thanks to the slowness of Asia Pictures' production, ironically, what had originally been created as its official organ, the *Asia Pictorial*, became a monthly current-affairs magazine—and was Chang's greatest contribution in TAF's eyes; *Asia Pictorial*, not his films, gave the strongest expression of Chang's anti-Communist crusade. Its look and style had a strong resemblance to Henry Luce's *LIFE* magazine, which should be no surprise. *LIFE* was the most popular US magazine at the time, and Luce was well known in Asia for his strident anticommunism and tireless support of the Chiang Kai-shek regime. Chang could model *Asia Pictorial* on *LIFE* also because he could afford it, with a TAF subsidy that was, for example, at least twice as much as that for *Chinese Student Weekly*. In 1956, *Asia Pictorial* received HK$13,800 each month, in addition to close to HK $50,000 of "non-recurring subsidy and administrative expenses" for Asia Press's publications (while *CSW* had HK $8,000 to $10,000).[30] Unlike Luce, who tried to publish his magazine for a mass audience cutting across racial and class backgrounds, however, Chang seem to have paid little attention to the business side and focused *Asia Pictorial* on winning over middle-class Chinese émigrés in Hong Kong, Taiwan, and Southeast Asia. With a clean, modern design on high-quality paper that distinguished it from the usually low-budget magazines in the Sinophone world, *Asia Pictorial* published beautiful pictures with minimal text and attracted readers with dazzling color covers featuring pro-Taiwan and Hollywood female stars and socialites. The periodical covered world events, celebrities, cultural information, Western science, and modern life with a blatant free-world slant. Especially indicative of its apocalyptic Cold War messages were many of its multipage "photo essays" on such stories as the plight of Eastern European refugees fleeing from Soviet rule or the happy life of Chinese mainlanders in Nationalist-ruled Taiwan. To attract an audience, similar to its US counterpart, the monthly also carried new stories of the frivolous and the salacious.[31] Boasting a circulation of thirty-five thousand across the region, and particularly popular in Taiwan, *Asia Pictorial* was one of the largest, most successful US weapons (along with *CSW* and *World Today*) in the struggle to attract Chinese in the early Cold War.[32]

Despite the wide circulation of *Asia Pictorial*, the unfulfilled promise of the well-funded Asia Pictures drew concerns about Chang's ability to take on cinematic propaganda warfare in Hong Kong as TAF was beginning to commit capital investment to rebuilding South Korea's cinema.[33] John Miller, the motion picture officer based in Tokyo, for example, expressed doubts whether Chang had the financial and management skills to effectively lead a media company through such a challenging business environment, and especially since he had already stretched himself too thin by taking up many difficult tasks all at once: film producer, book publisher, magazine editor, and news agency journalist. He was commended, however, for his commitment to "break down the old barriers of the old mode of [the] Chinese film production system" in order to catch up with the "world standard" of today and win back the "public's faith." Thus, should the United States be "giving the entire overseas Chinese motion picture industry to the Communists by default," as Miller posed the key dilemma to San Francisco, "or making what may turn out to be a costly effort to save it"?[34] Miller listed eight major problems of Hong Kong's émigré Mandarin cinema that anyone would take time to overcome, including lack of scriptwriters, lack of professional standards, lack of modern film equipment, trade restrictions (e.g., Taiwan's defense taxes riffs and tariffs and Thailand's quotas on imported films), and fluctuating currency rates.

Miller's comments actually pointed up the hidden agenda of Chang's anti-Communist entrepreneurship. Herein lay his fraught relationship with his American sponsor that led to the premature dissolution of the motion picture project. TAF sought to connect the global power conflicts with regional cultural mobilization by way of bolstering Hong Kong's strategic role as a hub of "free-world" film production in Asia. They expected Asia Pictures to produce a steady number of good-quality films with box-office appeal that would compete with and eventually destroy the transnational Communist influence across overseas Chinese communities. As fervent anti-Communist as he was, however, Chang appeared to have different, or a more aspiring, expansive plan for the company.

Among the three debut films Chang had initially proposed to TAF was *Fragrant Imperial Concubine* (香妃). Its original version was produced in Japanese-ruled Shanghai by S. K. Chang (張善琨) to allegedly project patriotic loyalty to Chiang Kai-shek's wartime government in exile (Chongqing). Chang wanted to hire S.K., who had long been lionized as the "king of Chinese cinema," "China's Darryl Zanuck," and a staunch opponent of communism, to produce an updated version of the film for Asia Pictures. Although the proposal did not get through (most likely because the Shanghai version was directed by Zhu Shilin (朱石麟), as mentioned in Chapter 1, now a leader of pro-Beijing cinema), it was clear that Chang was well informed about S.K. Chang's big dreams for creating a "Chinese Hollywood" in postwar Hong Kong.[35] Similarly, in 1954, Chang was appointed by Taiwan to sit on the board of directors overseeing the reorganization of the debt-ridden Yung Hwa, witnessing up close the crumbling of a once-glorious movie empire.[36]

It was indeed Chang's plan to seize the access to capital created by the US anti-Communist crusade to build a giant Hollywood-style film enterprise that would lead the Chinese cinema in exile to a new level of production standards and professionalism. And along the way, he would, just as C. S. Chang and T. Y. Lee had fervently tried to achieve in their careers, become the first producer ever to create a transnational Chinese cinema enjoyed by a worldwide audience, even though Asia Pictures was for the time being just one of the many independents without its own studio facilities and big stars under contract.[37] Thus he emphasized the importance of careful preproduction planning, especially in scriptwriting—and he insisted in sparing no expenses from his US-funded budget to pay good salaries to scriptwriters and have the best sets, costumes, and art designs for his debut projects: *Tradition, Heroine* (reminiscent of Yung Hwa's megabudgeted historical dramas *National Spirit* (國魂) and *Sorrows of the Forbidden City* (清宮秘史). Moreover, according to film journalist and historian Huang Jen, he unsparingly demanded that his cast and crew—from leads to minor technicians alike—observe the professional codes he adapted from Hollywood studios, such as being punctual and respecting directors' ideas on the set, and working only on one project at a time—instead of several, as commonly practiced in the industry.[38]

In a Rotary Club Island East speech of 1956, reprinted in *Asia Pictorial* and the English-language daily *Hong Kong Standard*, Chang cast himself in the leader's role to call on all major studio owners to be vigilant against "Communist threats." The most immediate challenge was, however, to address the lack of professionalism in the émigré film industry in order to avoid "imminent bankruptcy." Foremost among these problems included lack of integrity and punctuality and big stars commanding exorbitant salaries while directors and scriptwriters were "paid slave-like salaries," causing a shortage of good scripts and directors being "bossed around" by the stars on the movie set. He urged all non-Communist producers to join together to create an industry-wide code of ethics.[39]

Chang's high-cost and time-intensive method of production and his "Napoleonic" effort to professionalize émigré cinema raised suspicions and misgivings. "Chang merits the rank of General in the anti-communist force in Asia today," Robert Sheeks, a decorated Marine combat veteran and Kuala Lumpur representative who helped engineer the motion picture project, mocked. "At the present he is a Marine Corps–type General and the Foundation must supplement his leadership with the staff generalship!" The Union Press intellectuals, even half a century later, expressed contempt of Chang acting like a "[film] business tycoon" with a flashy, self-important air.[40]

Comparable with the Best Hollywood Sets

Chang promised to make six films in the first year. But he delivered only eight in five years before Asia Pictures shuttered in 1959. None of them, except the last one, *Three Sisters* (三姐妹, 1958), drew a good-sized audience. Chang refused to hire big female stars with proven box-office records, and invested instead on scripts, veteran directors, and what he called "uncompromising production values." For example, he flaunted in *Asia Pictorial* the long haul of making the period film *Heroine*, with all the meticulously researched sets and expensive costumes in order to re-create the historical environment of late Ming-Qing political intrigues (ca. 1600s–1650s). Moreover, Chang often submitted movie stories to the Nationalist government—as expression of his loyalty to Taiwan as the symbol of Free China in the global anti-Communist struggle as well as his company's key target market—for approval before shooting; all his films also, as noted, were supposedly subjected to reviews by TAF officers before public release. In fact, the first two projects Asia Pictures was planning (one on Sun Yat-sen's kidnapping in London and another S. K. Chang's *Fragrant Imperial Concubine*) were disapproved by Kuomintang officials because of the films' alleged political sensitivity. Similarly TAF had reservations about one of the directors' backgrounds. [41] It changed to *Tradition* and *Heroine* instead (See Figure 3.1).

Tang Huang's (唐煌) *Tradition*, and *Heroine*, directed by Evans Yang (易文) and Hong Shuyun (洪叔雲), were period dramas espousing the cultural ideals of loyalty and heroism. Reminiscent of a "using the past to allegorize the present" strategy (借古喻今), widely employed in Shanghai cinema to call for resistance against Japanese occupation during WWII, the films portray a thinly allegorized past to bring home the message of unremitting support of the exiled Chiang Kai-shek regime's continuous resistance against the "invasion" of "Red Imperialism." In *Heroine*, for example, Yang E (played by Liu Qi [劉琦]), a woman trained in martial arts, is transformed into a woman warrior during the Ming-Qing transition, plotting to assassinate a pro-Manchu general in order to save the Ming Empire. Though she fails, she is projected as a paragon of the virtues of loyalty and self-sacrifice in times of

Figure 3.1 Asia Picture publicity materials for *Tradition*

The Asia Foundation Collection, Box P-171, Hoover Institution Library and Archives, Stanford University

national crisis. An overt pro–Free China stance gave Asia Pictures the honor of holding an "international premier gala" for *Tradition* in Taipei in May 1954, while its actresses entertained the troops in a tour of the island, and being awarded a citation from Chiang Kai-shek honoring *Heroine*'s "morale-boosting" efforts.[42] The reaction from the opposite side of the Cold War divide was swift and harsh. In an internal document available to the local pro-Beijing cinema community, China's Ministry of Culture saw Chang as an enemy, condemning both films as "anti-people and reactionary," and the cultural tradition they claimed to espouse was merely "instruments [they] use to try to maintain [Chiang's] reactionary rule."[43]

It was possible that the colonial government intervened to try to avoid provoking the Communists, as Asia Pictures soon changed the style and message of its productions. There were no more historical subjects and overt pro–Free China expressions. Instead, the five projects after the release of *Heroine* centered around a common theme: how émigrés from the mainland wrestled with the agonizing dilemma of their attachment to home and the all-consuming pressures of adapting to new life in a "foreign land" (*yixiang*). For example, *Life with Grandma* (滿庭芳, 1955) deals with the prevalent problems of intergenerational gaps and changes of parental authority in wealthy émigré families, and *Half-Way Down* (半下流社會, 1955) probes the question of how struggling émigré intellectuals sustained their hope (of returning home to rebuild a new, democratic China or re-migrating to Taiwan) in spite of crushing poverty and all the temptations of urban vices. (Several TAF Hong Kong officers thought *Half-Way Down* "ideologically acceptable" and recommended adding a stronger closing scene to evoke nostalgia for home: showing "a bag carrying some earth from the homeland.")[44]

The most thoughtful of these émigré-themed dramas was *Long Lane*. Directed by Bu Wancang (卜萬蒼)—dubbed "China's Cecil DeMille" in prerevolutionary Shanghai—the evocative cinematography and soulful soundtrack of *Long Lane* bring a delicate touch to a traumatic experience widely discussed in the White Chinese community: orphanage. As many families broke up during the war and the mass flight to Hong Kong, the debate arose as to whether natural parents had the rights to reclaim their lost children now living in their adopted home.[45] In the same vein as MP&GI's song-and-dance classics *Mambo Girl* (曼波女郎, 1957, starring Grace Chang [葛蘭]) and Shaw Brothers' award-winning *Back Entrance* (後門, 1959), directed by Li Han-hsiang, *Long Lane* offered audiences a memorable orphan drama. Set in an unidentified city, it tells the story of a middle-aged couple,

Figure 3.2 The wife looks out to the long lane behind her house hoping her abandoned daughter might reappear.

played by veteran Shanghai actors Wang Yin (王引) and Chen Yanyan (陳 燕燕), who have already had three daughters when the wife gives birth to another girl. Worried that her husband would divorce her due to the patriarchal tradition, she secretly abandons the newborn girl near their house and picks up instead a baby boy from an orphanage. Many years have passed, and while all three daughters are filial and well educated, the boy, played brilliantly by future martial arts film auteur King Hu (胡金銓), has become a rascal, which deepens the wife's secret guilt. Every night she stands at the balcony for hours looking out on the long lane below and hoping somehow their daughter might reappear. The wife eventually confesses to her husband, entreating him toing the abandoned girl back (See Figure 3.2).

After roaming around for days in search of the girl, he collapses cold and exhausted near a house. When he wakes up, he realizes that he has been taken inside by no one but their lost daughter, now living in harmony with a woman she lovingly calls "Mother." In the next cross cut the audience sees both women chatting merrily in the kitchen, while the old man in the living room hesitates over whether he should reveal the girl's true identity and thereby destroy her happy adopted family (See Figure 3.3). He quickly leaves the house. The camera lingers behind him as he walks, slowly and forlornly, back home. He can't bring their lost girl back, yet his heart is somewhat at ease, knowing that "our daughter is safe and living well!" The old, ambivalent feeling of loss is underscored by the pensive music that plays under the concluding credits.[46] (See Figure 3.4)

Figure 3.3 The old man is shocked to see the close and happy (adopted) mother-daughter relationship.

Figure 3.4 The father decides not to take away the happiness of his daughter one more time by revealing her identity and, accompanied by the melancholy soundtrack, walks back home alone.

"Asia Pictures has since its founding made one expensive picture after another," a Hong Kong–based Nationalist journalist lamented. "It has consistently been losing money."[47] Featuring stars long past their prime or young actors lesser known to the public, and (except for *Long Lane*) with weak, inefficient plot development, Chang's projects lacked the entertainment values to draw audience to theaters. Learning the film-making business as he went along, and insistently enforcing professional behavior on the movie set (which antagonized several popular role actors), he knew he "could not hope to produce films all so well-received by the public."[48] However, he was confident that, with his loyalty to the Chiang government (as TAF officer L. Z. Yuen described euphemistically his political outlook, "narrow-minded as far as Taiwan is concerned"[49]), by capitalizing on TAF resources and acquiring the best new film technology, he could, sooner or later, break into new markets and build a Hong Kong–based Hollywood-style transnational Chinese film enterprise. It would serve both the cause of Free China in the anti-Communist propaganda warfare and the long-cherished dream of bringing Chinese films to a global audience. This explained why Chang continued to devote big budgets to sets and props (including, for the first time in Hong Kong, building an expensive *Half-Way Down* set in the refugee squatter slump in Diamond Hill), and constantly asked TAF for support of Asia Pictures' modernizing efforts in purchasing up-to-date cameras and recording and lighting equipment. For example, the company boasted a Mitchell BNC 35mm camera and a Westrex sound unit, both available for the first time in Hong Kong, as well as funding, also for the first time in the industry, for a special office for scriptwriting.[50] Chang also asked—on the strength of Hollywood personages Frank Borzage and Luigi Luraschi, whom he met at the Asian Film Festival—about sponsoring a visit of a Hollywood special-effects technician to help give an innovative edge in production values over pro-Beijing "Patriotic" cinema.[51]

At a time of enthusiasm in the Mandarin film industry for "opening the international market" and co-production, Great Wall executive Yuan Yangan (袁仰安) was widely rumored to be taking a trip to Europe to explore market opportunities and talk with Rank Corporation about showing films in China.[52] Chang tried to get TAF assistance, John Miller wrote to San Francisco, "putting him in touch with US distributors." The Tokyo-based officer reviewed *Heroine* and thought, while "not up to Hollywood standard" in narrative style and technology, its sets and props were "comparable with the best Hollywood sets." As an "Oriental product" its story was easily understood, and it was a disruption of the émigré film industry, "containing a 700 feet dream sequence in Eastman color." He went on to add a comment on the female lead, Liu Qi, rife with orientalist and sexist bias: for example, she had "more sex appeal than Anna May Wong during her best days." Thus, Miller recommended support of Chang's idea to distribute *Heroine* to the art house circuit as well as to US television networks.[53]

Chang Was "So Damned Good," But ...

Chang's trans-Pacific plan drew sharp opposition from Charles Tanner, TAF-Hollywood liaison, who articulated the TAF leadership's hardline strategy of aggressively containing communism within Asia. Tanner reiterated the TAF policy of sponsoring Asia Pictures for the sole purpose of strengthening the "anti-Communist voice in Chinese-language filming" so that it could "reach successfully the large mass of Chinese film goers" in Southeast Asia. Chang's mission was to produce more films to draw audiences away from the Communists, not to gain American market share or to "change the motion picture industry in Hong Kong." Leery of his unfulfilled promise and attendant logistical problems, Tanner wrote off the special effects assistance request altogether.[54]

Along the same vein, possibly wary of Chang's entrepreneurial agenda, Ivy was skeptical of *Heroine* going to America and opposed the idea of funding a Hollywood special-effects expert for Hong Kong. Ivy told San Francisco that Chang's immediate task was to strengthen his studio's financial management and develop a "definite program outline" in order to produce more and better pictures for overseas Chinese. But on the ground, Ivy was keenly aware of Great Wall's dominant presence and acceded to the importance of gaining a technical edge over the Communists. He recommended, instead, "taking advantage of other Asian technical advice." Ivy proposed sending Chang's crew to Japan for short-term training.[55]

Japan was Washington's most important ally in what international relations scholar G. John Ikenberry calls the American-centered anti-Communist postwar order in Asia. To combat Communist influences in the region, the United States provided Japan and other Asian allies with access to the American market, technology, and resources in exchange for their diplomatic and geopolitical support. Thus, especially after the onset of the Korean War, the United States aided in Japan's rapid economic reconstruction and helped expand its markets for exports (especially to Southeast Asia).[56] Just as the United States and Japan signed the San Francisco Bay Accord, which formally ended the postwar occupation, Japan's became the first Asian film industry to win big prizes at Venice. The success of *Rashomon* on the world stage, as film historian Michael Bassett documented, became "a model for emerging Asian nations" that sought to modernize and transnationalize their motion picture businesses.[57] In Hong Kong, for example, taking advantage of his personal connections to Japanese studio head Kawakita Nagamas, S. K. Chang took the lead in the mid-1950s to make a string of films in Japan with technical assistance (especially in color cinematography) from Towa Studio.[58]

According to the Tokyo-based US film journal *Far East Film News*, American Westrex executive Miles Goldrick suggested to Nagata Masaichi, producer of *Rashomon*, that it was time that the "Pacific War be forgotten" and "trade channels be reestablished" in the region.[59] Aiming to expand the market in the Southeast Asia, which had been part of the wartime Japanese "Greater East Asian Co-Prosperity Sphere," Nagata started the Federation of Southeast Asian Film Producers in 1953 in Manila and held out promises of technology transfer, technical support, and friendly exchange. The federation drew a clear ideological line by promoting unity and cooperation among non-Communist industry leaders. Indeed, it allowed membership only to US allies (the first group was Hong Kong, Japan, Malaya, the Philippines, Singapore, Taiwan, and Thailand) with strong national producers' associations. One of the strong advocates of Nagata's endeavor was Run Run Shaw (representing Malaya), known as a businessman "interested only in money," who quickly took advantage of the exchange relations to arrange for Nagata to bring along his new film equipment to shoot another Venice-bound spectacle, *Princess Yang Kwei Fei*, in S&S studio facilities, while sending the S&S film *New Madam Butterfly* (*Xin Hudie furen*) crew for on-site practice in the Daiei Studio (see chapter 4).[60]

At the start, TAF, like the Ford Foundation—which donated a coveted 16mm Mitchell camera for one of the film festival prizes—had high hopes for the Federation of Southeast Asian Film Producers, hoping that through cooperation and exchange its annual film festival would showcase the "ideological victory" of Free Asian cinema.[61] TAF actively involved in promoting and facilitating Nagata's transregional endeavor. The comity it hoped for, however, was not realized. In the context of decolonizing nationalism, postcolonial nation-building, business rivalry, and the history of Japan's pan-Asianist ideology and militarism in the region, the federation, as TAF representative Robert Grey described to San Francisco, quickly became "essentially a paper organization." Some member nations were suspicious of it as merely a springboard for Hollywood's expansion into Asia, and others demurred and began to challenge Japan's predominance.[62] As a matter of fact, Japan had snatched all the major prizes since the First Asian Film Festival in Tokyo (as a means, in their view, to gain market advantage), and Taiwan's cultural officials and Chinese-language film industry leaders were upset with Nagata's repeated disparaging remarks on the "backwardness" of Chinese products at the third festival in Hong Kong, which brought to mind the Japanese domination of China during World War II. Together, as Nationalist-affiliated studio executive Sha Yong-fong (沙榮峰) revealed, all ethnic Chinese film producers conspired to vote for each other's nominees at the expanse of Japan's.[63]

In 1954, TAF officers in Hong Kong and Taiwan were trying to promote the Mandarin film industry's cooperation and trade with Japan (buying films and film equipment) and facilitate the industry's participation in the Asian Film Festival. It was thus natural that Ivy turned to Japan for Asia Pictures' production upgrade. Chang, more than any Hong Kong studio head, was flamboyantly active in the Asian Film Festival. Cosmopolitan and fluent in English, he easily connected with film personages and business leaders who came to appreciate his energy and devotion to his cause. For example, he met two-time Oscar-winning director Frank Borzage (best known to Asian audiences for his *Seventh Sky*[64]) and Luigi Luraschi, the CIA-affiliated head of Paramount Pictures' foreign and domestic censorship, at the film festival. The two Hollywood "guests of honor" were impressed by Chang's efforts to beat Great Wall and offered him advice on creating an overseas film market, including getting a Hollywood special-effects artist.[65] Similarly, Chang was praised by Hollywood director William Seiter, who spent two months in Hong Kong in mid-1956 as a TAF consultant to the émigré film industry, for sole responsibility for the success of the Third Asian Film Festival.[66] As the festival executive secretary, Chang claimed that he also played a key lobbying role that helped make South Korea a full-fledged federation member, and in return, he landed a co-production deal with a Korean studio that would create new markets for the two Asian partners.[67]

Chang's leadership role in the Asian Film Festival did not divert TAF's pivot in its approach to the cinematic war in Asia. For one, while insisting on Japan's central role in "inter-Asian cooperation," TAF increasingly scaled down its work with the federation. In Hong Kong, at the same time, TAF took steps to phase out involvement in the Mandarin film industry, starting with discontinuing support of the "tri-dimensional" project.

TAF was unhappy with what they considered Chang's management problems and inefficiency in production. As early as 1954, some senior officials showed concern over Chang's problems with business finance. "What happens to the money which will come in from *Chuantong* and *Yang Er* and the other films as they are produced and released?" Charles Tanner questioned, for example, "We should know what plans have been drawn up concerning the income from Asia Pictures' films."[68] They also stopped support of one prong of Chang's tri-dimensional project—Asian News Service—because of its high price tag and uncertain benefits. The news service had a large staff, with unclear division of work, consisting of journalists who had recently fled from China. San Francisco was "conscious of his faults but he was so damned good—honest, sincere." Stewart discussed Chang with Ivy when they met in Hong Kong in August 1954 to review the programs. "Now we must urge him to prove effectiveness of his current staff." And they decided on "taking a firm stand with Fiction on his activities. . . . Take a firm line on budgetary matters."[69] They trusted Chang because of his ideological commitment. With his journalistic skills, he served also what can be considered a casual spy for the foundation. A detailed account of Burma and neighboring nations that he wrote for TAF in the mid-1950s—in which he detailed Beijing's ways of "instilling fear into the minds" of overseas Chinese and urged the United States to tighten its ideological and military grip in the region—was widely praised throughout the organization.[70] But the TAF officials were at the same time wary and dismayed by his independent streak and his penchant for doing things his own way, especially with regard to budgets and financial management. For example, Asia Pictures had a small studio on Hammer Hill Road, adjoining Yung Hwa (now under Cathay's management), with TAF subsidies. Chang furtively kept plowing earnings from his films back to expand the space and production facilities.[71] But this was precisely what Chang's anti-Communist entrepreneurship was about: he tried to capitalize on US Cold War funding and resources to fight the common enemy on the cultural front, while also dreaming of building a transnational Chinese film empire of his own in Hong Kong.

TAF representatives were also annoyed by Chang's troubling relationship with another of their major combat groups in Asia's cultural Cold War. As discussed in the previous chapter, Chang accused the Union Press group as holding a third-force line of anti-Nationalist rule and thereby betraying the US Cold War policy. "Some people still have to use Taiwan as an object of blame," he fumed, "out of their psychological necessity."[72] The young émigrés, on the other hand, complained about his flashy, arrogant, and domineering behavior. This mutual recrimination came out into the open in Rangoon,

Burma, when Chang and Maria Yen, both by TAF invitation, attended the CIA-funded Congress for Cultural Freedom meeting. Chang introduced himself as an "ambassador of Free Chinese culture" and blasted his Union Press colleagues everywhere he went. "Kuo-sin must act as big brother to the Union Press," Ivy slammed, at a time when infighting between émigré groups was rampant as a result of economic difficulties in Hong Kong.[73] Other officers sympathized with the young émigré intellectuals and thought Chang overly "narrow-minded" about the Nationalist regime in Taiwan. His criticism "weaken[ed] the contribution of our anti-Communist focus." Sheeks of Kuala Lumpur urged, "The fight has to be carried out by everyone who can be enlisted."[74]

A Partner in a Joint Enterprise for a Common Goal

On the heels of the Geneva Conference of 1954 and the Bandung Conference of 1955, US cultural officials and opinion leaders sounded alarms about the power of the "charm offensive" unleashed by Beijing in Asia. The phenomenal success in 1954 of the Shanghai-made opera film *Butterfly Lovers*, they pointed out, had brought a surge of pro-Communist nationalism in Asia's Sinophone communities.[75] "Commie 'Come Hither' to Industry," declared a headline in the influential *Far East Film News* in June 1956. It warned, in a feature titled "Communists Initiate Rapprochement with Movie-Makers of the Free World," that a campaign was underway in Japan to force studios to join the "Japan–Red China Fair" (a counterweight to the Asian Film Festival) to be held in Shanghai, and that "numerous cultural missions" from Southeast Asian countries were traveling to "Red China." Even Hollywood mogul Spyros Skouras planned to take a "look-see" trip to the Soviet Union.[76]

In this atmosphere, US information officers pressed for more Chinese-language visual media to win the support of overseas Chinese in Asia. However, despite its promise to "beat the Great Wall," Asia Pictures produced no more than two films a year, and none of them, as noted, did particularly well at the box office. In comparison, Great Wall and Phoenix released seventeen films in 1957 and eighteen the following year, many of them popular in Hong Kong as well as in Southeast Asia. Similarly, China rode on the opera film craze overseas to release *Marriage of the Fairy Princess* (天仙配) in 1956 and *Love in Academy* (搜書院) in 1957. Both attracted audiences in the millions across the region.[77] No wonder that TAF officers expressed deep concerns that the Communists were about "to squeeze out all non-Communist producers in Hong Kong" if they failed to bring up quality and increase production.[78] This seemed to be borne out by an intelligence account that concluded that "a great number" of actors and technicians switched sides because the "market of the rightist pictures became narrower every day."[79] Representative Robert Grey added to the sense of urgency in his memo to San Francisco that many highly skilled Hong Kong film technicians were promised a stable livelihood by the Communists if they would move north to join the Pearl River studio (founded in 1956) in Guangzhou, which was said to target the diaspora markets in Southeast Asia. This loss, he bemoaned, would further "cripple the local 'Free World' industry."[80]

In order to combat what they saw as the "danger of Communist domination" in the film industry, TAF set out grudgingly to take the matter into its own hands. We "provide the service of an experienced producer—a consultant to Free World producers," it announced, "to bring about the most constructive development of the industry in line with Free World objectives."[81] Apparently drawing from one of director William Seiter's recommendations, who believed that "Free World producers studios in Hong Kong needed to unite into a coherent front" to challenge the stronger, much better-organized Beijing-backed studios, TAF sought in 1956 to bring all non-Communist movie companies together to form the Association of Motion Picture Producers and Distributors (along the lines of the Motion Picture Promotional Corporation of Japan). TAF's objective was to help the émigré industry "restore confidence" by way of, among other tactics, reforming its "poor management" and providing models of "constructive standards."[82] These constituted, however, a mission impossible.

It was no secret that the postwar film business was like a war of fierce rivalries and cutthroat competition, where every studio and distributor, big or small, struggled to get ahead or just survive at each other's expense. Especially that TAF would not move forward with the initiative for fear of attacks of imperialist intervention, and the only person they could trust to take it up was Chang. However, he was in every sense an outsider, on the fringe of the film world. A self-made college graduate, a well-respected journalist with bilingual and bicultural skills, as film critic Huang Jen explained, he rarely socialized or mingled with people of the émigré film community, especially the business types. His proclaimed efforts as a US-sponsored studio head with no prior filmmaking background to reform and modernize the Mandarin industry along Hollywood standards raised suspicion

and ruffled many feathers—including of some actors who were fined for
being late to work. He made enemies in both camps. Indeed, contrary to his
high-profile involvement in the Asian Film Festival, Chang was not active
in the Nationalist-backed Hong Kong and Kowloon Free Film and Theater
Federation, nor did he take part in either the 1953 or 1954 Hong Kong "Free"
filmmakers' loyalty-pledging trips to Taiwan in celebration of Chiang Kai-
shek's birthday (see chapter 1). Instead, as noted, he took the *Heroine* cast
to the island-state, separately, in 1954 to celebrate Chiang's reelection to the
presidency.[83] The association of producers and distributors, not surprisingly,
came to nothing.

TAF did not take long in slashing aid to Asia Pictures. In the summer
of 1957, Hong Kong staffer L. Z. Yuen brought the budget news to Chang
in his Hammer Hill Road studio, which now boasted a sound stage and a
makeup room. Yuen discovered that an American Lux soap commercial was
in production and a 16mm animated short for USIS publicity was in preparation. Yuen told Chang that TAF from now on would cut the budget for all
the administrative and overhead expenses, and would finance no more than
50 percent of each new project, to the maximum of ten thousand dollars.
Also important was that all future earnings needed to be put into production,
not used for the studio's expansion. "I am not an agent implementing an enterprise for the foundation," Chang fumed, "but a partner in a joint enterprise
for a common goal!" The anti-Communist entrepreneur also revealed his ongoing plan for a co-production with Korea, as mentioned earlier, and to seek
collaboration with Hollywood on a "super-colossal production" about Qin
Shi Huangdi as a camouflaged attack of Mao's communism. The foundation
"won't support" them, Yuen flatly replied.[84]

TAF used the money saved to create a Motion Picture Production Fund.
The foundation claimed to have "acquired sufficient experiences" now to give
out funds "with good effects" to pro–Free World producers, who would otherwise have to turn to "Communist agencies" for loans and make "political
concessions."[85] As far as we can see, the Hong Kong office gave out only one
modest grant—of ten thousand dollars (in the form of an eighteen-month
loan with no interest—before it ceased functioning. The loan was to support
the production of *A Poor Child* (*Kuer liulang ji*) by the revered White Chinese
journalist Zhu Xuhua's [朱旭華] Kuo Phone Company [國風]. Adapted from
the French classic *San Famille*, the film had an impressive Shanghai emigre
cast that included the former Chinese movie queen Hu Die (胡蝶) and child
prodigy Josephine Siao (蕭芳芳), who won the Asia Festival Best Child Star

award in 1956 (and went on to become a Hong Kong film legend), and was shot in part in Japan, for its similarity to northeast China. Just like *Long Lane*, *A Poor Child* focuses on the problems of orphanage, except that it uses the orphan figure as also a political symbol to project the plight and determination of Chinese exiles from communism to reunite with their "Motherland." The film was distributed to Southeast Asia, but it lost money. The TAF cancelled Zhu's debt after the film was exhibited at the 1960 San Francisco Film Festival to showcase US support of the global anti-Communist crusade. Meanwhile, TAF around this time gave Chang full ownership of Asia Pictures, which was no longer functioning as a production company.[86] This brought to a close TAF's active Cold War campaign to politicize Hong Kong's film industry as well as the brief and yet significant history of Asia Pictures.[87]

The significance of Asia Pictures lies in Chang's attempt to leverage US Cold War intervention to build a transnational Chinese film enterprise in Hong Kong. Asia Pictures aspired to increase market share in Southeast Asia and reach audiences across the Pacific. Even after he lost American assistance, Chang continued to seek support for his ambitious *Qin Shi Huangdi* (秦始皇) project in the 1960s. He pleaded with the Nationalist regime for financial support. "Taiwan trusts Chang Kuo-sin's steadfast loyalty, and trusts his commitment to fight Communism and the Soviets," a Hong Kong–based Nationalist media officer sympathized. "But as poor as our government, it had no way to finance the picture and helped fulfill his cinematic dream."[88] Anti-Communist entrepreneur that he was, Chang insisted on investing as much capital and time as he could in each film project he made, in defiance of TAF's political needs. He promoted higher standards of professionalism and the importance of scripts at the risk of antagonizing many in the film community. However, his lack of filmmaking experience, business savviness, and stature in the émigré film world thwarted his efforts and made his Asia Pictures an abortive dream.

Similarly, the situation begged questions as to why TAF would trust someone as inexperienced in film production and unfamiliar with business management as Chang, other than his long-proved anti-Communist ardor, to take up arms to "beat the Great Wall." With most of its field staff lacking filmmaking experience, TAF was also—perhaps reflective of larger US policy toward China and Asia in the twentieth century—inconsistent and unrealistic in its dealing with Asia Pictures. It stopped support at the moment when Chang began to produce a film, *Three Sisters*, that ended up with box-office success in Hong Kong and Taiwan; moreover, he was in the middle of making a co-production deal with Korea due to his active role in the Asian Film Festival—just what TAF had been trying all along to achieve in Asia's cultural Cold War. These questions about TAF's investment in Chang's film enterprise need to be considered, nevertheless, in the broader context of the geopolitical uncertainty and industrial crisis of the émigré Mandarin cinema. In retrospect, with its capital investment, TAF played a trailblazing role in funding new film technology, promoting transregional marketing, and facilitating inter–Free Asian media cooperation—centering on Japan—that helped prepare the ground for British Hong Kong to become over the next two decades the regional hub of Chinese-language filmmaking and cultural production, when the Shaw Brothers took center stage.

4

Making "China" in Hong Kong

The Shaw Brothers' Movietown

The Shaw Brothers showed all kinds of movies without discrimina-
tion provided they are entertaining and acceptable to the censors of
the country [where] they're distributed.

William Goodwin[1]

I make movies only for entertainment—never politics.

Run Run Shaw[2]

It was very abstract, not because of blood relationship or land but
rather an ambiguous cultural concept. It was like a dream. . . . It was a
holistic Chinese influences.

Ang Lee[3]

It is a well-told story of how Hong Kong emerged from the postwar trade
embargo crisis to become an "economic miracle" in the 1960s. Similarly, its
film industry came off a series of crises to develop into a production hub
of Chinese-language motion pictures distributed to audiences around the
globe. Martial arts film auteur Chang Cheh (張徹), in his memoir, attributed
the emergence of the popularly dubbed "Hollywood of the East" to the business acumen and global vision of Sir Run Run Shaw (邵逸夫), arguably the
most celebrated cultural entrepreneur in the Chinese-speaking world of the
twentieth century. This "Great Man" theory, augmented by the media legend's
longevity—he lived to the age of 106—and much-celebrated philanthropy—
there is, for example, at least one Shaw Building on every university campus
in China and Hong Kong—has considerably shaped the prevalent narrative
of the history and cultural politics of Hong Kong media.

While no one can deny the extraordinary role that Run Run Shaw and his
"Movietown" occupied in the transformation of Chinese-language cinema,
this chapter suggests a complementary perspective that brings to light the

Hong Kong Media and Asia's Cold War. Po-Shek Fu, Oxford University Press. © Oxford University Press 2023.
DOI: 10.1093/oso/9780190073763.003.0004

contextual role the global Cold War played in the development of the Shaw brothers' film business empire. Based in Hong Kong, it ushered in what was to become a golden age of Mandarin cinema, yet, significantly, more than 90 percent of the people there had Cantonese as their first language. Indeed, Shaw Brothers was entangled in the émigré culture and politics of overseas Chinese markets that were at the forefront of Asia's cultural Cold War. Indeed, the global struggle between capitalism and communism for the hearts and minds of the Chinese diaspora had helped shape a Cold War media environment that included not just political suppression and ideological conflicts, as were commonly assumed, but also, among others, the lure of an open world economy, new supply chains, increased business competition and production, technology transfer and new technical innovation, increased production and profits, movement of ideas and talents, and various coproduction opportunities related to the Asian Film Festival.

In 1957, after building, with his brother, Runme (邵仁枚), a sprawling exhibition business in Southeast Asia, Run Run Shaw came to Hong Kong to reorganize the family's weak film production business. He seized many of the opportunities created by the Cold War media environment to expand the Shaw Brothers entertainment empire to such that its "SB" shield trademark became synonymous with show business in the everyday culture of this worldwide niche market: Chinese-speaking communities around the globe. Among the studio's best and most influential ones are those here: *Love Eterne* (梁山波與祝英台, 1962), *Come Drink with Me* (大醉俠, 1966), and *One-Armed Swordsman* (獨臂刀, 1967). All were historical films and huge box-office successes. The first two started the popular trend of Huangmei opera dramas; the third, the genre of so-called new-styled martial arts films.

Building on the rich literature on the Shaw Brothers, in addition to old magazines and archival materials, this chapter maps out Asia's Cold War media culture environment in the 1950s and 1960s, and the ways in which Run Run Shaw grappled and negotiated with it. The main strategy he embraced was to deemphasize the political in his culture making. He stated that he produced films to make money, creating popular entertainment to satisfy Chinese audiences' emotions and fantasies. His historical films of Zhongguowei (中國味; "Chinese flavors") whether in Huangmei music or in martial arts swordfighting, married cutting-edge Western technology and traditional Confucian values. Zhongguowei celebrated a pan-Chinese cultural nationalism at its front and center, an invented tradition, a shared idealized past, and a deterritorialized common heritage that brought ethnic Chinese to theaters for nostalgic solace.

Viewed historically, these were actually old strategies in a new geopolitical context. Shaw Brothers had its origin as a family enterprise in Shanghai in the 1920s and had developed determinedly through years of civil wars, foreign invasions, cultural crises, migration, and displacement as it moved its base to Hong Kong and Singapore and then back to Hong Kong. The family enterprise changed and expanded along the way into film distribution and exhibition. These travails had become an important part of the family business tradition and strategic outlook, shaping and inspiring continuously Shaw Brothers' depoliticized entertainment strategies and business goal in the Cold War environment. It is in the layering of diachronic and synchronic influences that we can gain a deeper and more nuanced understanding of the Shaw empire and Asia's cultural Cold War.[4]

The Rise of a Transnational Family Entertainment Business

The famous Warner Brothers–esque "SB" trademark that appeared in every Shaw Brothers picture dominated Chinese-language show business in the 1960s and 1970s. The studio started in Shanghai as the Tianyi, or Number One (天一) studio. Founded in 1925 by four Ningbo-born Shaw (Shao) brothers—Runjie (邵醉翁), Runde (邵邨人), Runme (仁枚), and Run Run (邵仁楞, more popularly known as Yifu)—Tianyi was a traditional family business, emphasizing hierarchy, a strong work ethic, and family management. While the eldest brother was the business leader making all decisions for the company—and the company's director—as film scholar Zhou Chengren described, "Each brother manages a different department. . . . Second brother Runde was the financial controller; third brother Runme and sixth brother Run Run were responsible for distribution . . . at home and overseas. The brothers coordinated their efforts in administration, while their talents were also given full display."[5]

Runjie Shaw was a shrewd businessman and a keen observer of box-office trends. He believed in making movies to make money, and movies appealed to people because they opened into a surprising and interesting world that they could also relate to their everyday lives. This pragmatism, profit motive, and emphasis on making what the audiences desired set the tone of Tianyi's production strategy and came to influence all the brothers' approach to filmmaking. In fact, even after some fifty years, Run Run Shaw would share this family business secret with American film director Hubert Niogret: "Audiences' tastes change all the times. However, all these changes do not go beyond a certain parameter."[6] The parameter he referred to was the customs and cultural values that came to constitute what popularly considered Chineseness (more later).

In the mid-1920s, when China was wracked by endless violence and social and cultural turmoil, Tianyi tried to distinguish its production strategy from other major Shanghai studios, which, echoing the May Fourth New Culture movement, defined their missions as modernizing the country and enlightening its people. Instead, the Shaw brothers claimed to bolster Chinese identity by promulgating the Confucian cultural tradition and "long-cherished ethical relationships" (固有倫理). To counter what they called a prevailing "Europeanization," they turned to folklore, traditional literature, myth, and unofficial history that had long been familiar to the urbanites. Some of them, such as *Liang Shanbo and Zhu Yingtai* (梁祝痛史, 1926), *Madame White Snake* (白蛇傳, 1927), and *Loyalty, Filial Piety, Chastity, and Virtues* (忠孝節義, 1926) were box-office sensations.[7] Shaw Brothers was also one of the first studios to dazzle audiences with the visual spectacle and physical skills of the female knight-errant (女俠) in the first wave of the martial arts film craze in 1927–1931. The woman warrior in *Lee Fei-Fei the Heroine* (女俠李飛飛, 1925) projects images of gender ambivalence (refashioned and remolded in Shaw Brothers' films of the 1960s as shown later): while she equals her male counterparts in spectacular power and valence, she fights to maintain the Confucian ideal of female chastity.[8]

Tianyi's rapid ascendency and backward-looking ideology, along with Runjie's allegedly hard-driving style, created many enemies in the industry, including notably the giant film companies Mingxing (明星) and Minxin (民新), which in response to the competition conspired to blockade Tianyi from lucrative overseas markets. In order to beat the rivals, in 1928 Runme ventured out to explore a new market in Singapore-Malaya, joined soon after by Run Run. This decision turned out inadvertently to change forever the fortunes of the Shaw family enterprise and Hong Kong film culture.

The two brothers initially encountered great difficulties in making entry into the Southeast Asian business world. Coming from Shanghai, they did not have the support of *tongxiang* (hometown) connections that was instrumental in forming business relationships in the Chinese diasporic communities, where most people were Cantonese or Hokkiens. They were not strangers to the adversity of migration. With their experiences as Ningbo migrants in Shanghai, they were quick to embrace what some scholars described as overseas Chinese traders' spirit of "adaptability," the emphasis on "inner resilience and a high level of family and clan solidarity."[9] Trying to reach audiences scattered all over the territory on their own, as the family lore went, they had to drive through many small towns surrounding Ipoh or Penang or Kuala Lumpur to set up film projectors in open areas to show Tianyi films. "There were no theaters there, and many of the Chinese workers were poor migrants working in tin mines or logging camps in re-mote places," Run Run Shaw told a group of young journalists many years later. "They couldn't go to the movies. So we took films to them." While these grueling experiences came to forge a corporate myth of "firm deter-mination" and "pioneering spirit," he recalled that his work as a traveling projectionist in close proximity to audiences had trained him to become es-pecially perceptive of what the market trend would be.[10] Run Run Shaw had an important advantage over many migrant businessmen in a colonial so-ciety, though: his English skills to deal with the colonial authority and non-Chinese businessmen, which he acquired at the Shanghai YMCA School. In fact, despite the initial handicap, the two Shaw brothers gradually developed boundary-crossing business connections and went on to build a circuit of over thirty movie houses and entertainment parks (which housed, among other entertainments, magic shows, Chinese operas, and Bansawan stages) around the Strait Settlement before the Second World War. Surely, this rapid development was due in no small part, as scholar S. Said documented about 1920s Indonesia, to the huge demands of overseas Chinese for movies that allayed their homesickness, and to the success of Tianyi's new Cantonese production strategy.[11]

In 1933, Tianyi released the first sound film in Cantonese, a movie ver-sion of the hugely popular Cantonese opera *Platinum Dragon* (白金龍). The film became an instant box-office sensation in the pan-Cantonese communities, especially across Southeast Asia. It was quickly followed by a string of Cantonese opera films; all brought in huge profits. The Shaw family decided to set up a production facility in Hong Kong to focus on making Cantonese films for the diapsoric markets. In 1936, after much family debate, Runde came to replace Runjie (whose aggressive business dealings caused criminal retaliation from other studio owners) to take charge of the Hong Kong production facility and later reorganized it as South Ocean (南洋, that is, Southeast Asia) to reflect its business strategy.[12] With Hong Kong serving as a connecting point in the supply chain of motion pictures and other entertainment business needs (such as dancing hall equipment and opera costumes from Shanghai and Guangzhou), Runme and Run Run continued to expand their theater chain and accumulate capital throughout the 1930s. Similarly, Runde depended on Singapore-Malaya for the steady cash flow and distribution circuit to produce films. Thus, thanks to their pragmatism, business flexibility, and relentless drive, the Shaw brothers took advantage of the British colonial trading ports and shipping routes, and overseas Chinese communities that linked Hong Kong and Southeast Asia, to build a transnational cultural enterprise.

From World War to Cold War

The Second World War struck a heavy blow to the Shaw businesses. It also brought to light the Shaw brothers' earlier pragmatic and flexible response to a political crisis.

On the eve of Singapore's fall, they made a plea to the overseas Chinese community highlighting the family enterprise's patriotic commitment. They emphasized to the press that they had shown a large number of "anti-Japanese films" and Nationalist newsreels, despite British and French censorship and transportation problems, in their theaters across Southeast Asia. They also, in addition to donating tens of thousands of dollars to the cause, while continuing business with all of their movie theaters, dance halls, and entertainment parks, made them available for free to local community organizations and patriotic groups as well as propaganda troupes from Shanghai, Wuhan and the likes to raise fund and rally support for the Chinese War of Resistance.[13] After the outbreak of the Pacific War, many of the Shaw brothers' properties (along with the Nanyang studio in Hong Kong) were seized by the Japanese army.[14] Probably trying to limit their losses, however, according to scholar Michael Baskett, the brothers also provided assistance to enable the enemy to "break into the film markets of Southeast Asia."[15]

While further research is needed to unravel the Shaw brothers' experiences under Japanese rule, they emerged from the Allied victory as big winners. Thanks to the postwar surge of demand for entertainment and their investments in rubber and tin, which saw a spike in global price, the Shaw family was flooded with cash.[16] Their businesses and investments greatly diversified and expanded exponentially as a result. By the late 1950s, according to *Far East Film News*, under the banner of the Shaw Organization

(邵氏機構), Runme and Run Run owned or controlled across Southeast Asia, among other places, 127 theaters, a chain of eight amusement parks and many nightclubs; a printing press (Shaw Printing Works) that published four film magazines in Chinese, English, Malay and Hindi that "circulated in nearly every town and city in Southeast Asia"; huge swaths of real estate and assorted other financial interests; a Malay film studio boasting new equipment acquired from Hong Kong and a stellar assembly of top Indian directors and Malay actors, whom Hollywood magnate Spyros Skouras felt obliged to visit during his business trip to Asia; and one of the world's largest film distribution companies, representing such global powerhouses as MGM and British Lions.[17]

Over the years of their rapid expansion, the Shaw brothers became known for their diplomatic skills and their apolitical pursuit of profits. For example, they never hid, if not openly broadcasted, their desires to squeeze as much money as possible out of their theater chains. They were said to put on movies of all kinds without regard to their political or social contents, "provided they are entertaining and acceptable to the censors of the country [where] they're distribute," mocked an American journalist.[18] Intelligence from the Asia Foundation (TAF) also revealed that the brothers made loans to small production companies (mostly in the form of pre-sales) in Hong Kong with interest rates as high as 18 percent. It was no surprise that the Kuala Lumpur representative Delmer Brown, frustrated with their distributing both pro–Free China and pro-Communist "Patriotic" films in the region, poured scorn on the Shaw brothers as "interested only in money."[19]

The Shaw brothers were known for their region-wide business networks and global connections in high places. "It is seldom that any world personality, whether prime minister, film producer or star, visits the Far East without calling on [them]," an American journalist observed.[20] They especially enjoyed understandably close ties with the British colonial authorities. For one thing, typical of wealthy overseas Chinese businessmen using philanthropy to increase their social capital, the brothers' high-profile Shaw Foundation, which made generous donations to "schools and community centers throughout the Commonwealth," and the escapism and commercial vitality of their entertainment business contributed significantly to the territories' social stability and financial strength. These factors were especially important after 1945 when Europe was in economic decline and political strife and anticolonial rhetoric in the region were increasing. They made available their amusement parks for the colonizing powers to hold regional

and international trade fairs as well as for military use, especially immedi-
ately after the war. That Runme made his first postwar business trip to Hong
Kong on board a Royal Navy cargo plane, for example, was thus no surprise,
and movies as well as various kinds of equipment he acquired from Hong
Kong were shipped to the Shaw enterprise by way of navy transport boats.
The Shaws also quickly got the Japanese-seized property back, in Singapore-
Malaya as well as in Hong Kong. Particularly important for the brothers'
business expansion, as director Chang Cheh revealed, starting in the 1940s,
they enjoyed limitless overdraft privileges and easy loan access at the Hong
Kong and Shanghai Banking Corporation Ltd., the British Empire financial
powerhouse.[21]

One problem the Shaw brothers had to deal with, however, was the constant slip of Nanyang's production quality. The chief accountant of the family
business since the 1920s, Runde Shaw was known as a penny-pincher. He
managed Nanyang, renamed Shaw Father and Sons (邵氏父子; SFS) in 1952,
with the emphasis on the bottom line, cutting cost whenever and wherever
he could. Thanks to the steady cash flow from Singapore, the second Shaw
brother was one of the city's leading non-Communist producers, boasting
under contract some of the most talented directors and actors. His studio
supplied a continuous stream of films to Southeast Asia—in both Mandarin
and Cantonese. Publicly, Runde often vowed to reform and modernize
postwar Mandarin cinema in order to regain public confidence, such as
claiming to experiment with 3-D movies in Natural Vision or to buy new
carbon lamps from the United States to make color films and introduce new
recording technology. And, as discussed in chapter 3, through their partnership in the Asian Film Festival (more later), Run Run arranged for Nagata
Masaichi's Daiei Studio to shoot two bug-budget historical spectacles,
Princess Yang Kwei Fei and *The Legend of the White Serpent,* at the Hong Kong
facility in order to push for better production practices. Runde's conserva-
tive spending habits, however, continued to give Shaw products a cheap, drab
look. According to Shen Jicheng (沈吉誠), who had worked for the family
since the early 1930s, Runde was preoccupied with managing the many real
estate properties he had brought mainly with money his two brothers sent
from Singapore.[22]

With some exceptions, such as Wang Yin's (王引) *Black Gloves* (黑手套,
1954) and Li Hanxiang's (李翰祥) *Springtime* (春光無限好, 1957), SFS's
Mandarin titles bore little resemblance to nonleftist, commercial films of
pre-1949 Shanghai. As veteran director and actor Wang Yin complained,

"Chinese films today are inferior in quality to those made [in the mainland] ten years ago. Our bosses care only about profits, not arts." An exodus of talent to the newly established MP&GI (see chapter 1) was to be expected. As industry insiders enthused, MP&GI brimmed with new "energy" and an "innovative spirit."[23]

Run Run to Hong Kong

Many scholars and critics have argued that it was the Shaw brothers' drive to beat their archrival dating back to at least the 1930s, Cathay Organization's (國泰機構) Dato Lok Wan Tho, that spurred Run Run to resettle in Hong Kong in 1957 to reorganize the family film production business. The two giant enterprises competed fiercely in film distribution and exhibition. While the Shaws had more theaters in Southeast Asia, the Cathay chain was better equipped overall. As Lok extended into production by forming MP&GI by taking over Yung Hwa facilities in 1956, whose sleek, modern imaginaries and young stars eclipsed S&S production in box-office receipts. The Shaw theater circuits needed better-quality pictures in order not to fall behind in market share. This made sense.[24]

I believe larger reasons were behind Run Run Shaw's reorganization efforts as well, including the Cold War that came to influence Asia's media environment. Well connected with world leaders and business figures, the Shaw brothers were aware of the bipolar global conflicts between the United States and the Soviet Union and the gradual decline of the European powers. At the same time, decolonization was rapidly developing in Southeast Asia and increasingly converged with the bipolar Cold War system. "US support was the main reason why the European colonial empires did not collapse in the 1940s. . . . All of the colonial countries were of course aware of this, and did their best to present their reluctance to decolonize as part of a common struggle against Communism," argued historian Odd Arne Westad.[25] Aiming to counter a domino effect following Mao's revolution, the Truman and Eisenhower Administrations created an anti-Communist security alliance in the region with a framework of capitalist democracy, technological modernity, and free trade. Cold War geopolitics and mounting regional tension created great challenges to the future prosperity of the family business, such as through increasing government censorship and disruption of film supply (e.g., the closing of China's market to capitalist countries), that called for astute and judicious management and continual innovation. But the US-centered "free world" market economy also created new opportunities to reform, upgrade, and modernize Chinese-language film and, especially important, facilitate its global expansion.

One important opportunity was cooperation with postwar Japan. As discussed in the previous chapter, Tokyo was the key player in the US anti-Communist alliance in Asia, so Washington mobilized huge resources to support Japan's economic reconstruction and technological upgrading. The US position was like that of a regional hegemon to lead the way in stimulating economic and cultural developments across the region.[26] In 1951, the success of Daiei Studio's *Rashomon*, and later also *Ugetsu* (1953) and *Gate of Hell* (1954), in the "free world" film festival circuit won many admirers among Asian filmmakers, even as popular opinion remained strongly anti-Japanese because of Japan's colonialism and wartime occupation. Closely connected to the Japanese government, Daiei president Nagata Masaichi formed the Federation of Southeast Asian Producers (FPA) in 1953, which had an annual (originally Southeast) Asian Film Festival as its main event, aiming to open movie markets especially in Southeast Asia. American cultural agencies, such as TAF, were also involved in the festival, endeavoring to make it a platform for technology transfer and regional cooperation under Japanese that brought all "free Asian" filmmakers into a power bloc against communism. Indeed, the FPA membership was open only to non-Communist countries.

The Shaw brothers saw the federations as a great opportunity for business partnerships with Japan and much-needed technological innovation. Indeed, for his strong support of Nagata's idea, Run Run was elected vice chairman in FPA's inaugural meeting in Manila in 1953. The group decided to hold the annual festival in different free Asian capitals to promote cooperation, cultural exchange, and access to new technology. Run Run bought a huge number of Japanese films and dubbed them into Cantonese, Mandarin, and Malay to fill the playing time of his theaters.[27] In return, Nagata brought the cast of Kenji Mizoguchi's historical epic *Princess Yang Kwei Fei*, along with some new gears and equipment, to shoot at the S&S studio as a way to demonstrate to the local Shaw employees up close how a high-standard color film was made. In the following year Run Run arranged for yet another blockbuster co-production deal with Japan, Toho studio's color costume picture *The Legend of the White Serpent*, which was adapted from a popular Chinese folktale and starring the legendary Yamaguchi Yoshiko, or Li Xianglan (李

香蘭). Again, it was aimed to expose S&S to the latest trend of moviemaking technology: color and widescreen. These co-production deals, while playing only a minor role, as we shall see, were clearly set up by Run Run as preparation for breaking new ground in the family business: to take Chinese films to the world stage.[28]

Hong Kong would be a good launching pad for the new business strategy. Under British rule, the Shaw brothers appreciated Hong Kong's free deep-water port, common law–based legal framework, sound financial and trade system well integrated with the global capitalist market, and a business-friendly government that believed in minimal intervention and low taxes. Unlike the chaos of the Cold War and decolonization in Southeast Asia, where "wars, insurgency and counter-insurgency . . . caused widespread fear and socio-economic disruptions,"[29] Hong Kong had arguably the most stable investment environment in Asia. In addition, the massive influx of refugees to Hong Kong after the Communist triumph in 1949 brought with it a large concentration of professional, entrepreneurial, literary, and artistic talents that was rarely seen in the region's history.[30] The British colony was also, American consular officer Syd Goldsmith noted, an "ultimate cheap-labor exploitation market."[31] In fact, with their capital and international business experience, Run Run's fellow Shanghai entrepreneurs and industrialists had taken advantage of the large reservoir of cheap labor and absence of labor protection to gradually transform the colony into a modern, export-oriented industrialized economy. If the film industry effectively organized and judiciously invested in new technology, would Hong Kong similarly be transformed into a film production hub serving a "free world" market?

It was probably in consideration of all these risks and opportunities, working on intersections of global, regional, and local levels, that the Shaw brothers decided to reorganize the film production business in Hong Kong. It must have invoked in them the memory of their youthful days in the 1920s when one of them stayed back in Singapore, the other drove around to surrounding small towns to explore market opportunities. If they used to carry a film projector around, now they had under command a distribution circuit that spanned the region. Runme would stay mainly in Singapore to look after their steadily expanding chain of theaters and amusement parks plus a myriad of businesses in tourism, banking, and real estate, and Run Run would live up to their own family business motto of "pioneering spirit" and "firm determination." He set out to Hong Kong to take over the slumping S&S from Runde (See Figure 4.1).

Figure 4.1 The Shaw brothers (*left to right*): Run Run and Runme Shaw

Run Run arrived in Hong Kong in 1957. After a series of family feuds (like those forcing Runjie to retire to Shanghai back in the 1930s), which were typical for family businesses in changing times, he took over the production business altogether under the new name of Shaw Brothers around 1959. As Runde moved to manage his own exhibition and real estate businesses, Run Run began to unfold his ambitious, expansive reorganization plan—which included, most significantly, purchase from the Hong Kong government a huge swath of land in Clear Water Bay to build the largest movie studio ever in Asia; a campaign to sign all the top émigré film talents he could recruit— among whom were stars Li Li-Hua (李麗華), Linda Lin Dai (林黛), and directors Yue Feng (岳楓) and Li Han-hsiang (李翰祥）and a plan to estab- lish a acting school to develop new talent. He also announced the production of a series of prestigious costume pictures featuring the "Four Beauties in an- cient China" (namely Imperial Concubine Yang Guifei [楊貴妃], Diao Chan [貂蟬], Wang Zhaojun [王昭君], and Xi Shi [西施]), all in widescreen and magnificent color.

The plans made it clear the key business strategies that Run Run used to define and guide the reorganization: big capital investment, technological modernization, and emphasis on cultural nationalism and historical themes. Scholars have often overlooked this strategic combination of modern technology and traditional subjects, which was, in some ways, a throwback to Runjie's Shanghai Tianyi strategy that, as discussed earlier, placed alleged emphases on promoting Chinese cultural values and customs, and drawing inspiration of its products from folktales, myths, and unofficial history. At the same time, this approach gave priority to continual technological innovation: Tianyi was one of the first Shanghai studios to hire foreign technicians to experiment with sound films and the recognized pioneer in Cantonese talkies. Run Run and Runme continued their interests in new technology in Singapore. As part of their exhibition empire, for example, they took special pride in arguably the largest and best maintained cinematograph and lighting equipment and engineering shop in Southeast Asia, and exclusive regional rights to the full lines of the American Simplex movie projector and theater sound system.[32] It is indeed important to pay attention to the continuities in the Shaw family enterprise strategy as it evolved in response to the changing Cold War media environment.

Film historian Law Kar argues that, echoing Tianyi's rivalry with the modern style-oriented Mingxin, Shaw Brothers' emphasis on traditional subjects was a strategic response to MP&GI's modernist ethos. It was, in other words, his product differentiation strategy.[33] Also important, however, was a competition in technology and production values. Although sleekly made, Loke's products, typical of the colony's film industry, were with a single exception (namely *Air Hostess*) in black-and-white and used the Academy ratios (1.33:1). The Shaw plan was to take the audience to the new age of color and widescreen, which had increasingly become the standard in Hollywood and most European production. This new technological upgrade further pointed to the Shaw brothers' ambition to follow the footsteps of Daiei and Toho to push their culturally themed products to the US-centered "free world." Color and widescreen would be the sine qua non for taking this ambitious step forward.

Here, besides the family business tradition of emphasizing traditional themes and folk cultures along with cutting-edge technology, the brothers might also likely be influenced by TAF debates (see the previous chapter) about the trajectory the non-Communist Mandarin film industry should take to reach a larger audience. For example, Tokyo-based Motion Picture expert John Miller and Hollywood director William Seiter had recommended a large-scale modernization of film production technology and equipment. They also found fault in the prevalent "Europeanized" trend and suggested instead putting historical figures and traditional stories on the silver screen.

"If they want their films to find markets outside of Asia," Miller gave his ardently orientalist suggestions to the film industry, "they must show Chinese traditions and customs, the farmer, the little merchant, the family life of the boat people and their small villages, the things that foreign audiences expect to find in China"[34]—that is, to sell to the non-Chinese audience what they imagined of a changeless China stuck in the past. These ideas appeared to be borne out by the great successes of Japan's *Rashomon* and *Ugetsu* or *The Tale of the White Serpent* in the European film festivals, and which had become part of the public discourse widely disseminated in pan-Chinese communities. As one of Asia's top show businessmen, the Shaw brothers would not be unaware of these ideas, and some of their top aides (more on this later) were closely connected to TAF. Hence, the rivalry with Loke's studio was an important, but certainly not the only, reason for Run Run to restructure the production base in Cold War Hong Kong.[35]

Movietown

Before moving into Clear Water Bay in 1961, when the "Movietown" was only partly completed, the Shaw brothers had already been recognized by the public as a major studio fighting neck and neck with MP&GI. As scholar Tino Balio defined it, based on the Hollywood experience, a major movie production company is characterized by volume production, national distribution, first-run exhibition, and a roster of one or two stars and a few hits. The Shaw brothers had all this except, instead of just national, it had region-wide distribution.[36] During the transition, Run Run Shaw had to rent studio space to start production.[37] They quickly made a splash. Its lavishly made color costume drama, Li Han-hsiang's *Kingdom and the Beauty* (江山美人, 1959), for example, became one of the first non-Japanese Best Picture winners at the Asian Film Festival. And the Shaws' first widescreen color film, *Les Belles* (千嬌百媚, 1961), a romantic comedy featuring American-style dancing and female fashion, introduced what soon became the signature of Shaw production: "Shawscope," which the United States Information Services (USIS) magazine *World Today* (今日世界) explained to its readers with reference to Hollywood renovation: "by adding an anamorphic lens and special microphones to the camera it revolutionizes film-watching experience by expanding 50% more vision than standard screen and with better, stereophonic sounds." Shaw Brothers' widescreen was a "new US-Japanese filming product," an American film journalist told his readers emphatically, "which has marked a turning point in Chinese filmmaking [in Hong Kong] in 1960."[38] Obviously American cultural agents tried to make sure to place the new Shaw project in the US-centered orbit in Asia.

The Shaws' "Movietown" indeed had the look of the Hollywood "Big Five" majors, and it clearly projected Run Run's ambition to transform Hong Kong film production with American technology and management technique. It sat on a massive 650,000 square feet of land in Clear Water Bay, which Run Run acquired (not rented, like T. Y. Lee of Yung Hwa) from the government. This was evident of his wealth, but also, most significantly, the colonial powers' support of his film enterprise. In early 1961 "Movietown" was officially open for business when its first phase of construction was completed. It had six sound stages and over the next five years expanded to fifteen, along with an array of new-styled office buildings, a Kodak-equipped color film development facility, a dubbing studio furnished with the latest Westex mixer and optical recorder, a permanent set in the backlot built in the model of traditional Chinese architecture and with the natural surroundings of the Lower Yangze region for shooting historical subjects, and an engineering and technical service department. Just as he did in Singapore, the mogul notably took pride in his new technology and allegedly treated his technicians better than most of his stars. For example, in the company's annual receptions he always shared the same table with all of his engineering and technical section chiefs.[39]

Movietown ran like a big assembly line, based on the US Fordist-Taylorist management system. It centered on the principles of rational management, cost efficiency, professionalization, and standardization of production in pursuit of profit maximization. "Boss Six" (六老闆), as Run Run's employees respectfully called him) oversaw every part of the production and made all decisions—from which scripts to use to when to release a film and who to make into stars—in the manner of what a British journalist called an "autocrat." And most of its seventeen hundred employees, except a few high-grossing stars and directors, were required to live in the company dormitory and subjected to a disciplinary regime of strict rules and contracts "notoriously weighted in the studio's favor." All this was possible largely because of the British colony's lack of labor protection legislations and union rights, which gave the studio the kind of power that "would surprise even Hollywood moguls of the 1930s," an American writer noted in amazement.[40]

Run Run had told actor-journalist Alex Ben Block that production in Movietown was "organized around scripts."[41] He had twenty-two full-time writers and he decided which scripts to use and assigned directors and the casts. But he also added that he made these production decisions "with the advice of trusted associates." These associates played a role comparable to what the sociologist Pierre Bourdieu calls cultural intermediaries, whose professional service in presenting and representing symbolic goods in cultural enterprises are intertwined with their own aesthetic tastes.[42] "Every week several directors (all veteran émigré directors from Shanghai) would join the Sixth Boss for dinner at his palatal mansion [above Clear Water Bay]," director He Menghua (何夢華) recalled. "Before the dinner all of them had first to report on the development of their current projects, the problems they had encountered, and new plans they had in mind."[43] Among these intermediaries, Run Run depended the most (up until the 1970s) on Raymond Chow (鄒文懷). Born in Hong Kong and a graduate of the elite Shanghai St. John's University, Chow was closely involved in the US information and cultural diplomacy community (as well as Union Press intellectuals such as Robert Hsi [奚會暲]) as he had worked since his return to the colony in 1949 as program manager for the USIS Voice of America, and his father-in-law was none other than TAF Hong Kong staffer L. Z. Yuen (袁能仁), who, as discussed in chapter 2, worked closely with *Chinese Student Weekly* (中國 學生週報) and Chang Kuo-sin's (張國興) short-lived Asia Pictures (亞洲電 影). Rising quickly from publicity director to powerful production director, Chow played an important role in talent management and reforming administrative practices to increase efficiency. He must have kept his boss abreast of the US cultural Cold War in Asia.[44]

Recall that the Shaw family business made its initial profits in the 1930s from Cantonese talkies. Run Run, however, focused most of the resources on Mandarin production, putting the Cantonese section on the sideline (literally outside of Movietown), with smaller budgets and indirect control. Why privilege Mandarin as its lingua franca? In contrast to Cantonese, which had been prejudiced as merely a vulgar local dialect spoken in the southern periphery, as discussed in earlier chapters, Mandarin was the official national language on both sides of the Taiwan Strait. It was fashioned into the national language (guoyu or Putonghua), the language that represented the modern nation-state of China. In fact, as Run Run Shaw knew by experience, one of the major agendas of the Nanjing government's nation-building project in the 1930s was to ban Cantonese cinema, which was held as the suspicious

other, if not a separatist threat, to the national body. Mandarin, from this nationalist perspective, embodied therefore the ethnic identity of Chineseness
to the world. It was the "Chinese" of "Chinese cinema." In his effort to modernize and push Chinese film to the world stage, a dream that had evaded
many ambitious movie entrepreneurs, from Luo Mingyou (羅明佑) in the
1930s to S. K. Chang, and T. Y. Lee (and to some extent, Chang Kuo-sin)
in the 1940s and 1950s, all of them champions of the "national language."
Mandarin naturally became the official language of the Shaws' productions.
The Cantonese-speaking British colony was first and foremost to the Shaw
brothers, like many émigré cultural entrepreneurs, a production base for
making and exporting Mandarin films to the world. For this purpose, Run
Run took advantage of the established Shanghai–Hong Kong nexus in the
motion picture business to recruit talent. As an émigré scriptwriter jok-
ingly recalled later, a Cantonese-speaker would have a problem surviving
in Movietown, as almost all the people there—from directors and stars to
technicians and managerial staff—were recent émigrés from Shanghai, and
few of them understood the local language.[45]

"A Firm Believer in Film Festivals"

Just as all émigré film business leaders came to realize that, without a home
market after the Communist victory, Mandarin films could not survive
without "restoring public confidence" and an expanded overseas market,
Run Run saw a strategic solution in an international film festival. He carefully cultivated an image of a "true believer in film festivals," as *Far East Film
News* lauded, by supporting Nagata's vision of a inter-Asian film organization
that promoted technology transfer and unity of regional non-Communist
industries. He formed business relations with Japanese majors Daiei and
Toho and began to hire their special-effects and camera technicians (just as
TAF officer J. Ivy advised Asia Pictures) to speed up production reforms. At
the same time, while US front organizations such as TAF had tried to politicize the FPA's Asian Film Festival along the lines of the Cold War rivalry in
Asia, the annual event increasingly became a platform for national competition and major studios' marketing and public relations campaigns. The Shaw
Brothers and MP&GI, in particular, fought neck and neck for major awards
to ramp up their market shares in the region. Along with this, as discussed
in chapter 3, came dissent against Hollywood's use of the event to "retard

the development of Asian industries" and unequal market access between Asian industries (such principally as Indonesia's Usmar Ismail, president of Indonesia Motion Picture Producers Association) and resentment against Japanese domination of the festival.[46] It had swept all major prizes year after year since 1954. In alliance with colleagues in Taiwan, South Korea, and others, Shaw Brothers snatched the Best Picture award for its first widescreen film, *La Belle*, in 1961 (its star Linda Lin Dai won Best Actress as MP&GI's Lucilla Yu Min did in 1958) and started Japan's decline of influence in the film festival. "Japan usually a forerunner in prizes collectively," the US magazine *Variety* gingerly applauded the Shaws' ascendency. It "had to take a back seat as the Asian picture is becoming more competitive."[47]

With success in the Asian Film Festival, Run Run eyed bigger and more important prizes if he wanted to bring Chinese films to a global audience. Clearly aiming at the largest film festivals of the "free world," he focused all Movietown resources in making two historical epics in widescreen and Eastman color: Li Han-hsiang (李翰祥)'s *The Magnificent Concubine* (楊貴妃, 1962) and *Empress Wu Tse-tien* (武則天, 1963), both starring Li Li-Hua and under the cinematographic direction of Nishimato Tadashi, who was hired from (New) Toho in 1959 to help specifically with widescreen production.[48] Also, Run Run made his first trip to Taiwan in 1962 to seek the Nationalists' blessing to represent "Free China" in major global competitions. It is important to note that, distinct from the émigré filmmakers' loyalty-pledging visits to Taiwan in 1953 and 1954 (see chapters 1 and 3), the mogul did not utter any public adulation of Chiang Kai-shek or statement against communism. Rather, he emphasized his diasporic "longing for the Motherland" and explained his mission in terms of cultural nationalism. "The purpose of our Shaw Brothers is to bring up the quality standard of Chinese films or *guopian* [國片]," he declared in the presence of Nationalist cultural and overseas Chinese affairs leaders, "in order to promote our traditional Eastern arts and bring glory to our country by way of gaining entry to international markets."[49]

Taipei did not participate in the Asian Film Festival in the first few years because of the low quality of Taiwan's state-controlled studios, and it mostly depended on small émigré film studios in Hong Kong to challenge the Communist domination (in return for market access or subsidies). It had kept a particularly wary eye on the popularity of Beijing's barrage of traditional love story–based opera films and their soft-power effects in the region's overseas Chinese communities. "They were meant to cultivate emotional attachment to the Communist regime on the mainland," a Nationalist document warned, "through connecting Chinese people to memories of their birthplace now under Communist domination."[50] With limited cultural resources, Taiwan tried to counter this connection by occasionally sending out theatre troupes to further the anti-Communist cause and by working with the US cultural diplomacy agencies to, with different degrees of success, pressure Southeast Asian states (notably Thailand and the Philippines) to ban distribution of Beijing's cultural products. Strategic cooperation with the giant Shaw Brothers to promote "Free China" as the sole legitimate bearers of the Chinese cultural tradition and the "Motherland" for overseas Chinese around the globe in the "free world" film festival circuit would thus bolster the Nationalist agenda.[51]

Lauded by Nationalist officials as signaling that "China–Hong Kong cinemas are like a family" (中港電影一家親), Run Run reached various co-production and trade deals with Taiwan and left for Cannes with *The Magnificent Concubine* cast members. The film was a spectacular story of tragic love and court intrigue adapted from the popular ninth-century poem *The Everlasting Regret*. Spending profusely in an effort to re-create a Tang-period "Oriental" atmosphere in the little French town, posters and handbills featuring the Tang beauty in a distinctly exotic setting were everywhere, and star Li Li-Hua was arranged to walk down the red carpet in an eye-catching Tang-styled costume (See Figure 4.2).

The Magnificent Concubine won just the minor Commission Superieure Technique for its sumptuous color and set design. Shortly afterward, Run Run took the film to show in the ROC Pavilion at the Seattle World's Fair. As the space race with the USSR was underway, the gigantic fair was aimed to showcase to the world US dominance in science, technology and economic power (with the US Science Pavilion, IBM's *New Paths to Knowledge* exhibit, and the soaring Space Needle, for example). It was also supposedly a showcase of the cultural diversity and prosperous modernity of the "free world" community under US paternalism. Included in this anti-Communist bloc were over twenty-five newly developing "free Asian" economies, including Taiwan, South Korea, Thailand, the Philippines, and Japan. Through exhibits and performances of traditional dance and music, the World's Fair official guidebook explained, these countries displayed the "faraway Oriental way of life" that was "unique" to their cultures. At the fair, Run Run met with Hollywood executives and various world leaders and came away with confidence in the future integration of Movietown into the "free world" market.

Figure 4.2 Run Run Shaw (*center*) and some of his top directors at a 1962 party with Li Han-hsiang, Yue Feng, and Ho Meng Hua on his right and King Hu and Yuen Qiufeng on his left, where he announced a new era of Shaw Brothers big-budget production focusing on historical dramas.
Southern Screen, n.59 (January 1963)

Indeed, he announced shortly afterward that his 1963 production plan would center on big-budget, high-tech "historical dramas that promote Chinese culture." "We make Chinese films," he proudly told his employees at the company's reception.[52]

However, the two mega-projects of Run Run in 1963 turned out to be disasters at the global film festivals. Again, he took the cast of Li Han-hsiang's *Empress Wu Tse-tien*—a huge-budget biopic of the only female emperor in Chinese history, which was often compared in the local press to Twentieth-Century Fox's *Cleopatra*—to Cannes with the expectation of a big prize. Yet it won nothing and was instead ridiculed by critics as looking more like "a comic strip." Later that year, the lavish Huangmei opera drama *Love Eterne* (梁山伯與祝英台), directed also by Li Han-hsiang, a phenomenal success in the pan-Chinese world, participated in the seventh San Francisco Film Festival. It came out, again, empty-handed. Worse still, mainstream American critics dismissed this "Chinese (Formosa) entry" for its "musical tradition of Chinese opera [that] lacks commercial appeal for Western audiences."[53]

Western critics recognized the "quality of fine Oriental art" in *Love Eterne* and *The Magnificent Concubine*. Few of them, however, mentioned the modern technologies and film techniques in which Run Run took much pride. In the Cold War context, "free Asia" was geopolitically and militarily a part of—and yet at the same time remained culturally and aesthetically apart from—the supposedly integrated "free world." Movietown was the "Oriental" other, relegated to the periphery of the US-centered hierarchy of cultural modernity in the global film market. After the Cannes and San Francisco debacles, Shaw Brothers appeared to concentrate instead on competitions and business networking within "Free Asia." Shaw Brothers took advantage of its increasingly central role in the Asian Film Festival to flex muscle at its business rivals and formed alliances and partnerships with other regional industries. At a time of protectionist trade policies associated with nation-building in postcolonial Southeast Asia, such as stringent censorship and heavy duties on what was called the "yellow culture" of Chinese films in Singapore and Indonesia, Shaw Brothers struck co-production deals with newly established studios (some with military backing) in Thailand and Vietnam—for example, usually with facilitation by local US cultural Cold War agencies that had been trying to strengthen local filmmaking. It provided creative and technological support in exchange for market expansion. South Korea studios, especially the Shin Company, became Shaw Brothers' longest-standing partner in the 1960s, because it provided access to abundant cheap labor, horses, and magnificent landscapes with traditional temples and pavilions that reminded audiences of the homeland—rugged north China. For many of its regional neighbors, indeed, Movietown's scale, glamor, and modern technology had taken on the prestige and popular imageries akin to those of the Japanese cinema of the golden age in the 1950s: the Hollywood of "Free Asia."[54]

Cold War Flexible Entrepreneurship

Nationalist Taiwan was the most important home market for all émigré Mandarin filmmakers. So it was for Run Run Shaw. By publicly identifying "Free China" as the "Motherland" of the Chinese diaspora, and representing it in the "free world" film festival circuit, moreover, he set up Movietown as the leading pro-Taiwan film production in the pan-Chinese world. However, the mogul did not conform to the binary logic of the cultural Cold War. Instead, he became emblematic of what can be called flexible entrepreneurship in the Cold War media environment: a border-straddling tactic of flexibility and an apolitical stance in navigating the pro-Taiwan–pro-Beijing and freedom-communism divides. Political ambivalences abounded as a result.

As noted earlier, Run Run and his brother approached their sprawling theater chain and entertainment parks in Southeast Asia just as running a big business. They had told everyone all along loudly and clearly their desire to make money. They showed any kind of movies as long as they could draw crowds into the theaters. And they, Run Run in particular, were known for their grueling travel to expand their global business networks transnationally in their tireless drive to accumulate wealth. In Hong Kong, Run Run continued to tell the world that he ran Movietown with the same apolitical approach. "I make movies only for entertainment—not politics," he told a *Time* magazine interviewer. His goal was, fitting with the stereotypical Asian familism, "to make my family comfortable for a few generations."[55] This strategic depoliticization in the Cold War context enabled the media mogul to claim neutrality and flexibly maneuver across ideological chasms in the region.

Taiwan was Shaw Brothers' principal market. Especially after the phenomenal success of *Love Eterne* in 1963, the studio dominated the film market there. As documented by media historian Liu Hsien-cheng, fifty out of one hundred top-ten films in Taipei between 1960 and 1970 were from Shaw Brothers. And the brothers also helped facilitate the Nationalist government's battle for hearts and minds by co-producing content with state-run studios and distributing Taiwan-made films and newsreels to Hong Kong and Southeast Asian markets.[56] Run Run was, moreover, a major backer of the quasi-Nationalist trade organization—the Hong Kong and Kowloon Film and Theater Workers Free General Association—which acted as a watchdog against Communist influences (see chapter 1), and he regularly took part in the annual Double Tenth National Day celebration with many of his top stars in tow. Shaw Brothers also brought clout and region-wide recognition to the Nationalist regime's major cultural warfare event—the Golden Horse Film Festival—by sending large delegations every year to participate and, starting with the Best Picture award for Li Han-hsiang's epic *The Magnificent Concubine*, took away most big prizes. Significantly, Taiwan had also become the key recruitment source for new talent since the 1960s—especially for directors, actors, and scriptwriters—as increasing numbers of émigré Movietown employees were approaching retirement age.

Seemingly to display his ideological neutrality and interest in only making films that audiences liked, Run Run, on the other hand, was constantly campaigning in public to recruit artistic talents from "Patriotic" studios. Unlike what Li Li-Hua, for one, had to go through—all the anti-Communist rituals when she switched sides to join S&S in 1953 (see chapter 1)—new converts signing up with Movietown almost never publicized their pro-Communist past. These recruitment campaigns, most notably all the press headlines about huge pay and film role offers for Great Wall star Moon Hsia and leading man Fu Qi, only, not surprisingly, further expanded the Communist position in the film world and drew criticism from pro-Nationalist critics. In this connection, some anti-Communist "Patriotic" studio employees, also complained about the increasing influences of American-style star power in their midst. Moreover, while the Shaw brothers continued to show "Patriotic" studios' pictures in their Southeast Asian theatre chains, they also often met quietly with pro-Beijing leaders to discuss market trends and exchange business favors. As Southern Film Corporation executive Xu Dunle (許敦樂) recently told scholar Lanjun Xu, "Run Run Shaw was our friend." Xu Dunle revealed that the brothers gave him advice on creating a star system and ways to attract audiences. Run Run also sought his assistance in gaining access to PRC (especially opera) films, and arranging for adaptation or distribution rights.[57] For example, the famous Yue opera *Dream of Red Chamber* (紅樓夢) gained a huge following when it was staged by a Shanghai troupe in Hong Kong; Movietown then remade it into Yuan Qiufeng's (袁秋楓) star-studded drama of the same title, and it became one of the top-ten box-office films in Hong Kong and Taipei in 1962.

The political ambivalence of Run Run's border-straddling flexible entrepreneurship provoked resentment and frustration on both sides of the divide. Many small independent producers in Hong Kong, for example, who depended entirely on the Taiwan market, complained about the Nationalist cultural establishment's unfair treatment as their films were banned if even one of the cast or crew members was judged to be a Communist sympathizer. And yet Shaw Brothers' pictures—which, while enjoying more tax and foreign currency remittance rate incentives, featured former "Patriotic" stars and writers—were given the green light to show across the island.[58] Similar controversy took place among the pro-Beijing establishment. As newly discovered Communist meeting minutes held in the wake of the Great Leap Forward campaign reveal, Beijing leadership tried to correct what in its view were the "ultra-leftist" mistakes of the local party apparatus—the Hong Kong and Macau Work Committee—which, among others, identified Shaw Brothers as the "bureaucratic-capitalist" (官僚資本家) enemy. Many local film cadres and studio heads tried to thwart business cooperation with it. Instead Beijing urged viewing the brothers as pragmatic businessmen "who would call her mother whoever let them suckle" (有奶就是娘), as the derisive political parlance went. Their business interests could help further the Communist cause on the cultural and propaganda front and therefore should be strategized as a key object for "United Front works." The Shaw brothers could and should be made "friends" to enhance the Party's propaganda warfare interests (This accommodating policy appeared to continue until the Cultural Revolution in 1966.)[59]

The Shaw brothers knew to use their wealth and clout to extend what some scholars called, typical of diasporic Chinese entrepreneurs in the region, their "fraternal business connections"—that is, "doing business man to man," to build various kinds of relations and partnerships with government officials and social elites.[60] For example, as Runme Shaw served on a wide array of government boards in Singapore and Malaysia, Run Run contributed various kinds of services to colonial authorities in Hong Kong and the British Empire—such as making newsreels to promote international trade and tourism. Their renowned philanthropy—through the Shaw Foundation and the Sir Run Run Shaw Charitable Trust—included what its official publicity called "return" money from their entertainment empire to society by donating tens of millions of dollars especially to education, cultural development, and public health. A journalist detailed the film mogul's approach to social service. In 1966, on the eve of the riot that was to rock the city, the Red Cross asked Boss Six for help. After he held a fundraising party with the rich and famous at his "palatial home on a crest above the studios," he discovered that ingrained superstition and feudal belief deterred many people from donating blood. Afterward he became chairman of the Red Cross and made blood collection a personal cause. Swordfight heroes and film starlets trooped out before the cameras to donate blood. So did wealthy businessmen and their wives, as did a swelling number of people as a publicity drive persuaded Hongkongers that giving blood was part of their commitment to society.[61]

The two brothers' philanthropic work and community service to the British Commonwealth and Hong Kong were especially appreciated at a time when the territory was rapidly developing its export trade and international finance while the colonial government had spent as little as possible on education, public service, healthcare, and welfare under the powerful financial secretary John Cowperthwaite's (1961–1971) noninterventionist policy.

Throughout the 1960s, Hong Kong had an average annual gross domestic product (GDP) of 9 to 10 percent, and exports increased 15 percent every year on average, while many people still lived in squatter huts or rooftops. Colonial officials urged its poor and disadvantaged not to expect any welfare support but rather to seek assistance from family and community leaders according to traditional Chinese practice.[62]

The Shaw brothers' contributions had therefore made the callous, unequal, "grey industrial world" of the colony appear a little less so.

Meanwhile, Run Run rode on the stability and rapid industrialization of Governor David Trench (1964–1971) to become the undisputed hegemon of Hong Kong cinema after Dato Lok Wen Tho's accident in 1964 that led to the decline of MP&GI. Boss Six led the way in transforming Hong Kong's media ecosystem. Big production budgets, color and widescreen offerings, new technology, a Western-style management system, in addition to special effects and other higher-cost entertainment values, had increasingly become the industrial norm. Many small Mandarin studios shuttered as a result. Similarly, Cantonese-language production, mostly in black-and-white and poorer quality, practically halted toward the close of the 1960s, as audiences increasingly preferred Shaw Brothers pictures, which they could now understand with the assistance of standard Chinese subtitles. Meanwhile, Movietown continued to expand with a new purchase of land in Clear Water Bay and increased production to about forty films a year. And as the Hong Kong population increased to almost four million, Run Run expanded the family's exhibition business to Hong Kong. Whereas there had been not even one theater focusing on Mandarin pictures in the early 1950s, the number increased to eight or ten in 1966, and some of them were downtown movie palaces comparable in luxury and prestige to first-run Hollywood movie houses. The tax revenues generated from the Shaw theater circuit and film exports bolstered the colony's public finance.[63]

In 1974 Run Run was awarded a CBE, and three years later, a knighthood from Queen Elizabeth II. These recognitions coincided with Hong Kong's economic takeoff and reforms by Governor Murray MacLehose's (1971–1982) to reform the colonial power structure and introduce extensive welfare programs.[64] The Shaw studios had by then completed their expansion plan and by the late 1970s had produced altogether somewhere between eight thousand and nine thousand films distributed to the pan-Chinese market. The Shaw brothers "worked in tandem with Hong Kong's development," as an industry insider commented discreetly on the studio's success. "So the

Hong Kong government has actually been paying close attention and providing indirect support to our motion picture industry."[65]

Sir Run Run Shaw also maintained intimate connections with different government agencies and corporation executives to expand his global connections. As the USIS press officer Syd Goldsmith recalled decades later, for example, "the mogul was everybody's favorite in the US Consulate General. He regularly invited us to private showings of his films before their public release. We learned to read the English subtitles fast enough to keep up with the action."[66] Indeed, just as he had done in Singapore-Malaya, the film mogul made Movietown a travel hotspot for the British royal family as well as "global stars such as Elizabeth Taylor and Sophia Loren, and [he] rubbed shoulders with other tycoons and financiers and with politicians" from around the world.[67]

Chinese Films Have to Have Zhongguo Wei

Shortly after Movietown began production in 1962, Run Run Shaw proclaimed that "as long as the production standard is good, Mandarin motion pictures will have no problems attracting audiences."[68] He tried to convince the public that his efforts should put to rest all the doubts and pessimism that had been prevalent in the émigré film community. Even with his setback on the global film festival circuit, Boss Six became increasingly confident—as demonstrated by the success of *Empress Wu Tse-tien* and *The Magnificent Concubine* in the Asian Film Festival and Golden Horse Festival—that films with new production technology and what he called "Zhongguo wei" (Chinese flavor, or sense of Chineseness) would bring Chinese audiences back to the theaters. "I make movies to satisfy the hope and desire of my audience," he told a *China Mail* journalist, "and the core of my audience is Chinese people."[69]

Run Run's emphasis on Zhongguo wei, as mentioned earlier, could be traced back to the Shanghai Tianyi strategy of reviving cultural values and customs in opposition to what it considered the Europeanized aesthetics of contemporary film studios such as Mingxing and Minxin. Tianyi had built a business on costume drama and Cantonese opera pictures. There was, however, a different contextualization of the cultural tradition. Whereas Runjie claimed to alter the cultural landscape by "championing the time-honored inherited virtues of China,"[70] Run Run emphasized instead the importance of providing spiritual sustenance to Chinese people living around the world. They "have missed the homeland they left behind," he once explained, "and the cultural tradition they are still cherishing."[71] As a member of the diaspora himself, he was keenly aware of the varied experiences of the overseas Chinese community; indeed, its support had been vital to the prosperity of his family entertainment business in Southeast Asia. The community had become larger and geographically more diverse as a result of the massive exodus from the Communist revolution. They represented what the cultural geographer Lily Kong terms a "global niche market," namely, a focused market that built around the (supposedly) connected experiences and shared tastes of ethnic Chinese scattered around the globe.[72]

In the fractured Cold War world, this global niche market was limited to the "free world," and the overseas Chinese community was internally divided along multiple dialects and opposing ideologies. To reach the largest audiences possible, the Shaw brothers privileged Mandarin, the guoyu, as the lingua franca in its productions and emphasized the cultural nationalism of Zhongguo wei—Chinese flavor—to virtually smooth over the linguistic and bipolarized ideological chasms. Its films, in fact, expressed Run Run's flexible, border-straddling entrepreneurship in focusing on a depoliticized, deeply romanticized world of traditional Chinese culture that appealed to Chinese people of opposing political positions. As noted earlier, Zhongguo wei was practically a cultural construction of Chineseness based on some stereotypical and essentialized ideas about Chinese traditional values and customs. Indeed, Run Run told an American filmmaker, as mentioned earlier, that Chinese audiences' tastes revolved around the cultural "parameter" of some time-honored beliefs.[73]

Just as Tianyi did in identifying Confucian tradition with costume film genres throughout the 1920s and 1930s, Movietown released many historical pictures in the 1960s featuring Chinese flavors, all drawing from folktales, unofficial history, traditional operas, legends, and mythology. Echoing the Tianyi business practice, Run Run emphasized a strategy that combined Hollywood-style management and new technology with Zhongguo wei. Indeed, Movietown had built a permanent set modeled after the classical gardens and traditional architecture of the Lower Yangtze region, which, as longtime film critic Shek Kei described, evoked a "film fantasy of [the] China dream."[74] The most successful among Shaw Brothers' depoliticized, high-tech Zhongguo wei pictures in the 1960s were Huangmei opera dramas (黃梅調電影) and martial arts films. *Love Eterne* in 1963 enabled the studio to conquer the Taiwan market, which had the largest audiences in the global niche market, thanks to the massive influx of mainland émigrés there after 1949, and *Come Drink with Me* and *One-Armed Swordsman*, in particular, extended its regional dominance in the "free world" through the second part of the 1960s.

As discussed in chapter 1, China exported a series of elegantly made opera pictures in the 1950s to Hong Kong and from there to Southeast Asia, including the Yue opera drama *Butterfly Lovers* (梁山伯與祝英台, 1953) and the Huangmei opera film *Marriage of the Fairy Princess* (天仙配, 1956). They had broken box-office records in many overseas Chinese communities. According to Xu Dunle, the catchy Huangmei tune had become a hit in Hong Kong. In order to seize the commercial potential, the Shaw brothers in 1959 launched *Empire and the Beauty* (江山美人), a folklore-based tragic romance between a playboyish emperor and a virtuous beauty from a lower-class background. Following its local box-office success came a few Huangmei opera dramas. In 1963 Li Han-hsiang's *Love Eterne* appeared. This was the latest of a succession of film versions of a well-loved folk tale about two lovers' devotion to each other that traced back to the fifth century—including the Shanghai Tianyi's *Tragic History of Liang and Zhu* (梁祝痛史). Some critics contend that the film adopts the viewpoint of the heroine, Zhu Yingtai, in offering a biting critique of the patriarchal order represented by her father, who refuses to let her go to school and later forces her to give up her true love.[75] This is true only to the extent that she tries to assert her agency.

Zhu's mother, portrayed by Shanghai émigré actress Chen Yanyan (陳燕燕) as a stereotypically "kind mother," serves to ameliorate the patriarchal excess of her "strict father." They let her go to school, after she feigns illness, as long as she disguises as a male student in order to maintain cultural norms. This sets up what came to be a selling point for the film: double cross-gendering and the many comedic moments that come with it. Zhu (played by Betty Lo Tieh [樂蒂]) dresses as a male, and Ivy Ling Po (凌波) plays the young scholar Liang Shanbo. It was at the boarding school that Zhu falls in love with her classmate in the disguise of "sworn brothers." When Zhu takes a leave from school to return home, Liang accompanies her down the hill in the "Eighteen-Mile Farewell" (十八相送) scene. Through a humorous series of culturally evocative references to classical poetry, history, and literary symbolism, Zhu tries to express her love to the oblivious young scholar. "If I were a woman," she slyly asks him, "would you marry me?" (See Figure 4.3)

Figure 4.3 The cross-dressing Zhu Yingtai tries to reveal her secret love to Liang Shanbo in an idyllic setting redolent with Zhongguowei.

After learning of Zhu's gender identity from the teacher's wife later, Liang rushes to her house to propose marriage. However, it is too late. Zhu's father has arranged for her to marry a rich man. An innocent, effeminate young student with no connections or ambition like most heroes in traditional "scholar-meets-beauty" narratives, Liang comes off as a personification of pure love and tragic loss. He passes away in sorrow shortly afterward. In grief, Zhu refuses to marry into a wealthy family unless she is allowed to dress like a mourner. This act of forced submission parallels her father's forced compromise, showing his concern for his daughter's feelings.[76] The confrontation leads to the dramatic climax. When the wedding party comes upon Liang's tomb, a huge storm blows up and cracks it open. Zhu quickly leaps into it. The storm then subsides and the lovers "transform into a pair of butterflies" (化蝶) flying up to the sky above (See Figure 4.4). The butterflies scene, as literary scholar Qin Yamen documents, represented in traditional performance arts as analogously a "happy ending," giving vent to audiences' compassion for the characters' virtues and sufferings.[77] Thus, Zhu's acts of transgression and escape to a mythologized realm represent the kinds of "small releases, small victories, and big releases, big victories" of female power that, just as Jeanine Basiger and other scholars have described Hollywood women's pictures, ultimately reconfirm the Confucian patriarchal order.[78]

Love Eterne was a box-office hit in Hong Kong and some Southeast Asian overseas Chinese communities, but it took Taiwan by storm. It shattered box-office records previously held by Hollywood pictures, which had dominated the market until then. How to explain this Liang-Zhu phenomenon? What

Figure 4.4 With the technical aid of Japanese special-effects technicians, *Love Eterne* enchanted the audiences with the reincarnation of the two tragic lovers into a pair of butterflies staying together freely forever.

appeared to appeal, first of all, to its large audiences (from housewives to intellectuals and students) was the film's modern technology and technique. Shot in magnificent Eastman color and Shawscope, it was a beautifully told love story laden with humor and melodious Huangmei tunes. Li Han-hsiang's masterful adaptation of Hollywood's camerawork (with the uncredited assistance of Japanese cinematographer Nishimoto Tadashi) and narrative style, especially constant tracking shots and continuity editing, to a long-cherished opera—plus the storm-blowing special effects and butterflies special effects (both were actually produced in a Tokyo facility)—made the film a thrilling and unforgettable experience for its viewers. "No one can say that foreign moon is rounder than the Chinese one," a journalist played on a nationalist cliché; Chinese film is now "in every aspect as sophisticated as the American one." [79]

The sumptuous cinematography and editing enhanced and magnified *Love Eterne*'s Zhongguo wei strategy—all in a luxuriant, evocative setting reconstructed in the manner of the cultural and artistic milieu of traditional Chinese literati. It was actually shot in the Movietown permanent set, as noted earlier, which was designed like a classical Chinese garden typical of those in the Lower Yangtze Delta region—with ponds, trees and flowers, prized rocks, artificial hills, and a multitude of pavilions all connected by zigzag pathways. Fluent segues took place between Huangmei songs and dialogues, all in clear Mandarin, and crafted (by Li Han-hsiang, who studied Western arts at Peking National Art Institute and a bibliophile and art connoisseur famous for his knowledge of Ming novels, along with his team of talented émigré songwriters, lyricists, and assistants) with rich cultural and poetic symbolism, historical references, and classical allusions. Especially memorable was the "Eighteen-Mile Farewell" sequence, which, with well-paced poetic songs alluding to Zhu's gender identity, was like a visualized presentation for many viewers of Chinese literary tradition.[80] These audio-visual elements created a supposedly authentic world of Zhongguo wei, one that conjured up a romanticized and gleefully depoliticized China of beauty and virtues.

The Zhongguo wei elicited in turn from the audiences' nostalgia and remembrances of their lost homeland. "*Love Eterne* allowed young audiences to have a fleeting flight into the realm of love and lust that were still very much a taboo in Taiwan society," as an ordinary housewife recalled her viewing experience. "Especially, watching the tragic love story unfolding in the darkness of the theater brought up for many older and middle-aged men and women the long-suppressed memories of their lost love, and sorrows about the life they had lived [back at home]." This might explain why Ivy Ling Po became a cultural icon overnight. If Zhu Yingtai fights for her agency in most of the film, her lover never seems to have a sense of agency at all. The Ling Po character—Liang Shanbo—is weak and totally helpless; he can only bear in silence the pain of his unfulfilled love, just like, symbolically, most ordinary Chinese people who had few choices but were just trying to survive the endless turmoil of wars, violence, family loss, and massive displacement in the mid-twentieth century.[81]

"It Was Very Abstract. . . . It Was Like a Dream"

Love Eterne, again, expressed the political ambivalence of Run Run's flexible border-straddling strategy. It became a battleground for the hearts and minds of Chinese people. In their fight to manipulate nationalism for political legitimacy, Beijing and Taipei struggled to claim the Liang-Zhu phenomenon for their respective causes.

In fact, Nationalist officials emphasized the traditional values enshrined in the film and its relations with Taiwan as the "free homeland" (自由祖國) for all Chinese people against communism. Deeply sympathetic to the nostalgic feelings the Shaw brothers had evoked among the millions of "Mainlanders [in Taiwan] who were longing for the homeland," for example, education minister Huang Jilu (黃季陸) pointed out that "Free China" was now the last bastion of Chinese culture, as traditional values and customs were being ravaged under Mao's rule.[82] Non-Communist intellectuals such as New Confucian philosopher Xu Fuguan (徐復觀), who was also a faculty member at the émigré New Asia College in Hong Kong, lauded the film for bringing forward the traditional ideal of "purity of love" (純淨之愛) in opposition to a chaotic and challenging world of "seven emotions and six desires" (七情六慾). What he seemed to imply in the contemporary context was a commitment to fight for freedom and agency.[83]

For the Communists, however, as Xu Dunle claimed, *Love Eterne* represented the success of the United Front policy that extended Beijing's cultural influences (such as *Butterfly Lovers* or *Marriage of the Fairy Princess*) through Run Run Shaw into enemy territories.[84] In fact, some of the Movietown Huangmei opera films were covert adaptations from opera pictures produced across the ideological boundary. For example, the first assignment for Shen Jiang, a new scriptwriter from Taiwan, was to rewrite a small-budget Teochew opera film by Great Wall into a splendid Huangmei opera drama, Gao Li's *Dawn Will Come* (雲斷奈何天, 1966), that aimed specifically for the Taiwan market, with Ivy Ling Po as the female lead.

The border-crossing movement of ideas and influences was, however, two-sided, demonstrating the ambivalence of film production in Hong Kong. In an effort to stay competitive in the rapidly changing film industry, pro-Communist studios intensified their efforts to add entertainment values to their production. As audiences flocked to watch Shaw Brothers' Huangmei opera films in color and widescreen, Great Wall and Phoenix countered with their own string of lavishly made color films adapted from different regional operas, including Li Pingqian's *Three Smiling Smiles* (三笑, 1964), Hu Xiaofeng's (胡小峰) *My Darling Princess* (金枝玉葉, 1964), and Huang Yu's (黃 域) *Emperor Takes a Holiday* (皇帝出京, 1965). Unlike Shaw Brothers' emphasis on tragic themes, the leftist opera-themed "pinkies," consistent with their other genres, were mostly comical and lighthearted, emphasizing the authenticity of the performance. These films were popular, enabling the pro-Communist studios to maintain market share in the region. Notably, according to Shanghai Municipal Film Bureau documents, all these lush color films not only received artistic assistance from mainland opera performers, they were actually developed by PRC technicians. In order to support its film propaganda in Hong Kong without overly increasing subsidies, which would otherwise have to come from London, Shanghai studios provided the technological assistance. Starting with further ideological control in 1965, the service required prior content review and approval by the PRC Foreign Affairs Ministry and Propaganda Ministry, and likely stopped altogether after the onset of the Cultural Revolution in 1966.[85]

At the same time, the romanticized and depoliticized Zhongguo wei of Shaw Brothers' opera films enmeshed with the colonial authority's political agenda during the Cold War (see chapter 1). Through such measures as media censorship and educational policy, as Wai-Man Lam and other scholars argue, the colonial authority had promoted a depoliticized community that "place[d] great value on cultivating a passive citizenship," in an effort to thwart creation of a local collective identity among the colonized that threatened its rule. In fact, in its claim for political neutrality, the colonial power aimed to depoliticize the media industry and make it more about entertainment as a way to deescalate the ideological rivalries between Communist China, Nationalist Taiwan, and the United States.[86] The Liang-Zhu phenomenon served thereby as a timely counterweight to the Trench administration fear of a Communist "monopoly of popular culture" in the region.

In fact, the breakout successes of Chinese opera pictures as well as visits of Chinese opera troupes to Hong Kong, which also attracted many Southeast Asian overseas Chinese tourists, raised alarms at Whitehall. The Colonial Office urged the governor to limit the number of visiting Chinese troupes in order "to prevent the Colony from becoming the cockpit of Communist/ KMT political conflicts: rivalry in cultural matters may on the face of it appear a good deal less objectionable, but one thing is apt to lead to another."[87] Around 1963, the colonial government had considered fending off the Beijing-initiated regional opera fad by promoting local Cantonese opera performance. The plan did not seem to follow through, though, probably because of concern for fomenting local identity, and of the popularity of *Love Eterne* and other Movietown opera films. It was thus no surprise that Governor Trench made it a point to often attend premiere galas of prestigious Shaw Brothers pictures.

The Liang-Zhu phenomenon had started a cycle in opera film and costume drama that ushered in what can be called a golden age of Mandarin cinema in the Cantonese-speaking British colony. Still, except in Taiwan, the genre gradually lost its lure in the mid-1960s, especially among the younger generation, who, unlike their refugee parents, were mostly born and raised in Hong Kong. Between the ages of ten and thirty-five, they had increasingly become an important audience demographic. They were drawn to the action movies and youth culture films imported from the "free world," such as Western flicks and the James Bond franchise, the Japanese Jidaigeki samurai dramas, and Sun Tribe youth films. In response to changing audience tastes, Movietown put out different types of films, including musicals and spy thrillers, as trial balloons to figure out the emergent trend. In 1965–1966, it set out to launch the new-styled martial arts films (新派武俠片), starting with, among others, King Hu's (胡金銓) instant classic, *Come Drink with Me* (1966), and Zhang Che's *One-Armed Swordsman* (1967). These knight-errant *wuxia* (武俠) films claimed to be totally different from the old types that featured supernatural elements and low-tech special effects (pervasive in Tianyi's Shanghai or Hong Kong Cantonese cinema) in modern technology and realistic violence. They put on display a bold, muscular, and heroic masculinity—in the name of yanggang (陽剛) or "staunch masculinity"— in place of the passive and feminine manhood that was prevalent, like the Liang Shanbo character, in Huangmei opera movies. The new-styled martial arts pictures quickly caught audiences' fancy. *One-Armed Swordsman* became the first film to gross one million dollars in Hong Kong. Movietown was turned shortly afterward into virtually a wuxia factory, producing one swordfighting film after another, which were also immensely popular in Thailand, Singapore, Malaysia, the Philippines, and Taiwan.[88] Shaw Brothers continued, before its declining influence in the early 1970s, to shape and transform the British colony's movie ecosystem with its innovation and new technology.[89]

Film critics and scholars such as Law Kar, David Bordwell, Po Fung, and Stephen Teo have discussed in varying depth the historical development, editing styles, and recording and cinematography techniques that brought out what Man Fung Yip terms the "sensory realism" of speed, impact, and masculine prowess that characterized new-styled martial arts films.[90] What needs to be pointed out in the Cold War context is the continuous theme of romanticized, depoliticized Zhongguo wei in them. Indeed, Shaw Brothers' official magazine, *Southern Screen* (南國電影), proclaimed in 1965 with rare reference to contemporary geopolitical conflicts, "In this age of wars and unrest, the trend of global film production was: 'action movies.' . . . Our 'action movies' have to tell wuxia stories in a way that is characteristically Chinese and traditional."[91]

These "Chinese and traditional" wuxia stories, just as with Huangmei opera dramas, were told through modern film technology and with Hollywood-inspired techniques, as well as the assistance of Japanese technicians.[92] Film critic Sek Kei, who was familiar with Movietown, commented that, like Li Han-hsiang of the Huangmei opera dramas, new-styled martial arts film masters King Hu and Chang Cheh were émigré artists "who took advantage of the Movietown's remarkable resources to give free rein to their respective 'dream of China.' . . . [Their wuxia worlds] were full of supra-realistic imaginations . . . and had diverse influences, but ultimately speaking, they were all drawn from Chinese ideas and cultural imagery."[93] Indeed, they in different ways turned their memories of home into projecting Zhongguo wei in some of Shaw Brothers' most influential pictures. A Beijing native, Hu was said to have taken classes at the National Peking Institute of Art before fleeing to Hong Kong in 1949. He was a deeply learned man well-known for his encyclopedic knowledge of Ming history and Peking opera, and enjoying close relations with New Asia College scholars. Struggling to make ends meet, he had worked for the USIS Voice of America, among various art-related jobs and low-level studio positions, before joining Li Han-hsiang's projects as his assistant (including on *Empire and the Beauty* and *Love Eterne*). Chang was a prolific writer and junior Nationalist official active in postwar Shanghai cultural circles, involved in evaluating occupation filmmakers. He moved to Hong Kong from Taiwan after a brief and frustrated stint as Chiang Ching-kuo's adviser and joined Movietown as its senior scriptwriter thanks to his influential press journalism.

The realistic action choreography and sensational violence of Shaw Brothers' martial arts films in the 1960s were undergirded by an amalgam of Confucian ideas of filial piety and loyalty, gender stereotypes, and folk legends of chivalric heroism. Set often in an unspecified time and place in old China, the knight-errant heroes (and sometimes, as in *Come Drink with Me*, heroines) emblematize these traditional values in their quests for vengeance and retribution to restore justice. In *Come Drink with Me*, for example, the woman warrior Golden Swallow (played by young Shanghai émigré star Cheng Pei-Pei [鄭佩佩]) is sent by her father—the governor—to rescue her brother, who is being held hostage by a band of outlaws connected with a renegade monk. Even with her almost fantastic martial arts prowess, as demonstrated in an exquisitely choreographed fight scene inside an inn reminiscent of a Peking opera setting, she is no match for the gang leader. It is the

Figure 4.5 Fang Gang's father sacrificed himself in protecting his Master from enemy attacks, who then adopts his son in recognition of his selfless loyalty.

beggarlike Drunken Knight (Yue Hua [岳華]) who, repeatedly and secretly, aids and rescues her, and, in the climax, kills the monster monk in a mystical waterfall hideout, who has actually murdered his master years ago. Golden Swallow's brother is released and justice restored as a result of both fighters' virtues and power.[94]

Similarly, loyalty and heroism frame *One-Armed Swordsman*'s violence-packed narrative. Fang Gang (played by Wang Yu [王羽]), an orphan whose father sacrificed himself in protecting Master Qi Rufeng (Tian Feng [田豐]), became his most trusted disciple. Out of jealousy, Qi's willful daughter (played by Pan Yin-tze) chops off Fang's arm (See Figure 4.5).

After recovering and relearning martial arts with one arm under a village girl's care, Fang is transformed into a super fighter. When Master Qi and his family are under mortal attack by a group of long-time enemies, the one-armed swordsman does not hesitate to put his life on the line to try to save them. Loyalty reigns supreme to him. In a series of emotionally charged fights—outside an inn, on a traditional stone arch bridge, inside a classical garden, all shot in the Movietown backlot—he kills all the attackers with his unique swordfighting style. After asserting his masculine virtues, the hero walks away from the brutal fighting world to live peacefully with the village girl (See Figure 4.6).

This stereotypical Chinese cultural tradition was attenuated by romanticized traditional Chinese settings. Just like Huangmei opera

Figure 4.6 The one-armed swordsman fulfills his sense of loyalty and honor by killing his Master's enemies one by one in a traditional setting underscoring the Chineseness of his heroic devotion.

pictures, these swordfighting films were shot in the same permanent set of Movietown that was designed to evoke a sense of nostalgia for the imagined homeland: with all sorts of traditional Chinese architecture and natural surroundings, including ponds, stone arch bridges, willow trees, bamboo forests, inns, temples, fishing boats, and elegant residential halls and pavilions with moon gates. Martial arts films conjured up for its audience an imagined cultural China. "The camera moves slowly to a close-up of the face of Golden Swallow looking to the side," as a *Chinese Student Weekly* author of émigré family background described a scene from *Come Drink with Me* that touched him deeply: "Her hair flows along with the breeze, with the window half open, she looks out contemplatively into the mist-covered garden and beyond." This cinematic Zhongguo wei invoked in him some deeply ingrained images of ancient Chinese poetry and prose that put him in a culturally nostalgic mood.[95] In Taiwan, future star director Ang Lee was also deeply moved by the Zhongguo wei of Movietown costume pictures. "People like me who grew up in Taiwan, receiving Chinese education, have lost touch with the Mainland"; he remembered how the movies came to shape his sense of cultural belonging. "I haven't really been to Mainland China. That's why I sometimes felt strange about my Chinese identity. This identity was obtained from Mr. [King] Hu and Li Hanxiang's movies. . . . It was very abstract, not because of blood relationship or land but rather an ambiguous cultural concept. It was like a dream."[96] (See Figure 4.7)

Figure 4.7 Golden Swallow in a contemplative moment in *Come Drink with Me*

Conclusion

Run Run Shaw took advantage of the Cold War media environment to build his film empire in Hong Kong. The technology transfer, concentration of Mandarin-speaking creative talents, film co-production, and transportation and trade networks, among other factors, were made possible largely by the US-centered anti-Communist alliance in the region. At the same time, using American-style management, modern Western technology, and new American and Japanese film techniques to tell dehistoricized traditional Chinese stories for a global Chinese niche market, the Movietown mogul played along with his flexible boundary-straddling entrepreneurship in the polarized context. Whether it was scholars-meet-beauties love stories in Huangmei opera or swordfighters killing villains to restore justice in wuxia pictures, he focused his production on entertaining his audiences with a dreamy cultural China, romanticized and distant from the contemporary turmoil of political conflicts and social problems. He openly declared that his business interests lay in profit maximization, not political engagement, trying to keep a distance from and not getting involved in side-taking politics.

In fact, the new-styled martial arts films came out at a time of Cold War turmoil in the region that included the escalating Vietnam War, Laos's political chaos, postindependence Malaysian and Indonesian racial conflicts, and the Chinese Cultural Revolution unleashed by Mao. In Hong Kong, two riots brought to focus its deep structural problems, especially the huge gap between the colonial power and the colonized (more discussion appears in the next chapter). The first riot started with a young activist's hunger strike against Star Ferry's fare hike in April 1966. It quickly led to violent demonstrations and property damage that resulted in the arrest of fifteen hundred people. The second one was the 1967 riot, which was, as journalist Gary Kar-wai Cheung argues, "a spillover from the Cultural Revolution."[97] It began as a labor strike at an artificial flower factory in May and was shortly transformed by local Communist leaders into an anticolonial, anticapitalist campaign. When the government fought back with force against the protests, extremists resorted to terrorist attacks and indiscriminate bombings that threw the city into chaos. By the time the riots subsided in December, fifty people were killed and about five thousand were under arrest. None of these global, regional, or local conflicts were registered in the dreamy world of Shaw Brothers romanticized swordfighting or opera romance (or other popular genre movies). One of its Southeast Asian–themed films, *No War in Saigon* (西貢無戰事), which was shot in Vietnam by the studio's Taiwan-based subsidiary, was a sentimental love story set against the backdrop of Saigon's nightlife.[98]

Despite his efforts to flexibly cross between the ideological divide in Hong Kong's cultural Cold War, with his unabashed pursuit of money and luxurious lifestyle, Run Run Shaw remained a paragon of "free-world" capitalist excesses in the cultural Cold War. He could be a friend when the moderate, pragmatic "Patriotic" film leaders were in control, but when the ultra-leftist policy prevailed in the Great Leap Forward and especially the Cultural Revolution, he became an enemy. Thus, during the 1967 riots there were strikes that threatened to close down Movietown and bombs planted in the vicinity of some of Run Run's movie theaters. Indeed, on balance, the Shaw brothers' popular, depoliticized productions and the tax revenues derived from them contributed significantly to the strength and power of the British colony. Moreover, as Shaw Brothers was gaining market share in Taiwan, Run Run Shaw contributed upgrading its media industry through co-production and technology transfer, and brought to Movietown from the island huge numbers of actors, directors, technicians, and especially scriptwriters. Most famous among them included box-office favorites Lily Ho (何莉莉), Li Ching (李菁), and Jenny Hu (胡燕妮). At the same time, the Shaw brothers' sprawling exhibition networks showed Taiwan studios' products in the region, notably including such big hits as Chiung Yao's (瓊瑤) romantic movies and Li Hsing's (李行) "Healthy Realistic" classic *Beautiful Duckling* (養鴨人家, 1965), which celebrated the strength of traditional values among the island's ordinary people (mainlanders). The popularity of these films and actors from Taiwan paved the way for streams of visiting Taiwan celebrities and entertainers, most notably star singer Theresa Tang (鄧麗君), who used Hong Kong as a launching pad for their career in Shaw Brothers' global niche market. Many of them became household names, and through all their *guoyu* songs (Mandopop), *guoyu* life performance, guoyu films, magazine interviews, and various fan clubs, they significantly increased the soft-power influences of "Free China" as the "free homeland" for all Chinese around the globe.[99]

5

Epilogue

"My City" in Flux

And you are young, you can create a beautiful new world according
to your dream.

Xi Xi[1]

The local born baby boomers were more Westernized than their
parents' generation on the one hand, and were more Hongkongized
as well on the other hand.

Chan Koon-Chung[2]

The British colony of Hong Kong was situated at the crossroads between
global Cold War conflicts and competing regional ideologies and identities.
It stood front and center in Asia's cultural Cold War. Right next to China's
southern province of Guangdong, across the Sham Chun River, and with
trade routes linking it to different parts of the world, the colony had long been
the world's gateway to China. As the Communists swept to power and established the People's Republic in 1949, a massive exodus of Chinese refugees
and exiles fled to different parts of the world. Among the many who found
refuge in Hong Kong were intellectuals, writers, and film professionals, many
of whom became in one way or another entangled in the battle between
Beijing, Taipei, and Washington for the hearts and minds of ethnic Chinese
in the Asia region.

The British colonial administration proclaimed political neutrality in the
Great Power conflicts, struggling to maneuver and negotiate between various opposing forces, while trying assiduously to avoid creating suspicions
in Beijing. The colonial authority kept a vigilant eye on American and
Nationalist political warfare and saboteur activities against the mainland,
and at the same time took an aggressive stance against Communist excesses

Hong Kong Media and Asia's Cold War. Po-Shek Fu, Oxford University Press. © Oxford University Press 2023.
DOI: 10.1093/oso/9780190073763.003.0005

when its governance was threatened. As previous chapters show, through a sprawling network of state-owned businesses and cultural organizations, China turned the British colony into its propaganda and United Front work base as well as an "international financial center."[3] Through films made by the "Patriotic" Chang-Feng-Xin (長鳳新) studios, and Chinese-made pictures distributed by the Southern Film Corporation, Beijing sought to win support of the overseas Chinese community in the region in its ideological war against the Nationalist claim for legitimacy and US containment along its periphery. After the 1953 confrontation with the colonial authority, pro-Communist productions began to shift from anti-imperialist, anticolonial radicalism to an increasing emphasis on uplifting entertainment with a didactic impulse in competition with studios allegiant to the "free world."

With a consulate in the British colony large than most embassies, the Truman and Eisenhower administrations intervened in Asia's clandestine ideological war by sponsoring and developing Hong Kong–based cultural productions to push back against the Communist influences in Asia. The Asia Foundation in particular, a nonprofit organization created by the CIA, bankrolled many media groups and higher education institutions in its effort to turn the colony into a propaganda base for mobilizing overseas Chinese support in Southeast Asia. TAF's largest investment was in former Associated Press journalist Chang Kuo-sin's Asia Pictures and the Union Press, established by a group of young émigré intellectuals affiliated with the liberal third-force movement. Asia Pictures received secret funding to counter the pro-Communist studios' domination among the ethnic Chinese audiences in the region. It failed to achieve the mission of "beating the Great Wall," even as it turned its fan magazine, *Asia Pictorial*, into a popular anti-Communist current-affairs weekly, and brought increasing awareness of the need to modernize and internationalize the production standard of the Mandarin film industry. The Union Press's flagship journal, *Chinese Student Weekly* (*CSW*), was enormously influential among émigré youths in the Sinophone world. In its first decade of publication, *CSW* championed an amalgam of cultural nationalism and diasporic identity in the "free world" language of liberty and individual autonomy. At a time of decolonization and ideological conflicts, *CSW expanded* transnationally into different parts of the region, connecting young readers and activists from Hong Kong, Taiwan, and Southeast Asia into a transnational community of imagined Chineseness in the cultural Cold War against Mao's revolution.

Taiwan also had a huge network of commercial enterprises and cultural organizations in the British colony to support its economy and its bid for legitimacy as the sole government for all China. Boasting the largest audiences of Mandarin films in the Sinophone world, the Nationalist state weaponized its market to mobilize Hong Kong film professionals for its anti-Communist crusade. Taipei did not control film production directly, like the Communists did with Chang-Feng-Xin. Rather, it won the loyalty of what was then called "free China" studios by regulating and politicizing access to its film market and promoting movement of Taiwan film talents to Hong Kong. Entertainment magnate Run Run Shaw, who had amassed a fortune along with his brother, Rume, in Southeast Asia, took advantage of the colony's Cold War media environment to expand and globalize the family's production base. Despite the lack of success in breaking into the core countries of the "free world," he gained access to Taiwan, which, together with Singapore and Malaysia, became the center of the Shaw brothers' global niche market catering to ethnic Chinese around the world. It modernized "free China" film production. Shaw Brothers' star-studded studio, big-budget historical spectacles, color and Shawscope widescreen productions, and Fordist-Taylorist management system had transformed the film industry's ecosystem, where only major film companies with resources for entertainment values could compete, and inaugurated a golden age of Mandarin cinema in the region.

The Shaws' Movietown was, however, fraught with Cold War ambivalence. Strategizing production that combined modern technology and technique with traditional subjects and imagery, Shaw's productions in the 1960s and most of the 1970s brought to the audiences a romanticized China that was as entertaining as it was discreetly depoliticized. The films projected the studio's efforts to keep a safe distance from Cold War power politics under the guise of "entertainment was for money." Leveraging its capital, business network, and market reach, Shaw Brothers was recognized as the leading "free China" film enterprise, while also collaborating with pro-Beijing "Patriotic" groups. During the 1967 riots, however, the studio had to fire more than one hundred technical employees accused of organizing strikes and replace them with Taiwan personnel. Yet a few months later, Run Run Shaw took a monthlong trip to Eastern Bloc countries, allegedly with a Singapore trade delegation. After his return he made a well-publicized visit to Taipei confirming his allegiance to the "free world." Since the mid-1970s, Shaw Brothers began to decline, with limited success in adjusting to the new consuming habits of young audiences and a shift of the family's business interests to television broadcasting.

Prosperity and Stability

Hong Kong experienced a series of seismic changes in the 1960s and 1970s that prompted a new, local-born generation to call into question and reshape the Cold War networks of émigré cultural production. Thanks to the capital and experiences of Shanghai entrepreneurs and a huge reservoir of low-pay, hard-working refugee labor, the colony had transitioned from entrepot trade to a booming export-oriented manufacturing economy, centering on the low-value-adding labor-intensive textile and garment (and later also toy and electronics) industries, and flush with foreign (especially US and Japanese) investments. Also important was the often overlooked Chinese role in Hong Kong's industrialization. In 1963, Premier Zhou Enlai made it a policy to supply the colony with ample food and, especially important, a water supply, which "reduced inflationary pressures . . . and helped to maintain the competitiveness" of the export industry. As an integral part of the US-centered capitalist world system, Hong Kong's economy experienced phenomenal expansion. Its annual gross domestic product (GDP) and GDP per capita increased around 8 to 9 percent in most years of the 1960s, and jumped to an average of more than 10 percent a year through the 1970s and 1980s.[4]

Underlying its rapid economic development, however, were massive social problems that came into public consciousness after the riots in 1966–1967. In pursuit of a laissez-faire policy of free capital flow and limited state intervention (and thereby "budgetary conservatism"), as former colonial official Leo Goodstadt wrote, "Hong Kong Government was openly biased in favor of businesses and the well-being of the rest of the community seems a secondary consideration." Under the influential financial secretary John Cowperthwaite (1961–1971), the colony became known for its free trade and low taxes, but it had no progressive tax, and government expenditure on public services and social welfare was minimal. It was "tragic that the prosperous 1960s had been frittered away," Hong Kong–based *Far Eastern Economic Review* editor Derek Davies lamented, "building up huge surpluses while spending a derisory 1.1 percent on social welfare, and providing its youth with hideously inadequate education."[5]

The swelling population as a result of the influx of refugees from the main-land made housing a humanitarian disaster for much of the 1950s and 1960s. As late as 1965, about half a million squatters were still living in crowded shantytowns with horrible sanitation and poached electricity on hillsides that were steep and dangerously prone to typhoon-induced landslides and huge fires (as immortalized in Richard Quine's *The World of Suzie Wong* and Allen Fong's *Father and Son* [方育平]). Like many rapidly developing countries in the mid-twentieth century regarding the international division of labor, colonial Hong Kong was an "ultimate cheap labor economy." There were no labor protection laws, no minimum-wage or health benefits, and old-age pensions were nonexistent. Critics such as Elsie Elliott decried the government's callous disregard of labor conditions, but their moral rage was a voice in the colonial wilderness; no significant change of labor protections occurred until the 1970s.

Hong Kong went through a huge demographic change in the 1960s and 1970s. It had increasingly become a young city. In the early 1970s, an estimated 40 percent of the total population of close to four million people were under eighteen years old.[6] Public expenditures on education, not to mention youth development programs, were small. According to one figure, only 18 percent of primary school graduates in 1965 could go on to sec-ondary schools. Lots of low-income and disadvantaged students were left out of the system, even after primary education became compulsory in 1971.[7] Concerns about idle youths and juvenile crime began attracting media atten-tion as Hong Kong slid into the chaos of the 1966–1967 riots.

In April 1966, despite public dissatisfaction, the Star Ferry, a popular pas-senger ferry across the Victora Harbor, between the Central District and Tsim Sha Tsui, increased its fares. In protest, twenty-seven-year-old Su Shau-chung (蘇守忠) staged a hunger strike in front of the Star Ferry Piers in Tsim Sha Tsui, the famous tourist district in Kowloon. It quickly attracted a large crowd. The police arrested him the next day, and many young sympathizers demanded his release by resorting to acts of violence. The few days of un-rest, which were not overtly directed against British colonialism, resulted in the killing of one protester and the arrest of around fourteen hundred youths. The ensuing inquiry commission underlined the significance of youth discontent in the riot and urged attention to "the underlying insecurity of lives in the Colony, resulting from international political and economic conditions, that create tensions which elsewhere would be more than suffi-cient cause for frequent disturbances."[8] The Trench administration ignored the warnings. Equally dismissive of youth discontent and "the underlying insecurity" of colonial life were, incidentally, the Communist-backed press and its foe, the US-funded *CSW*, both of which lent support to the government's suppression of the unrest for the sake of what it claimed to be the universal aspiration of the city: "peace and stability."[9] The term "peace and stability," or "prosperity and stability"—which become a popular political catchphrase in the colony especially after the late 1960s—originated in British rhetoric to justify the empire in the Asia region at a time of postwar anticolonialism. For example, Hong Kong's major English newspaper, the *South China Morning Post*, quoted a British Member of Parliament in 1947 to the effect that the colony had an important role in "Far Eastern prosperity and stability." Two years later, as Mao's forces were encircling Beijing, a local pro-Nationalist newspaper carried the British colonial secretary Arthur Creech-Jones's New Year's message that underscored the importance of prosperity and stability in Hong Kong and the region.[10]

Youth discontent flared up again in the bloody 1967 riots that rocked the territory. The actions were, as journalist Gary Kar-wai Cheung points out, "actually a spillover from the Cultural Revolution" that unleashed the Red Guard violence across China, and was organized and planned all along by the Communist leaders in Hong Kong (namely, the Hong Kong and Macao Work Committee). In May 1967, employees of the Hong Kong Artificial Flower Works in San Po Kong, an industrial area, went on strike against the brutal working conditions. Quickly the strike turned political, calling for an anti-British, anticolonial struggle, as crowds of neighborhood youths and students from pro-Beijing schools joined in and brawls with the police ensued. The Communists organized protests and rallies (including many outside the Government House, shouting anti-imperialist slogans and singing revolutionary songs), and called a general strike in June. With London's backing, Trench's administration stood firm in combating the rioters and, starting in July 1967, responded with increasing force. In August, to show solidarity with the anticolonial struggle in Hong Kong, Red Guards in Beijing laid siege to the British Embassy, accusing London of colluding with US imperialism. In the Cold War context, the 1967 riot was also a propaganda war. The Communists cast themselves as fighters for the global struggle against white imperialism and colonialism, while the colonial government presented the unrest as an attack on "capitalist prosperity and social stability." At the beginning of the riots, historian Elizabeth Sinn observed, especially among the young generation, "members of the public were ambivalent toward the labor dispute. . . . Some even thought that it was good to teach the colonial administration a lesson for its authoritarian style of government."[11] However, as the Communists shifted tactics in response to police aggression to encouraging young activists to disrupt traffic and plant homegrown bombs across town after July (which caused injuries to many innocent people, including children), the rioters lost public sympathy and, perhaps more important, Beijing's support (as Zhou Enlai allegedly regained control of the Foreign Ministry from the Radicals and continued the policy of using Hong Kong to generate foreign exchange) in toppling colonial rule. The six months of confrontation took a heavy toll on the colony: fifty lives were lost, at least two thousand people were arrested, and an exodus of capital took place. As rumors continued about People's Liberation Army (PLA) troop movements along the border and an imminent Chinese takeover, the people in Hong Kong threw their support to the colonial administration in quelling the riots. [12]

"Ironically, in the light of communist objectives," scholar Ian Scott observed, "the end-result of the disturbances was to increase the support for, and the legitimacy of, the existing order."[13] The biggest loser of the riots turned out to be the local Communist organization and young Communist sympathizers. The sprawling intelligence networks the Communists had built in the colony since the 1940s, especially those inside the colonial administration and related to Taiwan and Southeast Asia, were jeopardized. Its United Front efforts suffered a huge setback. The readership of its major newspapers, such as *Ta Kung Pao* (大公報) and *Hsin Wan Pao* (新晚報), plummeted, and the Beijing-backed "Patriotic" films lost their market influence. Moreover, many of the young strikers and activists who joined the riots because of their alienation from exploitative capitalism and colonial rule were thrown to jail or left out of work—and disillusioned. The turmoil of the riots, in particular, exacerbated the deeply entrenched "Communist phobias" of *konggong bing* (恐共病) and anti-Communist sentiments in the local community; people derogatively called the leftists "lefties" (左仔). Hong Kong's pro-Beijing camp spent the next decade largely in self-isolation.[14]

It was not a "love for the Hong Kong Government and its laissez-faire policies that did almost nothing for the huge struggling working class," American diplomat Syd Goldsmith—whose job was to study Hong Kong politics—argues, but fear and aversion to the havoc and turmoil on the mainland caused the local population to choose the "acceptance of a callous colonial regime" (and a strong US presence) to preserve prosperity and stability.[15] It was to get away from violence and turmoil that they sought refuge in the British colony in the first place. The colonial power also came to realize, nonetheless, that the enormous gap between the ruling elites and the colonized needed to be bridged, especially for the younger generation, whose active support was vital to the colonial authority's legitimacy. The incoming governor Murray MacLehose (1972–1982) expressed it well in his memo to the British Foreign and Commonwealth Office: "I still believe it would be possible . . . to hold the loyalty and attention of the population and build up a sense of local identity based on civic pride. . . . I thought this could be done by the implementation of extensive programmes of social reform, by greater responsiveness on the part of the Government."[16] By "civic pride," in retrospect, what MacLehose was suggesting was principally that the local people should be proud of their city's standard of living and quality of life comparable to those in developed capitalist countries, and in distinction from the developing economies in the region, especially the mainland. Hence, with the Financial Secretary Philip Haddon-Cave, the governor pushed forward a series of reforms in "housing and urban renewal, secondary and higher education, transport, social services, cultural development,"[17] including expansion of public assistance programs, extending free education to nine years, and construction of the Mass Transit Railway (MTR) and satellite towns (such as Shatin and Tsuen Wan) that virtually reshaped the territory's spatial economy. Even more significant in the public mind was the governor's creation of the Independent Commission against Corruption in 1974 to fight against corruption, especially the police force's abuse of power, which had long been an entrenched (if not unavoidable) evil in the colony's everyday life.

Along with multiple social programs, the MacLehose administration also introduced a slew of measures to promote "localization" that included adding new, local blood to the mid- to low-level civil service ranks, launching the annual Hong Kong Arts Festival in 1973 to promote local artists, and the "Trash Bugs" (垃圾蟲) campaign in 1978 to raise consciousness about making Hong Kong a distinctly clean living community. In 1974, after several years of internal debates and student protests, Governor MacLehose's administration adopted Chinese, in principle, as the official language. In fact, the governor was a skillful and savvy reformer with a mandate to make the colonial governance more efficient and responsive to public needs and try to narrow the gap between the governing elites and people on the street. Like all postwar governors before him, MacLehose was not a disruptor set on democratizing the colonial system. He had introduced limited political reforms during his rule. The governor's cabinet—the Legislative Council—remained under control of senior government officials and local business elites, and despite his call for localization, "the most senior and sensitive posts in the Civil Service were monopolized by expatriates until the last decade of British rule."[18] It is indeed no exaggeration that, as *Far Eastern Economic Review* journalist Richard Hughes mocked, "there is no nonsense about democracy in Hong Kong. Administration and legislation are conducted along unashamed colonial lines."[19]

The so-called MacLehose Decade was also a time of continuous economic development and increasing affluence, as discussed earlier, with estimated growth of more than 10 percent of GDP per capita in most years during the 1970s and early 1980s, thanks to expanding foreign trade and real estate and stock market booms (except for the 1973 stock crash). The geopolitical situation in the Asia region was also in a state of relative calm as the Vietnam War gradually ground to a halt and Cold War tensions between China and the United States abated after President Richard Nixon's visit with Mao in February 1972; Japan normalized its diplomatic relations with Beijing in September of the same year. The ideological landscape of the region shifted as a result. Washington decided to lift its two-decade-long trade embargoes against Beijing. And as China was preoccupied by its domestic turmoil and power struggles, relations with Great Britain were back on the right track in the wake of the embassy burning fiasco. Trade and cultural exchange between the two sides increased, and Prime Minister Edward Heath's Labour government, like American President Jimmy Carter did later, sought a normalization of relations with the PRC that included, among other policies, supporting Beijing's reintegration in the international community.

After several months of disruption during the riots that caused great inconveniences, Hong Kong was once again guaranteed a supply of food and water from the mainland at favorable prices, as it continued to serve China's foreign currency and economic development needs. In fact, beginning in 1971, amid all the political and economic turmoil, the Communist leadership needed to raise money to import new technology for military upgrades. The British colony was then to play an even more important role, and to be ever increasingly intertwined with the mainland political economy, when Deng Xiaoping came to power in 1978. He pushed forward an ambitious drive to speed up China's economic modernization that inaugurated a new era of "Reform and Open Up" that was to transform China into a manufacturing powerhouse. Special Economic Zones were created in 1978–1980 along the southeastern coast to attract investments from overseas Chinese communities to jump-start the export industries. Hong Kong entrepreneurs and investors took advantage of the business opportunities. Almost the entire traditional manufacturing sector had been relocated to the neighboring province of Guangdong in the latter part of the 1990s (giving way to financial and business services), which became practically the colony's "industrial hinterland," while the banking industry profited from the expanding import and export business.[20] By 1986, the mainland replaced the United States and Japan as the British colony's largest market and source of imports.[21]

In March 1979, confident about the colony's prosperity and its role in China's modernization drive, Governor MacLehose took a trip to Beijing with the intention of raising the question about the future of Hong Kong. In his meeting with Deng Xiaoping, the governor tried to press for an answer about China's view of post-1997 Hong Kong. The paramount leader was said to reply that China would resume sovereignty and rejected ideas of continuous British administration of the colony. There have been various interpretations of Deng's conversations with MacLehose, including that Deng might not have given much thought to the Hong Kong question as he was preoccupied at the time with the reunification with Taiwan, or perhaps with his impending visit to Washington about the normalization of Sino-American relations, and the invasion of Vietnam. In 1981, as believed, the Communist leadership came to a decision to take back the British colony with a "One Country, Two Systems" approach. This decision triggered economic and political conflicts and confrontations in the following decades that have come to reshape and disrupt the political life, social formation, and cultural identity of Hong Kong until today.

"Hong Kong Is Our City"

Accompanying Hong Kong's rapid economic development and changing political landscape, in the context of shifting Cold War dynamics, was the emergence of a new generation born after World War II. Born in Hong Kong or coming to Hong Kong as youngsters with their refugee parents, this was numerically a huge group (comparable to the American generation of baby boomers), which caused the colony, as discussed earlier, to stop being "a city of adults."[22] The postwar generation had no direct experience of wartime sufferings or everyday life on the mainland or the turmoil of the Communist takeover that gave rise to the massive exodus away from it. This generation's formative experiences were shaped instead by poverty and overcrowded living conditions, the 1966–1967 riots, the industrial takeoff of the 1960s, and increasing modernization of the colony's daily life. The rapid economic development since the 1960s created new career paths and job opportunities. Large numbers of young women in particular found work in the flourishing textile and garment industries to support their families, and their labor force participation began to disrupt longstanding patriarchal values and expectations of female submission inside and outside the home. The increasing public role for women was, in all likelihood, reflected in the character Zhu Yingtai's (祝英台) demand for a voice in her education and marriage in Li Han-hsiang's Huangmei opera film *Love Eterne* and the "fan phenomenon" of Cantonese idol Connie Chan, whose 1960s film roles of what sociologist Janet Salaff calls dutiful "working daughters" connected with the dreams and frustrations of her young factory girl admirers.[23]

Moreover, with the astonishing speed of new technological changes (e.g., rice cookers, the telephone, television and portable radios, Shaw Brothers' color and widescreen movies), the expanded networks of cultural and educational institutions, and the increasing opportunities for studying and travelling abroad, the new generation came into a new world where the rules and values of their seniors were up for debate. An important contributing influence to this cultural change was the new global youth culture, which started in the core economies of the "free world." The 1960s in the West was a period of youthful rebellion and mass movements: the demonstrations against the Vietnam War and American imperialism in the United States and Europe, the Paris revolts of May 1968, the Italian "hot autumn" of 1969, the Woodstock 69 that used music as protest, and the social movements for justice and equality of the marginal people that went along with them—the women's movement, the US civil rights movement, and labor strikes. They signified large-scale alienation, dissatisfaction with capitalist inequality, and the desire for personal liberation in developed Western economies. "The new 'autonomy' of youth as a separate social stratum," historian Eric Hobsbawm explains, gave shahese astonishing developments.[24] Their countercultural expressions gave rise to a new iconic lifestyle of blue jeans, rock and roll music, protest songs, long hair, and indie cinema, which almost instantly became the symbols of hip and modern youths worldwide.

The Beatles performed two concerts in Hong Kong in 1964. The mainstream press was hostile to the ensuing Beatlemania among the young fans, who emulated the long mod hairstyles and formed rock bands of their own, pejoratively calling the English group "Crazy People" or the "Long-Haired Four." The US-funded *CSW* was ambivalent about how to react to the rock music phenomenon. The youth-oriented magazine was in a state of uncertain transition. The Union Press leadership, all émigrés from the mainland, continued to see *CSW* as a bridge linking ethnic Chinese across generations and geographical boundaries into a transformative force of cultural nationalism in opposition to Chinese communism.

CSW's new editors saw a different world. Joining *CSW* full-time around the same time in the early 1960s, Law Kar (羅卡; penname of Lau Yiu-kuen [劉耀權]), Loke-Lay (陸離; LokeHing-chun [陸慶珍]), and Ng Ping (吳平) played key roles in shaping editorial trends during the 1960s. Luk graduated from New Asia College, studying with New Confucian masters Tang Junyi and Mou Zongsan (牟宗三). A multitalented writer famous for her passion for Francois Truffaut, Loke-Ley brought a witty, humanistic touch to her editorial work in the areas of arts and culture. Her *MAD* magazine–influenced Hong Kong–focused humor and satire section, "Happy Valley," enjoyed a huge audience. Along with Ng, a hard-working literary editor, they encouraged and mentored many new talents from the postwar generation, such as Xi Xi (西西) and Yuanyuan (圓圓), to replace the domination of émigré and Taiwan writers, marking a new, youthful, and localized trend in *CSW* (See Figure 5.1).

In his first job after graduating from college, Law spent a year learning the ropes before being asked to take over the movie section in 1962. He quickly changed the emphasis from covering news and brief reviews of non-Communist Mandarin films (especially those from MP&GI) to introducing European avant garde cinema and new cultural trends. Under his deft editorship, in barely two years, a group of young film enthusiasts began to coalesce around the movie section, discussing and arguing with each other about countercultural movements in Western film culture, especially the French New Wave and Italian Neorealism, that turned it into a beacon of inspiration for those who saw in it a unique window to absorb new ideas and cultural experiences from the developed world. Law recalled decades later that the antiestablishment culture also allowed the young generation to vent their frustration about parental control, the bleakness of colonial life, and their uncertain futures. After 1965, the movie section also turned its attention to use

Figure 5.1 Law Kar (*center*) at a *CSW* editorial staff meeting in the early 1960s
Courtesy of Law Kar

its newly acquired perspectives to lash out at local film production—especially in their view "the money-worshipping" Shaw Brothers—and called for radical change. They dreamed of creating a new Hong Kong cinema; they pooled their resources to make 8mm experimental films to capture true life. "Great films will come out of Hong Kong one of these days," one of them said. "If we can't do it, there will be 'you,' and if you can't, there will be 'them' who come after in the future to come."[25] Along with Law, some of this cohort of film enthusiasts, including Law Kar, Shek Kei (石琪), who was to become a most-respected film critic, Yofan (楊凡), and future action film legend John Woo, went on to play significant roles in Hong Kong cinema. Regarding the movie section's enormous influence among the postwar generation, Loke-Ley Lei attributed it to a confluence of material developments in the increasingly globalized city of the 1960s: in particular, the opening of the modern twelve-story city hall in the Central District in 1962, equipped with a public library and a concert hall, quickly became what scholar Leo Ou-fan Lee describes as "a favorite gathering place for all kinds of civic activities."[26] One was a European expatriate group called Studio One, which showed avant garde movies from around the Western world—particularly French New Wave and Italian Neorealism. In the meantime, the American library and a variety of English bookstores provided easy access to major English-language film journals such as *Sight and Sound*, *Movie*, and *Film Culture*, which offered key information for the young fans to make sense of the ideological and aesthetic contexts of these unconventional works.[27] (See Figure 5.2)

Law's success prompted attacks from *CSW*'s archival rival, the Communist-backed magazine *Youth Paradise* 青年樂園. They lambasted the movie section's tendency to "worship and have blind faith in everything foreign." There were also other emulators vying for writers and readers. At the same time, early generation of Union Press 友聯leaders expressed displeasure with its inadvertent shift of audience to college students because the contents were overly esoteric for secondary school adolescents, who might not even have heard of the films in discussions. They thought all the frivolous

Figure 5.2 Law Kar (*center rear*) and *CSW* film section colleagues Xi Xi and Luk Ley met with director Chang Cheh in Movietown (*front, left to right*)
Courtesy of Law Kar

talks about avant-garde visual cultures, moreover, diverted from *CSW*'s mission of enlightening its readers with Chinese cultural nationalism and Cold War agenda. Thanks to the Lin Yueheng 林悅恆, Taiwan University-trained editor-in-chief known for his liberal leadership, who took pain to defend the film section's large following among young readers, both college and some precocious high school students.[28]

The movie section and the localization efforts of Loke-Ley and Ng contributed to keep *CSW* one of the best-selling periodicals for the young generation in the first part of the 1960s. According to a survey of literary youths of the sixteen- to twenty-year-old age group, it was voted second most-read magazine.[29] Shortly after the 1967 riots, Law Kar quit and joined a left-leaning cultural magazine and took part in various radical movements before leaving, in 1971, for Rome to study filmmaking. Among his reasons for leaving *CSW* was his clash with UP's hard-line anti-Communist stance. Similar to many young intellectuals of the time, the movie section editor was sympathetic to the labor strikes in San Po Kong, where the *CSW* office was located, and he walked past the workers everyday. He argued for an editorial policy regarding the disturbance that would take into account the public's discontent with colonial injustice. He recalled half a century later that senior management rejected it on the grounds that nothing was more urgent during this political crisis than upholding the organization's "pro-government" and "anti-Communist" priorities. To criticize the colonial authority for disregard of the workers' plight would only legitimize the Communist-led riots.[30]

CSW had started a precipitous decline in sales and influence around 1967–1968. The main problem was funding. TAF, which had bankrolled the UP and *CSW* for over a decade—helping fuel its rapid expansion despite low prices and lack of advertising revenues—began to draw down its involvement in Hong Kong's cultural Cold War in the mid-1960s. *CSW* lost funding around 1967, which resulted in cuts of staffing and extracurricular interest groups, which had been an important source both of recruiting volunteers and expanding readership, and possibly depended on the UP offices in Singapore and Malaysia to keep it afloat. As discussed earlier, many UP founders and early activists had resettled in Singapore and Malaysia since the 1950s and used their strong connections with the postcolonial governments to build up profitable enterprises with a constant stream of revenues from Chinese-language textbooks (with emphasis on traditional Chinese cultural virtues) and printing businesses. They were in a strong position to shape the transnational organization's policy, which tended to be out of sync with Hong Kong's changing situations.

After Law Kar and other editors had left, Loke-Ley and Ng handled all the editorial work. Loke-Ley now took charge also of the movie section, extending her range to covering television and other new cultural and social changes. Ng tried to add content that reflected the rising tides of social activism. The overload quickly caused burnout. This was, however, a time of intense competition in the publishing industry, as the cultural marketplace was crowded with periodicals (aside from the Communist-sponsored *Youth Paradise*) in similar formats, but with more radical, locally engaged styles and sensibilities, including most notably *Hong Kong Student Weekly* (香港學生週報), *Youth Weekly* (青年週報), *Secondary School Students Weekly* (中學生週報), *New Weekly* (新週報), *Workers Weekly* (工人週報), *Panku* (盤古), *The Seventies* (七十年代), and *70s Biweekly* (70年代雙週刊), vying for both writers and readers from the new generation. In 1974, the struggling *CSW* shut down.

Besides its budget shortfalls, CSW had an image problem. Socially conscious young readers increasingly saw it as old-fashioned and out of touch. The mood and sensibility of the new generation shifted around the turn of the 1970s. Two major cultural trends paralleled and intertwined with each other that ran counter to what *CSW* had represented. They were an emergent consciousness of *becoming* a community as distinct from the crisis-ridden Chinese nation state across the border, and the development of campus radicalization and social activism.

CSW continued through most of the 1960s to champion the "unyielding spirit," like that of a "tree" in times of what philosopher Tang Junyi allegorized as a crisis of "scattered flowers and fruits." It strove to perpetuate an imagined diasporic identity that was framed around the notion of "returning" to an ethnic homeland.[31] At a time when the British colony was undergoing rapid economic changes in addition to the Trench and MacLehose administrations' efforts to engineer a sense of "local community" (such as by starting the Hong Kong Festival or an anticorruption campaign), these sentiments seemed irrelevant and at times even bred dogmatic intolerance in some circumstances. Margaret Ng (吳靄儀), an elite English-medium high school student and future pro-democracy legislator, complained to *CSW* that she had been called a "traitor" for not going to a Chinese-medium school.[32]

Increasingly, a sense of local belonging and emotional attachment—that Hong Kong was, after all, "my city," as writer Xi Xi intimately called it—while mostly continuing to embrace Chinese ethnicity began to emerge.[33] A "civil identity" was, indeed, in the making. "The population of Hong Kong came to identify themselves as 'Heung Gong Yan,'" observed Hong Kong–based anthropologist Matthew Turner in 1995, "an ambiguous construction that was more that of a 'resident,' less that of a 'people.' Hong Kong identity was rather the identity of life-style, a shared recognition of similar self-images, real or desired, of existential choices, from food to education."[34] This lifestyle or self-image has been characterized by various critics, journalists, and scholars as "go-getting and highly competitive . . . not British or Western . . . not Chinese in the same way that the citizens of PRC are Chinese,"[35] or "*Homo economicus,*" believers in the so-called Central District values (the Central District is Hong Kong's downtown business center) who were driven by capitalist values of profits, efficiency, and prosperity.[36] Cultural scholar Rey Chow, on the other hand, called this an identity of "compulsory logic," that chasing after money was (and still is) the only alternative for the people of Hong Kong, who had been denied "something essential—political power."[37] Actually, all these characterizations point to one of the key legacies of the Cold War in Hong Kong. As this book tries to argue, the Great Power rivalry and propaganda and psychological warfare reinforced and intensified the efforts of the colonial authority (and its big business allies) to tighten its political grip and to depoliticize educational system and cultural production and make it more entertaining, championing the laissez-faire policy of prosperity and stability.

It was therefore no surprise that there was a gap between the writings in *CSW* about the anxiety about China's future and the importance of reinforcing Chineseness by "studying more about China's philosophy, arts and history," and the young generation's emergent local attachment. In a 1969 roundtable discussion about high school students' view of Double Tenth National Day, for example, a student taunted, "I don't know how the older generation thought about the national day. It is of no interest to me. . . . Other celebrations in Hong Kong such as the Christmas holiday are more popular and ubiquitous, we have food, and we have days off. As for the Chinese National Day, I think it is of relevance only to a handful of people." Another teenager expressed her alienation: "We are of the generation mostly born after 1950. We have never ever experienced life on the mainland before the regime change. Every time when I saw people celebrate the Double Tenth National Day or the October One National Day, I felt nothing but weird and bizarre. At the same time, I also felt sad. We have two national days, and yet

I don't feel like belonging to either of them."[38] On the other hand, in celebration of the first Hong Kong Festival in 1969 sponsored by the Trench administration, which featured a variety of activities and entertainment programs across the city, students of the elite Belilios Public School decorated the premises festively along the theme of "Hong Kong, Our City, B.P.S., Our School."[39]

This new local consciousness was in constant flux, always evolving and in contestation through the coming decades. In 1973–1974 the city as a focus of local belonging was captured by Xi Xi, a young émigré writer from Shanghai, in her influential novel *My City*. In a lighthearted, playful tone, it tells the story of a new generation of hard-working, nonideological, Westernized, highly educated youths taking pride in the only home they know: Hong Kong, with all the markers of capitalist modernity. Yet they were also, somehow, remotely conscious of their ethnic-national connections with China: "It doesn't matter if you speak Mandarin, or Cantonese, our country is like a crabapple tree leaf on the map."[40] Around the same time, pop singer Sam Hui (許冠傑), sang "Eiffel Tower above the Cloud" (鐵塔凌雲) in Cantonese on the trailblazing television show *Good News from Double Stars* (雙星報喜), hosted by his brother Michael Hui and himself. Just as Xi Xi's character exclaims, "God bless Hong Kong," after traveling away from the city, the song's protagonist calls Hong Kong home after returning from an around-the-world trip.[41] The great success of the song paved the way for the Cantopop boom in the 1980s and 1990s that overturned the domination of Taiwan-influenced Mandarin pop song culture. Similarly, the term "Hong Kong Chinese" (香港的中國人) became widely used in the media in the decades leading up to the 1997 handover.

On the other hand, in 1976, Chan Koon-Chung (陳冠中), son of a Shanghai émigré steeped in Marxist humanism, cofounded the hip *City Magazine* (號外), which tried at first to emulate *CSW* and *New Yorker* magazine in targeting students and promoting Western New Journalism while delving into the colony's hidden history. Instead of the stylized homesickness prevalent among the older émigré writers, the magazine created a new style of what can be called a nostalgia of the local, rediscovering the human meanings of Hong Kong's rapidly disappearing neighborhood life and cultural style (such as former child star Peter Dunn's (鄧小宇) evocation of MP&GI and Shaw Brothers' star culture) in the face of modernization that had little connection to China. Seeing himself as a Xianggangren (香港人), or Hongkonger, Chan went so far as to lament there was no special anthem for Hong Kong, which drew ridicules for imagining Hong Kong independence.[42] Also, poet Kun Nam (崑南) created a small magazine titled *Hong Kong Student Weekly* (in defiance of the "Chinese" in *CSW*), which, with its overt display of Hong Kong identification and radical discussion of global avant-garde music, quickly became *CSW*'s big rival.

The first half of the 1970s was also a period of student radicalization. Under the influence of the worldwide counterestablishment protests, and especially the influence of the transnational Chinese protest against the Diaoyu (or Senkaku) Islands dispute, many Hong Kong youths were radicalized. Considered by some as analogous to the Berlin crisis in the early Cold War, the Diaoyu Islands generated enormous geopolitical problems between China, Japan, and the United States that have threatened to destabilize the South China Sea and impair the US alliances in Asia. In 1970, Washington announced the reversion of the islands to Tokyo along with Okinawa.[43] The decision stirred nationalist fervor among Chinese students (mostly from Taiwan) in the United States. Several massive demonstrations were launched in 1971, and eminent scholars such as historian P. T. Ho (何炳棣) and mathematician Shiing-Shen Chern (陳省身) sent a petition to the Nationalist regime urging opposition to the US-Japanese agreement. College students in Taiwan also organized protests in the face of government suppression. In the colony, students and some non-Maoist left-wing groups—most notably the Trotskyite-Anarchist collective, whose journal *70s Biweekly,* which contained political essays and radical film and art reviews centering on local problems, was at the forefront of the anticolonial and antiestablishment foment in the 1970s—responded to the anti-Japanese nationalist movement with enthusiasm. This started the "Protect Diaoyu Islands Movement" (保釣運動) in solidarity with those in the United States and Taiwan. More than thirty rallies and demonstrations were held during 1971 and 1972 to demand the return of the islands to China. They resulted in scores of arrests and injuries by the colonial administration, which was afraid that the nationalistic fervor would turn into another 1967 riot. Initially the protestors saw the Chiang Kai-shek regime as the sole representative of Chinese sovereignty. Taipei's high-handed reaction to student protests, and the high-profile meeting of Zhou Enlai with US Baodiao leaders and other scholars—and especially the news of President Nixon's impending trip to China—radicalized the movement, shifting the allegiance to Mao's anti-imperialist revolution and the call for cross-Strait unification.[44] (See Figure 5.3)

The Baodiao movement energized social movement in opposition to colonial injustice and Cold War power politics. Radical nationalism became the

Figure 5.3 The May 1971 cover of *70s Biweekly* featuring a Baodiao protest
70s Biweekly, n.20 (May 1971)

order of the day. A US-returned student, Pao Cho-shek (包錯石), published a series of essays in 1972 that became enormously influential among college students and young intellectuals. Borrowing languages from American modernization theories, Pao heaped scorns of derision on, in his opinion, pro-American New Asia Confucian scholars and émigré intellectuals (implicitly such as those of the Union Press and *CSW*) for their anti-Communist rhetoric and called for "reunification" and reengagement with the contemporary Chinese society. All these intellectuals were "located in between foreigners and the native Chinese," he condemned, "who look Chinese but have the heart of foreigners."[45] Radical nationalism became the order of the day. Activists were generally divided into two major camps, which reflected the tension in identity between the local and the national: namely, the "social action group" (社會派), which prioritized changes of local structural inequality and grassroots mobilization, and the so-called national interest group (國粹派), which emphasized promoting identification with Mao's China. Centering around campus student associations and the influential leftist magazine *The Seventies*, the Communist establishment was allegedly behind some of the latter group's activities, including cultural exhibitions on college campuses, public forums on reunification, and "study trips" to China. The Maoists' group lost legitimacy, however, with the arrest of the Gang of Four in 1976 and exposure of all the barbarism and political evils of the Cultural Revolution. Right after graduation its leading members took up management jobs in multinational firms to do trade with China. Inspired by New Left and community organization ideas, throughout the 1970s, many social activists involved themselves in grassroots movements and became social workers or labor organizers. Protests and demonstrations also occurred frequently during this decade, demanding, to name a few issues, government action against police corruption, adoption of Chinese as the official language, more public housing, and more social services. Radical intellectuals also organized demonstrations against US imperialism in Indochina and the colony's role in the Vietnam War: provision of rest and recreation for American service members. The social action movement began to wane in the latter part of the 1970s with Hong Kong entering a new phase of China–Hong Kong relations.[46]

In 1978, the new leader, Deng Xiaoping, proclaimed the start of "Reform and Open Up" policies that were destined to change China and global geopolitics forever. A year later, China established four Special Economic Zones that included Shenzhen and Zhuhai, neighboring British Hong Kong. Soon afterward, as mentioned earlier, Governor MacLehose visited Beijing and was told that China would take the colony back. However, when he returned home the governor only conveyed the Chinese leader's message to local investors: "to set their hearts at ease."[47] It also coincided with the normalization of Sino-American relations, signaling post-Mao China's openness to a capitalist free-market economy and the emergence of a new global constellation.

Similar to the British regime's long-held views, Hong Kong became to Beijing an "economic city," privileging its neoliberal capitalist emphasis on profit, stability, and efficiency. It was to serve as the "model for the PRC's export industries and as the most accessible source of funding for its industrial takeoff." Many local entrepreneurs and investors looked to the mainland for business opportunities, and by 1997 almost the entire manufacturing sector had been moved to the neighboring province.[48] By 1986, China was the colony's second-largest market, trailing only the United States. As the economies on both sides of the Strait inched closer, the Sino-British negotiations that led to the Joint Declaration on the Question of Hong Kong (1984) and Basic Law (1990) were volatile. The prospect of returning to China stoked long-standing fear and suspicion of communism and pessimism about Hong Kong's future. Despite Beijing's promise of "One Country, Two Systems," the uncertain future touched off a wave of emigration, and the overwhelming majority of those who stayed on, according to various opinion surveys by popular media, preferred no change to the status quo. However, a group of college student leaders and former social activists advocated "democratic reunification" (民主回歸) after the announcement of the British National Act of 1981, which provoked a sense of betrayal. Central to their belief was an attempt to combine anticolonial nationalism with ideas of Western-style democracy, embracing China's recovery of sovereignty while placing hope in the development of a democratic China. It has now been discovered that some of these advocates were under the influence of the Chinese Community Party's United Front works that emphasized China's sufferings under Western imperialism and Cold War anti-China containment.[49] The hope of "democratic reunification," as evidenced by the Tiananmen Square incident of 1989 that brought half a million people in Hong Kong to take to the streets in a show of solidarity, as scholar and former student leader Law Wing Sang remarked, turned out to be at best a "wishful thing" at a time of crisis of confidence.[50]

While Hong Kong's future was uncertain, the emergent local consciousness was now reworked and extensively contested in the popular media as people became ever more identified with the city they called home and tried to re-story how it came into becoming "our city." Films, in local language, turned into a popular vehicle of this identity making. As director Michael Hui told Golden Harvest, which was to displace Shaw Brothers' hegemony with its flexible subcontracting system, "The Cantonese-speaking population of Hong Kong would really welcome films and songs which spoke the language of the common people."[51] After more than two decades of the Mandarization of the Hong Kong entertainment industry, Cantonese films made a comeback in the mid-1970s with the Hui Brothers' (Michael and Sam) record-shattering comedies, *Games Gamblers Play* (鬼馬雙星, 1974), *The Private Eyes* (半斤八兩, 1976), and *Security Unlimited* (摩登保鑣, 1981). Filled with almost nonstop gags and trying-to-get-rich-fast stock characters, they contained exaggerated (but also innocuous) satirization of capitalist inequality and the rat-racing, status-seeking consumerism of colonial Hong Kong. The theme songs of Hui Brothers' films by Sam, combining playful Western tunes and colloquial Cantonese lyrics, became instant Cantopop classics as well. Also immensely popular were movies (e.g., the family comedy *Mr. Coconut* of 1989 [合家歡] and black comedy *Her Fatal Way* of 1990 [表姐,妳好嘢]) and TV series (e.g., *The Good, the Bad, and the Ugly* of 1979 [網中人], starring Chow Yun-Fa [周潤發]) that invariably otherized mainland Chinese as uncultured and greedy poor cousins. The commercial success led to a plethora of TV dramas and innovative film genres that catapulted Hong Kong to the position of the world's second-largest movie exporter. They included gangster films (e.g., Leung Po Chi's [梁普智] *Jumping Ashes* of 1975 [跳灰] and John Woo's [吳汝森] shengunfighting classic *The Killer* of 1989) and kung-fu comedies (e.g., Yuen Woo-ping's *Drunken Master* of 1978 and Sammo Hung's [洪金寶] action comedy *My Lucky Star* of 1985 [福星高照]), which subverted the ethnic and nationalist mystification of martial arts films (like those by Cha Che and Bruce Lee) while paradoxically continuing to borrow ideas and motifs from Chinese folk culture.[52]

It was in these years of increasing identification with "our city," global market expansion, and artistic and technological innovation that the so-called New Wave directors emerged in 1979 and early 1980, such as Ann Hui (許鞍華), John Woo, Tsui Hark (徐克), Allen Fong, Yim Ho (嚴浩), and Jacob Cheung (張之亮). Many of them were US- or UK-trained, bringing new film techniques and sensibilities to bear on their deep attachment to Hong Kong in which their roots lie. Unlike the early generation of émigré filmmakers such as Li Han-hsiang, King Hu, or Zhu Shilin, and Li Pingqian, who were obsessed with their Chineseness and the fate of China, as Law Kar and Sek Kei point out, the New Wave directors saw the British colony of Hong Kong, with all its problems and defects. as their home. Their works represented the "birth of local consciousness" in Hong Kong cinema.[53]

The new directors paid little regard to any remaining Cold War antagonism and restrictions in taking on projects for both Taiwan-financed and Beijing-backed film companies, even as the Nationalist regime continued to battle with Beijing for legitimacy as the sole representative of China after Taiwan's

1971 ouster from the United Nations. Some of their influential works were actually supported by the Sil-Metropole Organization (銀都機構), which was formed in 1982 under the control of the new PRC State Council Hong Kong–Macao Affairs Office. Due to the stringent ultra-leftist intervention from Beijing during the Cultural Revolution and the loss of artistic talent (e.g., Moon Hsia migrated to Canada) and audiences after the 1967 riots, Chang-Feng-Xin had trouble reconnecting to the new generation when they became active after 1978. In order to maintain a strategic position in the new media ecosystem, the three studios merged into Sil-Metropole and recruited young filmmakers, including New Wave directors, to make films that could bring audiences back to their theater circuits.[54]

Some of the New Wave directors' best films during the 1980s brought out the ambivalence of Hongkongers about their homeland across the border. An example was Yim Ho's *Homecoming* (似水流年, 1984), one of the earliest films shot on the mainland and produced by a Sil-Metropole subsidiary, which won a slew of top awards at the 1984 Hong Kong Film Awards, including for Best Film. In a lyrical, nostalgic mood, *Homecoming* tells the story of a thirty-something Hong Kong woman, Shanshan (played by Josephine Koo [顧美華]), whose cross-border journey of escape from family strife and the alienation of the money-is-all capitalist lifestyle to her ancestral home, a rural town near Chaozhou, that she left more than twenty years before. Instead of finding a spiritual refuge, she slowly comes to realize that the idyllic, peaceful life of her homeland is only a product of her wishful thinking. All of her childhood friends are now married, burdened with families to support and a changing economy to navigate, as Deng's modernization campaign is now touching the countryside in southern China. Her intrusion as a wealthy, fashionable, long-lost cousin into their lives only stirs up jealousy and conflicts in their families and breaks the rhythm of local community life. Although deeply attached to the lush rural landscape and some disappearing local traditions, Shanshan returns to Hong Kong. Framed by luscious shots of the area that are evocative of traditional Chinese landscape paintings, her former best friend taunts Shanshan if she would come visit again soon. With an uncertain, self-mocking look, she retorts, "Perhaps in a year?" The nostalgic mood deepens as a sad, soulful song (of the same title) plays out with the rolling of the closing credits (See Figure 5.4).

Produced by Taiwan's Central Motion Corp., Ann Hui's semi-autobiographical family drama *Song of Exile* (客途秋恨, 1990), on the other hand, invites the audience to see the ambiguity of local identity through

Figure 5.4 Shanshan bids farewell to a childhood friend before returning to Hong Kong.

Huien's (played by Maggie Cheung [張曼玉]) transnational passage of home-coming and family reconciliation. Huien has just graduated from a London college and had encountered racism in her first job interview. She then agrees to go back to her native Hong Kong to attend her estranged sister's wedding. Through a series of evocative flashbacks, her passage connects colonial Hong Kong to London, World War II–era Manchuria, Portuguese Macao, small-town Japan, Canada, and the mainland during the Cultural Revolution, which brings to light the increasing internationalization and cosmopolitanism of the city in the 1970s and 1980s. We discover as the film continues that Huien was brought up in a traditional family closer to her grandparents, who immersed her in traditional Chinese culture, than to her own mother (Lu Hsiao-Fen [陸小芬]), always looking grim and aloof. Then, during their trip to Japan, Huien comes to realize her mother is Japanese and has only recently began to feel comfortable with the cultural values and lifestyle in Hong Kong. They become closer (See Figure 5.5).

As Huien begins to feel at home in Hong Kong, working as a television journalist involved in the crusade against corruption and colonial injustice in the early 1970s, she feels obliged to take a trip to Guangzhou to see her ailing grandparents. The couple had left Macao to return to the mainland because of nationalist devotion. Just a few months earlier, Huien's grandfather suffered a brutal Red Guard attack when he bought a Song dynasty poetry collection as a gift to her. The film draws to a sorrowful close as the old

Figure 5.5 Mother and daughter get closer together during their Japan trip in *The Song of Exile*.

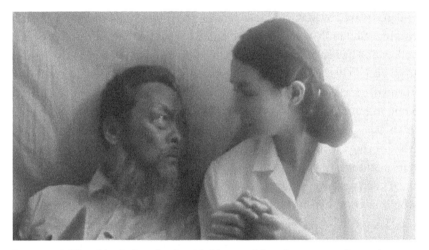

Figure 5.6 The old scholar pleads with his granddaughter not to give up hope on China.

scholar struggles to tell her, "Don't give up on China. Its future lies on you." Though shattered by Mao's political madness, he places his hope on the new generation of an unbroken bond and nationalist commitment with China. The camera lingers on Huien as she looks, with tears rolling down her face, at her grandfather falling to sleep (See Figure 5.6).

Released a year after the 1989 Tiananmen tragedy, it is difficult not to read *Story of Exile* as a metaphor for the inescapable and embittering relations between China and "our city." Unlike Shanshan, who simply slips away back to Hong Kong after feeling betrayed by her romanticized imagining of the mainland, Huien is left to confront the unavoidable tension between her new home and her grandfather's dream of an unbroken bond with the homeland. These romanticized images and ideas of cultural nationalism, as discussed in earlier chapters, were articulated, disseminated, and popularized by émigré artists, intellectuals, filmmakers, and entertainment businessmen— including *CSW*, Asia Pictures, Great Wall, the Southern Corporation, and the Shaw brothers—entangled with the cultural and ideological warfare in the British colony. Their influences on the younger generation continued after the gradual decline of Asian Cold War conflicts and the increasing prevalence of local consciousness in the 1970s and 1980s. From this baby boomer generation emerged some leading voices of democratic reform and nationalist devotion—such as barrister Margaret Ng who as a high school student wrote for *CSW*, that helped shape the 1997 handover story. These voices championed, among other civil rights, free elections and individual freedom under "one country, two systems." Up until 2019, in fact, Hong Kong was the only place on Chinese soil that continued for thirty-two years to hold annual vigils commemorating the crackdown on the 1989 pro-democracy movement. Now, with the striking transformation of the former British colony as a result of the Beijing's intervention in the massive crackdown of the 2019 the COVID-induced economic meltdown, and surging emigration among especially well-educated young people, it would probably be Huien's turn, like her grandfather did in *Song of Exile*, to struggle to tell the younger generation: the future of China and Hong Kong lies within you.

Notes

Preface

1. Melvyn Leffler and Odd Westad, eds., *Cambridge History of the Cold War*, Cambridge: Cambridge University Press, 2010.

2. Quoted from Odd Arne Westad, "The Cold War and the International History of the Twentieth Century," in *Cambridge History of the Cold War*, pp. 2 and 6. See also in that volume Jessica Gienow-Hecht, "Culture and The Cold War in Europe," v.1 pp.398–420; Rosemary Foot, "The Cold War and Human Rights," v.3 pp.445–465, Nicholas Kull, "Reading, Viewing, and Tuning In to the Cold War," v.2 pp.438–459. For similar publications, see, for example, Elaine May, *Homeward Bound: American Families in the Cold War Era*, New York: Basic Books, 2018; Akira Iriye ed., *Global Interdependence: The World after 1945*, Cambridge, MA: Harvard University Press, 2014; Nick Cullather, *The Hungry World: America's Cold War Battle against Poverty in Asia*, Cambridge, MA: Harvard University Press, 2010; Thomas Bostlemann, *The Cold War and the Color Line: American Race Relations in the Global Arena*, Cambridge, MA: Harvard University Press, 2003; Frances Saunder, *The Cultural Cold War: The CIA and the World of Arts and Letters*, New York: New Press, 2000; Richard Immerman and Petra Goedde eds., *The Oxford Handbook of the Cold War*, Oxford: Oxford University Press, 2013.

3. Federico Romero, "Cold War Historiography at The Crossroads," *Cold War History*, v.14 n.4 (2014), p.686.

4. For examples, see Christina Klein, *Cold War Cosmopolitanism: Period Style in 1950s Korean Cinema*, Berkeley: University of California Press, 2020; Jadwiga Mooney and Fabio Lanz eds., *De-Centering Cold War History: Local and Global Change*, London: Routledge, 2013; Taomu Zhou, *Migration in the Time of Revolution: China, Indonesia, and the Cold War*, Ithaca, NY: Cornell University Press, 2019; Tuong Vu and Wasana Wongsurawat eds., *Dynamics of the Cold War in Asia: Ideology, Identity, and Culture*, New York: Palgrave Macmillan, 2009; Hal Brands, *Latin America's Cold War*, Cambridge, MA: Harvard University Press, 2010; Chen Jian, *Mao's China and the Cold War*, Chapel Hill: University of North Carolina Press, 2001; Zheng Yanwen et al. eds., *The Cold War in Asia: The Battle for Hearts and Minds*, Boston: Brill, 2010; Odd Arne Westad, *The Global Cold War: Third World Interventions and the Making of Our Times*, Cambridge: Cambridge University Press, 2011; Manu Bhagavan, *India and the Cold War*, Chapel Hill: University of North Carolina Press, 2019; Timothy Scarnecchia, *Race and Diplomacy in Zimbabwe: The Cold War and Decolonization, 1964–1984*, Cambridge: Cambridge University Press, 2021; Hal Brands, *Latin America's Cold War*, Cambridge, MA: Harvard University Press, 2012; Patrick Iber,

Neither Peace nor Freedom: The Cultural Cold War in Latin America, Cambridge, MA: Harvard University Press, 2016.

5. For examples of Hong Kong history during the Cold War and earlier period, see Elizabeth Sinn, *Pacific Crossing: California Gold, Chinese Migration, and the Making of Hong Kong,* Hong Kong: Hong Kong University Press, 2012; Law Wing Sang, *Collaborative Colonial Power: The Making of the Hong Kong Chinese,* Hong Kong: Hong Kong University Press, 2009; Ming K. Chan ed., *Precarious Balance: Hong Kong between China and Britain, 1842–1992,* Armonk, NY: Sharpe, 1994; Priscilla Roberts and John Carroll eds., *Hong Kong in the Cold War,* Hong Kong: Hong Kong University Press, 2016; Chi-kwan Mark, *Hong Kong and the Cold War: Anglo-American Relations, 1949–1957,* Oxford: Clarendon, 2004; Catherine Schenk, *Hong Kong as an International Financial Center: Emergence and Development, 1945–1965,* London: Routledge, 1990; Grace Chou, *Confucianism, Colonialism, and the Cold War: Chinese Cultural Education at Hong Kong's New Asia College, 1949–1963,* Boston: Brill, 2011; Ian Scott, *Political Change and the Crisis of Legitimacy in Hong Kong,* Honolulu: University of Hawaii Press, 1989; Steve Tsang, *Democracy Shelved: Great Britain, China, and Attempts at Constitutional Reform in Hong Kong, 1945–1952,* Hong Kong: Oxford University Press, 1988.

6. Tony Shaw and Denise Youngblood, *Cinematic Cold War: The American and Soviet Struggle for Hearts and Minds,* Lawrence: University Press of Kansas, 2010, pp.3–5. For examples of Cold War cinema studies, see Lary May, *The Big Tomorrow: Hollywood and the Politics of the American Way,* Chicago: University of Chicago Press, 2000; Tony Shaw, *Hollywood's Cold War,* Amherst: University of Massachusetts Press, 2007; Daniela Berghahn, *Hollywood behind the Wall: The Cinema of East Germany,* Manchester: Manchester University Press, 2005; Josephine Woll, *Real Images: Soviet Cinema and the Thaw,* London: I. B. Tauris, 2000; Ronnie Lipschutz, *Cold War Fantasies: Film, Fiction, and Foreign Policy,* Lanham, MD: Rowman and Littlefield, 2001; J. Hoberman, *An Army of Phantoms: American Movies and the Making of the Cold War,* New York: New Press, 2012; Homer Pettey ed., *Cold War Film Genres,* Edinburgh: University of Edinburgh Press, 2018; Robert Cober, *Cold War Femme: Lesbianism, National Identity, and Hollywood Cinema,* Durham, NC: Duke University Press, 2011.

7. Examples of pioneering works include Kyoko Hirano, *Mr. Smith Goes to Tokyo: Japanese Cinema under the American Occupation, 1945–1952,* Washington, DC: Smithsonian Institute Press, 1992; Tony Day and Maya Liem eds., *Cultures at War: The Cold War and Cultural Expression in Southeast Asia,* Ithaca, NY: Southeast Asian Program, Cornell University, 2010; Theodore Hughes, *Literature and Film in Cold War South Korea: Freedom's Frontier,* New York: Columbia University Press, 2014. For the most recent books on Hong Kong cinema and the Cold War, see Wong Ain-ling and P. Lee eds., *Lengzhan yu Xianggang dianying* [The Cold War and Hong Kong cinema], Hong Kong: Hong Kong Film Archive, 2009; Vivian Lee, *The Other Side of Glamour: The Left-Wing Studio Network in Hong Kong Cinema in the Cold War,* Edinburgh: University of Edinburgh Press, 2020; Jing Jing Chang, *Screening Communities: Negotiating Narratives of Empire, Nation, and the Cold War*

in Hong Kong Cinema, Hong Kong: Hong Kong University Press, 2019; Sam Ho, *Wenyi renwu: Xinliang qiusuo* [Literary and arts mission: Sun Luen's quest], Hong Kong: Hong Kong Film Archive, 2011.

8. Po-Shek Fu, *Between Shanghai and Hong Kong: The Politics of Chinese Cinemas*, Stanford, CA: Stanford University Press, 2013, p.xii.

Chapter 1

1. "Hong Kong's Ten-Year Miracle," *LIFE*, international edition, December 7, 1959, quoted from Richard Hughes, *Borrowed Place, Borrowed Time: Hong Kong and Its Many Faces*, Singapore: Toppan Printing Co., 1976, n.p.

2. Prime Minister's Lok Sabha speech, November 19, 1956, quoted from Odd Arne Westad, *The Cold War: A World History*, New York: Basic Books, 2017, p.274.

3. See Elizabeth Sinn, *Pacific Crossing: California Gold, Chinese Migration, and the Making of Hong Kong*, Hong Kong: Hong Kong University Press, 2012;

4. Syd Goldsmith, *Hong Kong on the Brink: An American Diplomat Relieves 1967's Darkest Days*, Hong Kong: Blacksmith Books, 2017, p.37.

5. James Lilley, *China Hands: Nine Decades of Adventure, Espionage, and Diplomacy in Asia*, New York: PublicAffairs, 2004, pp.84–85. The author did not, however, include among the Chinese of all stripes in Cold War Hong Kong the Chinese affiliated with the US government organizations.

6. Kenneth Osgood, *Total Cold War: Eisenhower's Secret Propaganda Battle at Home and Abroad*, Lawrence: University Press of Kansas, 2006, pp.7–35.

7. Quoted from Kevin Peraino, *A Force So Swift: Mao, Truman, and the Birth of Modern China, 1949*, New York: Crown 2017, p.258.

8. P-Shek Fu, *Between Shanghai and Hong Kong: The Politics of Chinese Cinemas*, Stanford: Stanford University Press, 2003, pp.1–50.

9. See, for example, Yu Mo-wen, *Xiangang dianying shihu* [An informal history of Hong Kong cinema], Hong Kong: Subculture, 1998, v.3, pp.161–170.

10. Zi Fu et al., "Women zheyang kan Guohun" [Our view of Guohun] *Huashang bao*, September 12, 1948.

11. Zhou Enlai told the CCP leadership in December 1946 that "Hong Kong has become increasingly important not just for Guangdong-Guangxi and Southeast Asia, also important for works with European and American. . . . We have to reorganize our leadership structure in order to centralize our overt and covert work." Quoted from Christine Loh, *Underground Front: The Chinese Communist Party in Hong Kong*, Hong Kong: Hong Kong University Press, 2010, p.276, footnote 79.

12. Chen Jian and Chen Qijia, *Xia Yan zhuan* [Biography of Xia Yan], Beijing: China Theater Press, 2015, pp.397–447; Wang Weiyi, *Nanwang de suiyue* [My unforgettable memories], Beijing: Zhongguo dianying, 2006, pp.103–108; Yip Hon Ming and Choi Po King argue that the Communists had established a cultural hegemony in Hong Kong during the civil war period; see their "Zhimindi yu geming wemhua

baquan: Xianggang yu sishi niandai houqi de Zhongguo Gongchanzhuyi yundong" [Colony and revolutionary hegemony: Hong Kong and the Chinese Communist movement of the late 1940s], *Journal of Chinese Studies*, v.10, 2007, pp.191–218. See also Su Tao, *Fucheng beiwang: chonghui zhanhou Xianggang dianying* [Rewriting postwar Hong Kong cinema], Beijing: Beijing daxue chubanshe, 2014, pp.3–23. For the 1930s Shanghai leftist realist style, see Chris Berry, "Chinese Left Cinema in the 1930s: Poisonous Weeds or National Treasure," *Jump Cut*, no.34 (March 1989), pp.87–94, and Laikwan Pang, *Building a New China in Cinema: The Chinese Left-Wing Cinema Movement, 1932–1937*, Lanham: Rowman and Littlefield, 2002.

13. For a description of the public attitude to the People's Liberation Army (PLA)'s possible seizure of Hong Kong, see Wang Weiyi, *Nanwang de suiyue*, pp.112–115.

14. See, for example, Kong Kwan-sheng, *Zhonggong zai Xianggang* [Communist China in Hong Kong], Hong Kong: Cosmos Books, 2012, v.2, pp. 25–36; Christine Loh, *Underground Front*, pp.79–83; Chi-Kwan Mark, *Hong Kong and the Cold War: Anglo-American Relations, 1949–1957*, Oxford: Oxford University Press, 2004.

15. Jin Raoru, *Xianggang wushinian yiwang* [Remembering Hong Kong in the last fifty years], Hong Kong: Jin Raoru Memorial Foundation, 2005, p.33; Kevin Peraino, *A Force So Swift: Mao, Truman, and the Birth of Modern China*, New York: Crown, 2017, pp.200–203. For the two powers' differences of opinions, see also Fredrik Logevall, *Embers of War: The Fall of an Empire and the Making of America's Vietnam*, New York: Random House, 2012, pp.313–316.

16. "Wushi tian Zhengfeng huiyi jilu" [Fifty days of Rectification Meeting minutes], in Cheng Xiang, *Xiangang Liuqi baodong shimo* [History of Hong Kong 1967 riots], Hong Kong: Oxford University Press, 2018, pp.470, 476, 478–479.

17. Leo Goodstadt, "Economic Relations between the Mainland and Hong Kong: An 'Irreplaceable' Financial Center," in Gary Luk ed., *From a British to a Chinese Colony: Hong Kong before and after the 1997 Handover*, Berkeley: Institute of East Asian Studies, 2017, pp.195–196.

18. Quoted from Christine Loh, *Underground Front*, p.84.

19. In his semiofficial account of the CCP's policy toward Hong Kong, Li Hou contends that Hong Kong's Communist establishment had committed three major "ultraleftist" mistakes that deviated from the CCP pragmatic policy and caused havoc—namely, the "March 1 Incident" of 1952–1953, the "Great Leap Forward" in 1958, and the 1967 riots. See Li'shis *Huigui de lichen* [The journey to return to China], Hong Kong: Joint Publishing Co., 1997. For a vivid memory of the anticolonial sentiment among Hong Kong's Communists, see Ludang Xiaozhou, "Liushi niandai 1967 yizai fansi" (Rethinking 1967 riots), https://1967.hk.com/tag/%E4%BD%99%E6%B1%9D%E4%BF%A1/.

20. Quoted from Leo Goodstadt, "Economic Relations between the Mainland and Hong Kong," p.191.

21. Richard Hughes, *Borrowed Place, Borrowed Time*, p.13.

22. See Leo Goodstadt, *Uneasy Partners: The Conflict between Pubic Interests and Private Profits in Hong Kong*, Hong Kong: Hong Kong University Press, 2005, especially pp.1–15; Ming K. Chan ed., *Precious Balance: Hong Kong Between China and Britain*,

1842–1992, Hong Kong: Hong Kong University Press, 1994; and Chan Lau Kit-ching, *From Nothing to Nothing: The Chinese Communist Movement and Hong Kong, 1921– 1936*, Hong Kong: Hong Kong University Press, 1999).

23. Richard Hughes, *Borrowed Place, Borrowed Time*, pp.42–43.

24. Syd Goldsmith, *Hong Kong on the Brink,* especially pp.143–149.

25. Quotation by famous businessman "King of New Territories" Cheung Yan Lung, from Christine Loh, *Underground Front*, p.93. Governor Alexander Grantham allegedly made his trip in 1954 to the United States with the aim to "correct the impression that Hong Kong provided a route to circumvent America's sanctions on China." See Neil Monnery, *Architect of Prosperity: Sir John Cowperthwaite and the Making of Hong Kong*, London: London Publishing Partnership, 2017, p.104.

26. See, for example, James Lilley, *China Hands*, Chi-Kwan Mark, *Hong Kong and the Cold War;* Steve Tsang, "Strategy for Survival: The Cold War and Hong Kong's Policy towards Kuomintang and Chinese Communist Activities in the 1950s," *Journal of Imperial and Commonwealth History*, v.25 n.2 (1997), pp.294–317; Tsang, *Democracy Shelved: Great Britain, China, and Attempts at Constitutional Reforms in Hong Kong, 1945–1952*, Hong Kong: Oxford University Press, 1998.

27. Alexander Grantham, *Via Ports: From Hong Kong to Hong Kong*, Hong Kong: Hong Kong University Press, 1965, p.148.

28. Unlike the rest of the British Empire, Hong Kong had started to enjoy a wide range of political and financial autonomy since at least 1947–1948 as an official acknowledgment of its reliance on China. London gave Hong Kong even more administrative autonomy in 1958 when it stopped reviewing its annual budget. It became free to create its own tax policies, foreign exchange transaction rules, and social welfare programs. This autonomy allowed "the colony to function as its own administrative and economic entity." It could participate independently in various international organizations and felt no obligations to defend the pound sterling against devaluation in the 1950s. John Carroll, *A Concise History of Hong Kong*, Lanham: Rowman and Littlefield, 2007, p.171, and Leo Goodstadt, "Economic Relations between the Mainland and Hong Kong," pp.188–191. Also, for a study of the British Cold War strategy, see Anne Dighton, "Britain and the Cold War," in Melvyn Leffler and Odd Arne Westad eds., *Cambridge History of the Cold War*, Cambridge: Cambridge University Press, 2010, v.1, pp.112–132.

29. Quoted from Michael Ng, "Rule of Law, Freedom of Expression and the Anxiety of Empire: Press Censorship in British Hong Kong," unpublished manuscript, 2016, p.29. My thanks to the author for sharing it with me.

30. Richard Hughes, *Borrowed Place, Borrowed Time*, p.13.

31. For the humanitarian crisis and social discontent, see Zhou Yi, *Xianggang zuopai douzheng shi* [A history of the Hong Kong leftist resistance], Hong Kong: Nice News Publishing Co., 2008, pp.49–153; John Carroll, *A Concise History of Hong Kong*, pp.143–146; Edvard Hambro, "The Problem of Chinese Refugees in Hong Kong," *Phylon Quarterly*, v.18 n.1 (1957), p.13.

32. Carol Jones, "A Ruling Idea of the Time? The Rule of Law in Pre- and Post-1997 Hong Kong," in Gary Luk ed., *From a British to a Chinese Colony*, pp.112–126; Christine

Loh, *Underground Front*, pp.75–77; Chi-Kwan Mark, *Hong Kong and the Cold War*, pp.15–18; Zhou Yi, *Xianggang zuopai douzheng shi*, pp.36–38.

33. Zardas Shuk-man Lee, "From Cold Warrior to Moral Guardianship: Film Censorship in British Hong Kong," in Gary Luk ed., *From a British to a Chinese Colony*, pp.146–150.

34. Su Tao, *Fucheng beiwang*, pp.10–18.

35. Q. Mccfadyen, "On Interview of 19-6-1951, to Hon. C.L. [Commissioner of Police]," Box TU/260/2, 1951, Hong Kong Public Office.

36. For the leftist view, see Xu Dunle, *Kenguang tuoying* [Developing cinema], Hong Kong: MCCM, 2005, pp.43–50. For the US complaint, see Zardas Shuk-man Lee, "From Cold Warrior to Moral Guardianship," pp.150–152.

37. Thomas Gill, "Hong Kong," *Far East Film News Special Supplement: Pacific Asian Trade List, 1960–1961*, 1962, p.24.

38. Jing Jing Chang, *Screening Communities: Negotiating Narratives of Empire, Nation, and the Cold War in Hong Kong Cinema*, Hong Kong: Hong Kong University Press, 2019, p.38. Her argument is based on Wai-man Lam's broad concept of a "culture of depoliticization" prevalent in Hong Kong from British colonialism to post-1997 rule. See *Understanding the Political Culture of Hong Kong: The Paradox of Activism and Depoliticization*, Armonk: M. E. Sharpe, 2004.

39. Adapted from Yan Lu, "Limites to Propaganda: Hong Kong's Leftist Media in the Cold War and Beyond," in Zhang Yangwen et al. eds., *The Cold War in Asia: The Battle for Hearts and Minds*, Leiden: Brill, 2010, p.95.

40. Guy Searls, "Red China Switch to Love, Soft-Pedal Marx to Sell Movies," *Wall Street Journal*, September 26, 1957.

41. See Li Yizhuang and Zhou Chengren, *Xianggang yinmu zuofang* [The left side of Hong Kong cinema], Hong Kong: Diatomic Press, 2021, pp.50–52; Wang Ailing, *Lixiang niandai: Changcheng yu Fenghuang de rizi* [Age of idealism: The days of Great Wall and Phoenix], Hong Kong: Hong Kong Film Archive, pp.111–117.

42. See, for example, John Carroll, *A Concise History of Hong Kong*, pp.142–143; Chen Jian and Chen Qijia, *Xia Yan zhuan*, pp.436–446.

43. Su Tao, *Fucheng beiwang*, pp.26–28.

44. Kong Kwan-sheng, *Zhonggong zai Xianggang*, v.1, pp.71–74.

45. See, for example, Toby Rider, *Cold War Games: Propaganda, the Olympics, and US Foreign Policy*, Urbana: University of Illinois Press, 2016, Chapter 2.

46. "Wushi tian zhengfeng huiyi jilu," p.471.

47. Sue Dawnson, "But Where Are the Love Scenes?" translated into Chinese in *Changcheng huabao*, n.28 (May 1953), p.22.

48. John Miller, "Memorandum to the President, CFA," June 25, 1954, AFC Box P-56.

49. Raymond Hsu, "New Scheme of the Great Wall Motion Enterprise," January 14, 1955, AFC Box P-56.

50. Sue Dawnson, "But Where Are the Love Scenes?" pp.22–23.

51. See Donna Chu, "Chu Hung," in Wong Ailing ed., *An Age of Idealism*, pp.238–248; Sam Ho ed., *Wenyi renwu: Xinlian qiusuo* [Literary and artistic mission: Xinlian's quest], Hong Kong: Hong Kong Film Archive, 2011, pp.150–188.

52. "Extract of the *Ta Kung Pao*," 1960, Box TU/260/6, Hong Kong Public Record Office.

53. Chen Jian, *China's Road to the Korean War: The Making of the Sino-American Confrontation*, New York: Columbia University Press, 1994, pp.26–28; Taomo Zhou, *Migration in The Time of Revolution: China, Indonesia, and the Cold War*. Ithaca: Cornell University Press, 2019, Chapter 3.

54. Liao Chengzhi, *Liao Chengzhi wenji* [Collected works of Liao Chengzhi], Hong Kong: Joint Publishing Co., 1990, v.2, pp.215–219, 275–279, 323–325. See also Xu Lanjun, "The Southern Film Corporation, Opera Films, and the PRC's Cultural Diplomacy in Cold War Asia," Modern Chinese Literature and Culture, v.29 no. 1 (Spring 2017), pp.243–246. For discussion of China, the overseas Chinese community, and Southeast Asian governments, see Meredith Oyen, "Communism, Containment, and the Chinese Overseas," in Zhang Yangwen et al. eds., *The Cold War in Asia*, pp.57–93.

55. Chen Huangmei, "Tan zhiyun nongye, Gangpian, kejioa pian, waiguopian wenti" [On problems of assisting agricultural film, Hong Kong film, scientific education film, foreign film], November 17, 1962, B177–1-21, Shanghai Municipal Archive.

56. The confrontation, which was known later as the "March 1 Incident" of 1952, started with a fire in Tung Tau Village that left at least twenty thousand homeless. It should be seen as part of the rising radicalism and labor activism in the early 1950s as activists saw Mao's victory as a call for decolonialization in Hong Kong. For the incident and radicalism, see Kong Kwan-sheng, *Zhonggong zai Xianggang*, v.2, pp.51–60; Zhou Yi, *Xianggang zuopai douzheng shi*, pp.49–118; Christine Loh, *Underground Front*, pp.91–93.

57. "Wushi tian Zhengfeng huiyi jilu," pp.464, 476–478.

58. Su Tao, *Fucheng beiwang*, pp.36–58.

59. "Wushi tian Zhengfeng huiyi jilu," p.467.

60. "Liao Yiyuan," in Sam Ho, *Wenyi renwu*, p.152. For a study of leftist film aesthetics, see Sek Kei, "Gangchan zuopai dianying ji qi xiaozichan jieji xing" [Hong Kong-produced leftist cinema and its petit-bourgeois outlook], *Chinese Student Weekly*, no. 740 (September 23, 1966).

61. *Yijiu wuyi nian Changcheng gaizu yinian lai gongzuo zongjie yu jinhou de zhanwang* [The 1950 summary of the Great Wall production after one year of reorganization and its future plan), 1951, n.p., Special Collection, Hong Kong Film Archive.

62. Qun Yang, "*Yi ban zhi ge* guanhou" [*The wall in between* review]. *Quanmin bao* (Singapore), September 7, 1952.

63. "Huang Yi," in Sam Ho, *Wenyi renwu*, pp.168–169.

64. "Survey of and Statistics in the Mandarin Motion Picture Industry in Hong Kong," 1956, AFC Box P-58.

65. Lanjun Xu, "The Southern Film Corporation, Opera Films, and Cultural Diplomacy in Cold War Asia," pp.243–263.

66. Guy Searls, "Red China Switch to Love."

67. Xu Dunle, *Kenguang tuoying* [Developing cinema], Hong Kong: MCCM, 2005, pp.35–39.

68. Guy Searls, "Red China Switch to Love."

69. "US Treasury Dept. Names HK Designated Nationals," *Far East Film News: Special Supplement: Pacific-Asian Trade List, 1960–1961*, p.6.
70. Lanjun Xu, "The Southern Film Corporation," pp.266–268.
71. "A Review of Government Achievements in Taiwan," *Taiwan Review*, November 1, 1951, https://taiwantoday.tw/news.php?unit=4&post=6678.
72. See Sha Rongfeng, *Binfen dianying sishichun: Sha Rongfeng huiyilu* [Forty cinematic years: Memoirs of Sha Rongfeng], Taipei: National Film Archive, 1994, pp.9–18.
73. David Wang, *The Monster That Is History: History, Violence, and Fictional Writing in Twentieth-Century China*, Cambridge: Harvard University Press, 2004, p.157.
74. Ibid.; quoted from Li Tianduo, *Taiwan dianying, shehui yu lishi* [Taiwan cinema, society and history), Taipei: Yatai tushu, 1997, pp.83, 90–93.
75. *See* Chiang Ching-kuo, *Jinag Jinguo zishu* [Diaries of Jiang Jinkuo], Changsha: Hunan chubanshe, 1992; Liu Yongxi, *Jiang Jingguo zai Tai sanshi nian* [Thirty years of Mr. Jiang in Taiwan], Hong Kong: Dalian, 1985. For Taiwan's overall anti-Communist propaganda, see Gary Rawnsley, "Taiwan's Propaganda Cold War: The Offshore Islands Crisis of 1954 and 1958," in Richard J. Aldrich et al. eds., *The Clandestine Cold War in Asia: Western Intelligence, Propaganda and Special Operations*, Portland: Frank Cass, 2000, pp.82–104.
76. Chiang Ching-kuo, "Xiang fangong fuguo de ben zhanchang jinjun" [Let's march to fighting back and restore nation], 1959, *Chiang Ching-kuo xiansheng quanji*, Taipei: Government Information Office, 1991, pp.2004–206.
77. Sha Rongfeng, *Binfen dianying sishichun*, p.27.
78. "Survey and Statistics in the Mandarin Motion Picture Industry in Hong Kong," 1956, AFC Box P-58.
79. Gong Deyuan, "Yinse huiguang changzhao Baodao" [Treasure Island under the silver lights], *Xinwen tiandi*, no. 329 (June 5, 1954), pp.10–12; Yi Yan, "Ying Xianggang ziyou yingjuren lai Tai" [Welcome "free" makers of film and drama to Taiwan], *Lianhe bao*, May 19, 1954.
80. Chiang Kai-shek, *Chiang Kai-shek Diaries, 1917–1972*, Stanford: Hoover Institution Archives, Stanford University, n.d. For Chiang Ching-kuo's role, see Huang Ren, "Gangjiu dianying xiju shiye ziyou zonghui de jiaose he yingxiang" [The role and influences of HKFFGA], in Wong Ailing eds., *Lengzhan yu Xianggang dianying*, Hong Kong: Hong Kong Film Archive, 2001, 72–75.
81. For the film, see Xu Shumei, *Zhizuo "youda": zhanhou Taiwan dianying Zhong de Riben* [Making "Friends": Japan in postwar Taiwan cinema], New Taipei City: Daoxiang chubanshe, 2012, pp.181–199.
82. See Yue Qing, *Wanzi qianhong: Li Li-hua* [A Sparkling life: Li Li-Hua], Beijing: Zhongguo dianying chubanshe, 2015, pp.123–169.
83. "Liao Yiyuan," in Sam Ho, *Wenyi renwu*, pp.153–154.
84. Chia LeeNi, interview with author, December 12, 2014, New York City.
85. Li Li-hua, "Wo de zizhuan" [My autobiography], *World Today*, no. 46 (February 1, 1954): 8–9
86. Ma Xingkong, "Xianggang yingcheng tuihong nian" [The year of Red fading in Hong Kong film community], *Xinwen tiandi*, no. 309 (January 16, 1954), pp.9–11;

Shao Mingchun, "Xianggang yingtan tuihong nian" [Red fading year in Hong Kong cinema], *Xinwen tiandi*, no. 309 (January 16, 1954), pp.9–10.

87. Quotation about Xia Yan from Chen Jian and Chen Qijia, *Xia Yan zhuan*, p.393. Film Bureau, "Xianggang dianying yu dianying jie qingkuang cankao ziliao," quoted from Su Tao, *Fucheng beiwang*, pp.76–77.

88. See Zuo Gueifang and Yao Liqun eds., *Tong Yuejuan [The Life of Tong Yuejuan]*, Taipei: National Film Archive, 2001, pp.143–150; Huang Ren, "Gangjiu dianying xiju shiye ziyou zonghui de jiaose he yingxiang," pp.75–79; Huang Zhuohan, *Dianying rensheng: Huang Zhuohan huiyilu* [Cinematic life: Memoir of Huang Zhuohan], Taipei: Wanxiang tushu gufen gongsi, 1994, pp.69–82.

89. George, "Hong Kong," *Far East Film News*, v.3 n.16 (October 7, 1955), p.22; "Guoyu dianying jinri dianying de kunnan" [Difficulties of Mandarin cinema today], *Guoji dianying*, n.1 (October 1955), pp.50–51; "Film Producer Urges Hong Kong Producers to Collaborate with Taiwan," unidentified newspaper clippings, March 29, 1956, AFC P-58.

90. See, for example, Lu Haitian, "Chonggao de lixiang" [A lofty ideal], *Guoji dianying*, n.3 (December 1955), pp.10–11.

91. Sha Rongfeng, *Binfen dianying sishichun*, pp.30–31, 35–37; Huang Ren, "Gangjiu dianying xiju shiye ziyou zonghui de jiaose he yingxiang," pp.73–76.

92. Chia LeeNi, interview with author, March 18, 2022, and Chia LeeNi, *Stories from My Album*, New York: Shiny Printing, 2021, v.2, pp. 436–438.

93. For a discussion of the film and the MP&GI, see Po-Shek Fu, "More Than Just Entertaining: Cinematic Containment and Asia's Cold War in Hong Kong, 1949–1959," *Modern Chinese Literature and Culture*, v.30 n.2 (Fall 2018), pp.1–55.

94. Gao Shanyue, "*Kongzhong xiaojie* bieyou yongxin" [The secret motive of *Air Hostess*], *Ta Kung Pao*, June 10, 1959.

95. Chen She, "Zhengfu yao zhuyi de" [The government should pay attention], *Lianhe bao*, July 23, 1959.

96. Kenneth Osgood, *Total Cold War*, pp.88–103, quotation from p.102. See also Wilson Dizard, *The Strategy of Truth: The Story of the United States Information Services*, Washington, DC: Public Affairs Press, 1961.

97. Logevall Fredrik, *Embers of War*, pp.221–259.

98. Kenneth Osgood, *Total Cold War*, pp.53–60.

99. Syd Goldman, *Hong Kong on the Brink*, p.61. This Mandarin vs. Cantonese or Hokkienese rivalry continues today. See, for example, Stephen Chu, *Found in Transition: Hong Kong Studies in the Age of China*, Albany: SUNY Press, 2018, pp.91–116, and Rey Chow, *Writing Diaspora: Tactics of Intervention in Contemporary Cultural Studies*, Indianapolis: Indiana University Press, 1993.

100. Johannes Lombardo, "A Mission of Espionage, Intelligence and Psychological Operations: The American Consulate in Hong Kong," in Richard Aldrich et al. eds., *The Clandestine Cold War in Asia*, London: Frank Cass, 2000, pp.69–70.

101. Wilson Dizard, *The Strategy of Truth*, pp.138–139.

102. Shan Dexing, *Fanyi yu mailuo* [Translation and contexts], Taipei: Shulin chuban, 2009, pp.117–158.

103. Grant Advertising Inc., "A Survey of the Reading Habits of the Chinese in Hong Kong," 1953, AFC Box P-169.

104. Jack O'Brien, "Richard McCarthy," Association for Diplomatic Studies, 1998, url:https://www.adst.org/OH%20TOCs/McCarthy,%20Richard%20M.toc.pdf accessed August 26, 2018.

105. "Memorandum of Discussion at the 447th Meeting of the National Security Council," 1960, *Foreign Relations of the United States*, https://history.state.gov/historicaldocuments/frus1958–60v06/d528.

106. For example, see Fredrik Logevall, *Embers of War*, pp.313–316.

107. James Lilley, *China Hands*, pp.80–85.

108. Johannes Lombardo, "A Mission of Espionage, Intelligence and Psychological Operations: The American Consulate in Hong Kong," p.69.

109. See ibid., pp.68–73.

110. See, for example, *Ta Kung Pao*, December 6, 1957.

111. Frances Saunders, *The Cultural Cold War: The CIA and the World of Arts and Letters*, New York: New Press, 2001.

112. See "Committee for a Free Asia, December 13, 1951," declassified and released by Central Intelligence Agency Sources Methods Exemptions 302B Nazi War Crimes Disclosure Act Date 2007, https://www.cia.gov/library/readingroom/docs/DTPILLAR%20%20%20VOL.%201_0085.pdf; and "The Asia Foundation (1952–1953)," AFC Box-P55; Robert Blum, "The Work of the Asia Foundation," *Pacific Affairs*, v.29 n.1 (1956), pp.46–49.

113. Emma North-Best, "The Stolen History of the CIA and the Asia Foundation," November 2, 2017, MuckRock, https://www.muckrock.com/news/archives/2017/nov/02/taf-1/; Kevin Peraino, *A Force So Swift*, pp.150–155.

114. Grace Chou, *Confucianism, Colonialism, and Cold War: Chinese Cultural Education at Hong Kong's New Asia College,* Leiden: Brill, 2011.

115. "Dai Tian" and "Lin Yueheng," in Lo Wai-luen and Hung Chi Kum eds., *Xianggang wenhua zhongsheng dao* [Multiple voices of Hong Kong culture], Hong Kong: Joint Publishing Co., 2014, v.1 pp.174–213.

Chapter 2

1. See Kenneth Osgood, *Total Cold War: Eisenhower's Secret Propaganda Battle at Home and Abroad*, Lawrence: University Press of Kansas, 2006, p.81.

2. William Colby, *Honorable Man*, New York: Simon and Schuster 1978, p.103.

3. Grace Chou, *Confucianism, Colonialism, and the Cold War: Chinese Cultural Education at Hong Kong's New Asia College*, Leiden: Brill, 2011; Zhang Yang, "Cultural Cold War: The American Role in Establishing the Chinese University of Hong Kong," in Priscilla Roberts ed., *The Power of Culture: Encounters between China and the United States*, Newcastle: Cambridge Scholar Publishing, 2016, pp.148–169; Shuang Shen, "Empire of Information: The Asia Foundation's

Network and Chinese-Language Cultural Production in Hong Kong and Southeast Asia," *American Quarterly*, v.69 n.3 (September 2017), pp.589–610; Xiaojue Wang, *Modernity with a Cold War Face: Reimagining the Nation in Chinese Literature across the 1949 Divide* (Cambridge: Harvard University Asia Center, 2013).

4. See "Interviews with "Robert Hsi," "Wang Jianmin," and "Sun Shuyu" in Lo Wai-luen and Hung Chi Kam, *Xianggang Wenhua zhongsheng dao*, v.1, pp.48–81, 106–173. Quotations from pp.133 and 164.

5. *Xianggang nianjian* 1952 (Hong Kong) (Hong Kong 1952), Hong Kong: Wah Kiu Yat Po she, 1952, Part I, p.I.

6. Alexander Grantham, *Via Ports: From Hong Kong to Hong Kong*, Hong Kong: Hong Kong University Press, 1965, p.112.

7. Quotation from Christopher Rand, *Hong Kong: The Island between*, New York: Alfred A. Knopf, 1952, p.66. For details of the refugee crisis, see Helen Zia, *Last Boat out of Shanghai: The Epic Story of the Chinese Who Fled Mao's Revolution*, New York: Ballantine Books, 2019, pp.328–338, 387–396, and Zheng Zhuyuan, *Zhangbi zuo tianya: Zheng Zhuyuan huiyilu* [Memoir of Zheng Zhuyuan], Taipei: World Journal LLC, 2017, pp.139–168.

8. Yu Yu (余予), "Zuanshishan sumiao" [A sketch of Diamond Hill], *World Today*, n.5 (May 15, 1952), p.12.

9. Daniel Kurtz-Phelan, *The China Mission: George Marshall's Unfinished War*, New York: W.W. Norton & Company, 2018, pp.138–156; Odd Arn Westad, *Cold War and Revolution: Soviet-American Rivalry and the Origins of the Chinese Civil War*, New York: Columbia University Press, 1993.

10. Daniel Kurtz-Phelan, *The China Mission*, pp.256–258.

11. For studies of the Chinese third-force movement, see Roger Jeans, *The CIA and Third Force Movements in China during the Early Cold War: The Great American Dream*, Lanham: Lexington Books, 2018; Carsun Chang, *The Third Force in China*, New York: Bookman Associates, 1952; and Lyman Van Slyke, *Enemies and Friends: The United Front in Chinese Communist History*, Stanford: Stanford University Press, 1967, pp.169–259. For third-force activities in Hong Kong, see Liu Shaotang, "Pu Shaofu zege ren" [This man, Pu Shaofu], Taipei: Yuanjing chuban shiye gongsi, 1983, pp.72–79, 250–253; Jiao Daye, "Di sanpai liushi hang maimai," (The Secret Deals of the Third Force) *Xinwen tiandi*, n.294 (October 1953), pp.6–9; Li Hanji and Li Minghui eds., *Xu Fuguan zawen bubian* [Miscellaneous essays of Xu Fuguan], Nangang: Zhongyang yanjiuyuan Zhongguo wenshize yanjiusuo choubeichu, 2001, vol.6, pp.28–47, 60–82; Lin Bowen, "Yijiusijiu nian hou de Xianggang disan shili "[Hong Kong third force after 1949] http://www.difangwenge.org/read.php?tid=9591, accessed July 18, 2017. For a study situating Chinese liberal thought in historical context, see *Andrew Nathan, Chinese Democracy*, New York: Alfred Knopf, 1985, pp.45–86.

12. Historian Lyman Van Slyke points out that *White Papers* had enraged Chiang, and incited Mao to publish a series of damaging essays denouncing the hypocrisy of American imperialists as well as all the pro-American, "short-sighted, muddle-headed liberals" in China. Lyman Van Slyke, "Introduction," in *The China White*

Paper 1949, Stanford: Stanford University Press, 1967. It includes the Original Letter of Transmittal to President Truman from Secretary Dean Acheson. For a study of NSC-48 and Truman's view of "indigenous Chinese elements," see Kevin Peraino, *A Force So Swift: Mao, Truman, and the Birth of Modern China, 1949*, New York: Crown, 2017, pp.102–126, 246–252; Hong Zhang, *American Perceived: The Making of Chinese Images of the United States, 1945–1953*, Westport: Greenwood Press, 2002.

13. See J. Lilley, *China Hands: Nine Decades of Adventures, Espionage, and Diplomacy in Asia*, New York: Public Affairs, 2004, pp.78–85, 135–138; Christopher Rand, *Hong Kong: The Island Between*, pp.118–122. US political officer Ralph Cough called these refugees "peddler[s] of information" and so much of their information was "phon[y]" and always "hard to spot." See Charles Stuart Kennedy, "Ralph Clough," 1990, in "Association for Diplomatic Research and Training: Hong Kong, A Reader" (hereafter ADRT). https://adst.org/OH%20TOCs/Clough,%20Ralph%20N.toc.pdf.

14. See "Biantai xinli xia de Disan shili wenti" (The Abnormal Psychology of the Third-Force, originally published in November 1950), in Li Hanji and Li Minghui eds., *Xu Fuguan zawen bubian*, v.2, pp.60–68. Qian is quoted in Yu Yingshi, "Zhongguo ziyou ahishiren" [Chinese liberal intellectuals], *Mingbao yuekan*, n.5, July 2018, p.19.

15. Chen Zhengmou, "Wushi niandai Xianggang disan shili de zhuyao tuanti Zhongguo ziyou minzhu zhandou tongmeng shimo," (The Main Third Force Group of the 1950s Hong Kong) *Bei Taiwan xuebao*, n.34 (June 2011), pp.439–442. For backgrounds, see also J. Lilley, *China Hands*, chapter 6; Christopher Rand, *Hong Kong*, pp.121–128

16. Guo Shi, "Ziyou chubanshe cangsang shi" [History of Freedom Press], *Xingshi yuekan*, v.1 n.1 (January 1963), pp.8–9. However, we should note that historian Yu Ying-shi believes that Xie secured American support because his wife was a Chinese American. See his "Yu Ying-shih's Reminiscences of His Life and Times," trans. Michael Duke, unpublished manuscript, pp.191–192. [This manuscript was at the time under consideration for publication by Columbia UP.]

17. Gup Shi, Op cit. See also Chen Zhengmao, *Wuling niandai Xianggang disan shili yundong soumi* [Hong Kong third-force movement], Taipei: Xiuwei zixun keji gufen, 2011.

18. One of the emissaries was a well-known liberal intellectual, Lei Zhen, who later ran afoul of Chiang. See Chen Zhengmou, *Shiqu de hongying: Xiandai renwu shuping* [Study of modern personnel], Taipei: Xiuwei zixun keji gufen, 2011, pp.211–212.

19. "Yu Ying-shih's Reminiscences of His Life and Times," trans. Michael Duke, p.192.

20. See Wu Chao, "Du Shiping *ziyou zhanxian* hou de wojian," (My View of *Frontline of Freedom*) *Ziyou zhanxian*, v.6 n.8 (August 10, 1951), p.16.

21. Editorial, "Women yao xiang xinsheng dadao maijin," (We Should March Forward to Freedom) *Ziyou zhanxian*, v.2 n.1 (April 16, 1950), pp.19–20; Editorial, "Women de jibeng xinnian," *Ziyou zhanxian*, v.3 n.3 (October 10, 1950), pp.4–5.

22. Edward Dillery, "Harvey Feldman," ADRT, 1999, https://www.adst.org/OH%20TOCs/Feldman,%20Harvey.toc.pdf. [Harvey Feldman was interviewed by Dillerey]

23. Alexander Grantham, *Via Ports: From Hong Kong to Hong Kong*, Hong Kong: Hong Kong University Press 2012, pp.111–112.

24. Ibid., pp.131–139.

25. Ibid., pp.163–168. For earlier colonial government claims of neutrality with regard to China, such as during the First World War and the early phase onset of the Japanese invasion of China in the 1930s, see Michael Ng, "Rule of Law, Freedom of Expression and the Anxiety of Empire: Press Censorship in British Hong Kong," unpublished paper, 2016.

26. Zheng Shusen, "Zhimin zhuyi, lengzhan niandai ye bianyuan kongjian: Lun sishi niandai xianggang wenxue shengcun zhuangtai" [Colonialism, Cold War period, and marginal space], Suye wenxue, v.52 (April 1994), pp.20–23.

27. Richard Hughes, Borrowed Place, Borrowed Time: Hong Kong and Its Many Faces, London: Andre Deutsch, 1968, pp.39–40.

28. Syd Goldsmith, Hong Kong on the Brink: An American Diplomat Relives 1967's Darkest Days, Hong Kong: Blacksmith Books, 2017, pp.143–145.

29. Richard Hughes, Borrowed Place, Borrowed Time, pp.39–43, and Syd Goldsmith, Hong Kong on the Brink, pp.90–93. See also John Carroll, A Concise History of Hong Kong, London: Rowman and Littlefield, 2017, pp.176–177, 305–333.

30. Daniel Kurtz-Phelan, The China Mission, p.104.

31. Jack O'Brien, "Interview with Richard McCartney," ADST, 1988. https://www.adst.org/OH%20TOCs/McCarthy,%20Richard%20M.toc.pdf, p.5.

32. L. Z. Yuen, "Memorandum to Ivy," April 20, 1955, Asia Foundation Collection, Hoover Institution Archives, Stanford University (hereafter, AFC), Box P-55.

33. The incident and its aftermath were documented by Kong Kwan-sheng, Zhonggong zai Xianggang [Communist China in Hong Kong], Hong Kong: Cosmo Book, 2012, v.2, pp.82–92, 102–106. For the Chinese intelligence apparatus, see, for example, James Lilley, China Hands, pp.135–151; Christine Loke, Underground Front: The CCP in Hong Kong, Hong Kong: Hong Kong University Press, 2010, pp.79–98.

34. Syd Goldsmith, Hong Kong on the Brink, pp.121–122.

35. Lewis Schmidt, "Interview with Earl Wilson," ADST, 1988, https://tile.loc.gov/storage-services/service/mss/mfdip/2004/2004wil12/2004wil12.pdf, p.69.

36. Charles Stuart Kennedy, "Interview with Charles Cross," ADST, 2001, https://www.adst.org/OH%20TOCs/Cross,%20Charles%20T.toc.pdf https://www.adst.org/OH%20TOC, p.4.

37. James Lilley, China Hands, pp.83–89, 136–148.

38. Quoted from Kwong Chi Man, Eastern Fortress: A Military History of Hong Kong, 1840–1970, Hong Kong: Hong Kong University Press, 2014, p.245.

39. "Memorandum of Discussion at the 447th Meeting of the National Security Council," Foreign Relations of the United States, 1958–1960, China, Washington: United States Government Printing Office, 1996, v.19, p.2.

40. Cheng Chu-yuen, Zhangbi zou tianya, pp.132–136.

41. Charles Stuart Kennedy, "Charles Cross," ADST, 1997, https://www.adst.org/OH%20TOCs/Cross,%20Charles%20T.toc.pdf; Jack O'Brien, "Richard McCarthy," ADST, 1988. For a well-documented discussion of the important influence of the translation series in Taiwan cultural and literary circles in the 1950s-1970s, see Shan Dexing, Fanyi yu maile [Translation and Context], Taipei: Shulin chuban youxian gongxi, 2009, pp.117–158.

42. Cheng Chu-yuen, *Zhangbi zou tianya*, p.139, and Yu Ying-shih, "Yu Ying-shih's Reminiscences of His Life and Times," trans. Michael Duke, p.195.

43. "Subject: Committee for a Free Asia," December 13, 1951, declassified and released by Central Intelligence Agency Sources Methods Exemptions 302B Nazi War Crimes Disclosure Act Date 2007, https://www.cia.gov/library/readingroom/docs/DTPIL LAR%20%20%20VOL.%201_0085.pdf.

44. Emma North-Best, "Robert Bum, the Spy Who Shaped the World, Part 1," August 17, 2017, MuckRock, https://www.muckrock.com/news/archives/2017/aug/17/robert-blum-spy-who-shaped-world-part-1/.

45. Christina Klein, *Cold War Cosmopolitanism: Period Style in 1950s Korean Cinema*, Berkeley: University of California Press, 2020, pp.29–30.

46. "The Asia Foundation Hong Kong (1953)," AFC Box-P55.

47. Robert Blum, "The Work of the Asia Foundation," *Pacific Affairs*, v.29 n.1 (March 1956), pp.46–47.

48. Quoted from Fredrik Logevall, *Embers of War: The Fall of An Empire and the Making of America's Vietnam*, New York: Random House, 2014. p.232.

49. "The Asia Foundation: Hong Kong," 1952–1953, AFC Box P-55; "Youth and Related Activities," 1956, AFC Box P-58; "Social and Economic Groups: Cultural," 1952–1953, AFC Box P-55.

50. YUDC, "A Memorandum," October 1951, AFC Box P-55.

51. Yu Ying-shih, "Yu Ying-shih's Reminiscences of His Life and Times," pp.195–197.

52. Biographical information gathered from Lo Wai-luen and Hung Chi-kam, *Xianggang wenhua zhongsheng dao*, "Yu Ying-shih's Reminiscences of His Life and Times," pp.195–203.

53. William Hsu, "Letter to Ivy," December 13, 1951, AFC Box P-55.

54. YUDC, "A Memorandum."

55. Maria Yen, "Letter to Ivy" May 4th, 1952, AFC Box P-55.

56. Yue Xin, "Huiyi Xuesheng bao de dangsheng" [Remembering the birth of *CSW*], *CSW*, n.470 (July 21, 1961).

57. See Pierre Bourdieu and Jean-Claude Passeron, *Reproduction in Education: Society and Culture*, Beverly Hill: Sage, 1977.

58. "Public Open Space Celebrated Historical Links of the New Asia College," October 31, 2016, Urban Renewal Authority, https://www.ura.org.hk/en/news-centre/feat ure-stories/public-open-space-celebrates-the-historical-link-of-the-new-asia-college.

59. See Zhang Yang, "Cultural Cold War," pp.148–169, and Grace Chou, *Confucianism, Colonialism, and the Cold War*.

60. "Yu Ying-shih's Reminiscences of His Life and Times," p.200. See also "Robert Hsi," in Lo Wai-luen and Hung Chi-kam, *Xianggang Wenhua zhongsheng dao*, v.1, pp.48–81.

61. See "Ho Chen-yah" and "Robert Hsi," in *Xianggang Wenhua zhongsheng dao*, v.1, pp.8–80.

62. See J. Ivy, "Hong Kong Communication No. 15, Subject: Chinese Student Group," October 25, 1951, AFC Box P-55; Hsu Tung Pien, "Letter to J. Ivy," November 13, 1951, AFC Box P-55.

63. Chen See-ming, letter to Arthur Hummel, October 9, 1954, and letter to Mr. Harrington, October 9, 1954, "Hong Kong U.S. Counsel General, Hong Kong," RG 84, Box 2, National Archives.

64. See J. Ivy, "Letter to J. Stewart, HK-2," June 2, 1952, AFC Box P-55.

65. "Gu Mei," in *Xianggang Wenhua zhongsheng dao*, v.1 p.89.

66. J. Stewart, "Letter to J. Ivy," June 3, 1952, AFC Box P-55.

67. "Yu Ying-shih's Reminiscences of His Life and Times," p.195.

68. In a 1954 meeting between J. Stewart and J. Ivy in Hong Kong, the Asia chief was alarmed that the Beijing-backed Chung Hwa Book Company was putting out such a series. "Do people on our side have any comparable series?" The answer was no. To neutralize Communist domination in the field, the *UP Loose-Leaf Reader* was launched. "Discussion Note: J. Stewart and J. Ivy, Hong Kong," August 24, 1954, AFC Box P-55.

69. "Youth and Related Activities: Students," HK108, 1953, AFC Box P-55.

70. See Bob Crawford, "Report on the Union Press," July 9, 1957, AFC Box P-57; "Social and Economic Cultural (HK)," HK-26, n.d., AFC Box P-57. For UP members' memory of the USIS connection, see, for example, *Xianggang Wenhua zhongsheng dao*, v.1, pp.23–26, 181–183.

71. Jessica Gienow-Hecht, "Culture and the Cold War in Europe," in Melvyn Leffler and Odd Arne Westad eds., *Cambridge History of the Cold War*, Cambridge: Cambridge University Press, 2012, v.1, pp.398–399.

72. Dekuan, "Mangchang de xingcheng" [Long road ahead], *CSW*, n.53 (July 24, 1953).

73. Editorial, "Women de daolu" [Our path], *CSW*, n.53 (July 24, 1953).

74. Editorial, "Fuqi shidai de zeren" [Take up the responsibility of our time], *CSW*, n.1 (July 25, 1952). See also Editorial, "Women dui Kongzi de taidu" [Our attitude toward Confucius], *CSW*, n.6 (August 29, 1952), and Dekuan, "Mangchang de xingcheng."

75. Ann Byington, "Letter to J. Ivy," August 14, 1952, AFC Box P-172.

76. Qian Mu, "Jinggao liuwang haiwai de Zhongguo qingnian men" [A plea to Chinese youths in exile overseas], *CSW*, n.36 (March 27, 1953). See also Xiao Sao, "Qian Mu xiansheng yu Xinya xueyuan" [Mr. Qian Mu and New Asia College], *CSW*, n.69 (November 13, 1953).

77. Tang Jungyi, *Shuo Zhonghua minzu zhi huaguo piaoling* [On the scattered fruits and flowers of Chinese people], Taipei: Sanmin shuju, 2005, pp.22–27; Thomas Frohlich, *Tang Jungyi: Confucian Philosophy and the Challenge of Modernity*, Boston: Brill, 2017.

78. Editorial, "Gei haiwai duzhe he tongunyuan de hua" [To our overseas readers and reporters], *CSW*, n.457 (April 21, 1961).

79. J. Stewart, "Memorandum for the Record," September 1, 1954, AFC Box P-55; J. Ivy, "Letter to Robert Blum," September 3, 1954, AFC Box P-55. For a vivid description of the Special Branch relationship with US agencies, see J. Lilley, *China Hands*, especially pp.80–86.

80. Chia LiNi, interview with author, New York, December 23, 2014.

81. P. C. Liu, "Memorandum to J. Stewart," July 30, 1952, AFC Box P-172; Ann Byington, "Letter to J. Ivy," August 14, 1952, AFC Box P-172; L. Z. Yuan, "Memorandum to M. Lintner," [n.d.] 1952, AFC Box P-172.

82. "Agreement of Financial Assistance to the Chinese Student Weekly," November 20, 1952, AFC Box P-55; "Agreement between Yu Tak-Foon and CFA," June 20, 1953, AFC Box P-55; "Agreement," June 30, 1954, AFC Box P-55.

83. "Letter to J. Stewart," marked "private and confidential," August 27, 1952, AFC Box P-55.

84. See, for example, Yang chijun (楊熾均), "Wode liangshi yiyou" [My mentor and friend], *CSW*, n.470 (July 21, 1961).

85. Fuyao, "Women zhenyang dakai xiaosu" [How did we increase sales?]), *CSW*, n.53 (July 22, 1953).

86. Delmer Brown, "Memorandum to the President," June 22, 1953, AFC Box P-55; J. Ivy, "Memorandum to Field Representatives, CFA," September 1, 1952, AFC Box P-55.

87. J. Ivy, "Letter to Patrick Judge, " October 7, 1954, AFC Box P-55.

88. See, for example, Robert Hsi, interviews with author, November 2014 and January 2016; . Chia LiNi, interview with author, December 2014.

89. Robert Hsi, "Letter to TAF," December 23, 1954, AFC Box P-55; J. Ivy, "Memorandum to the President," January 3, 1955, AFC Box P-55; "Agreement No.1," January 1, 1955, AFC Box P-55.

90. William Hsu, "Letter to Ivy from Hsu," April 4, 1956, AFC Box P-57; L. Z. Yuen, "Memorandum to the Representative, Hong Kong," August 28, 1957, AFC Box P-57.

91. "107: Chinese Student Weekly," Hong Kong Representative, July 31, 1958, AFC Box P-57; "Hong Kong Office Memorandum," November 30, 1957, AFC Box P-57; "AP-4301," period March 31, 1961, AFC Box P-57.

92. J. Ivy, "Letter to Judge," October 7, 1954, AFC Box P-55.

93. Wu Kangmin, *Wu Kangmin koushu shi* [An oral history of Wu Kangmin], Hong Kong: Sanlian shudain, 2011, pp.64–66.

94. Leung Mo-han, *Wo yu Xianggang dixia dang* [My life in Hong Kong's underground Communist Party], Hong Kong: Open Books, 2012, pp.3–13.

95. Lo Wai-luen, interview with author, January 3, 2022.

96. See Shih Zhongying, "Women renshi de *Qingnian leyuan*" [The youth paradise we know], in Guan Yongqi and Wang Zicheng eds., *Women zouguo de daolu* [Our paths], Hong Kong: Cosmos Books, 2015 pp.72–99.

97. Yang Xiaoliu (杨萧流), "Huanle jinri" [Enjoy today], *CSW*, no.263 (August 2, 1957). For a discussion with *Bixue hua* [Flower in Blood] in wartime Shanghai, see *Passivity, Resistance, and Collaboration: Intellectual Choices in Occupied Shanghai*, Stanford: Stanford University Press, 1993, pp.89–90.

98. "Letter to J. Stewart H-62," July 25, 1952, Box P-55.

99. Zhao Guoxiong, "Changlvshu yu qingnian de gouge" [Evergreen tree and young diaspora], *CSW*, n.470 (July 21, 1961).

100. J. Lilley, *China Hands*, pp.88–89.

101. Delmer Brown, "Memorandum to the President," February 17, 1954, AFC Box P-55. The TAF provided $250 monthly for a year to support the Indonesian edition.

102. "Excerpts from Yu Tak-foon's Letters, December 22, 1954-January 5, 1955," AFC Box P-57.

103. Ibid..

104. See Lo Wai-Luen and Hung Chi Kum eds., *Xianggang Wenhua zhongsheng dao*, v.1, p.60.

105. Brian Stewart, "Winning in Malaya: An Intelligence Success Story," in Richard Aldrich et al. eds., *Clandestine Cold War in Asia: 1945–1965*, New York: Routledge, 2000, pp.267–283; Souchou Yao, *The Malayan Emergency: The Essays on a Small, Distant War*, Honolulu: University of Hawaii Press, 2016.

106. Lo Wai-Luen and Hung Chi Kum eds., *Xianggang Wenhua zhongsheng dao* v.1, pp.60–62, 93–96, 152–156; and Kychia, "Taiji de liangyi" [Two sides of Taiji], April 8, 2018, https://www.sinchew.com.my/20180804/%E9%9B%85%E8%92%99-%E2%80%A7-%E3%80%90%E5%AD%A6%E5%8F%8B%E8%BF%BD%E5%BF%86%E5%B0%91%E5%B9%B4%E6%A2%A6%E5%AE%8C%E7%BB%93%E7%AF%87%E3%80%91%E5%A4%AA%E6%9E%81%E7%9A%84%E4%B8%A4%E4%BB%AA/.

107. See Lo Wai-luen and Hung Chi-Kum eds., *Xianggang Wenhua zhongsheng dao*, v.1, pp.56–63, 89–93.

108. "Office Memorandum, Hong Kong," November 30, 1957, AFC Box P-57.

109. "Cultural Program Designed: Attachment," n.d., AFC Box P-55.

110. J. Stewart, "Letter to J. Ivy," SX-HK-882, February 3, 1955, AFC Box P-55; "107—The Chinese Student Weekly," July 31, 1958, and "107—The Chinese Student Weekly," March 21, 1959, AFC Box P-57.

111. See Kenneth Yung, "Diaspora of Chinese Intellectuals in the Cold War Era: From Hong Kong to the Asia-Pacific Region, 1949–1969," unpublished manuscript, pp.18–19. Thanks to the author for sharing this with me.

112. For example, in 1956 *CSW* launched a rooftop "free primary school" in the working-class neighborhood of Wong Tai Sin. The TAF made it a condition for funding to register properly with the Education Department and strictly follow all its rules. See J. Ivy, "Letter to Robert Blum," September 3, 1954, AFC Box P-55; "Attachment No. 3 to Basic Agreement between J. Ivy and William Hsu, Dated July 1, 1956," AFC Box P-57.

113. See, for example, "Huainian minzu de kutong" [Remembering national sufferings], *CSW*, n.362 (June 26, 1959); Qiu Zhengli, "Gei Zhongguo qingnian de yi feng xin" [To Chinese youths], *CSW*, n.356 (May 15, 1959).

114. Tang Junyi, *Shuo Zhonghua minzhu zhi huaguo piiaoling*, pp.66–67.

115. Bernard Luk, "Chinese Culture in the Hong Kong Curriculum: Heritage and Colonialism," *Comparative Education Review*, v.35 n.4 (November 1991), pp.667–668. See also John Carroll, *A Concise History of Hong Kong*, pp.148–150.

116. Chen Shu-tong, Tu Yun-fei, and Hsiao Mu, "Letter to Arthur Hummel, USIS," June 10, 1954, Hong Kong US Consulate General, RG 84, National Archive.

117. See L. Z.Yuen, "Memorandum to J. Ivy," April 20, 1955, AFC Box P-55; Robert Sheeks, "Memorandum to Hong Kong Representative," May 11, 1955, AFC Box P-55. For the UP and CSW lifestyle and work ethic, see, for example, Lo Wai-Luen and Hung Chi-kum, *Xianggang wenhua zongshengdao*, pp.50–73 and 106–138.

118. After lashing out at Mao's "destruction of Chinese culture," for example, Qiu Zhenli blasted Taipei for losing China and yet remained "selfish. . . . Never push forward

with democracy." "Tangtang de zuo yige Zhongguoren" [Be a proud Chinese], *CSW*, n.253 (May 24, 1957).

119. Bob Crawford, "On the Union Press," July 9, 1957, AFC Box P-57; L. Z. Yuen, "Letter to John Sullivan," June 13, 1962, AFC Box P-57; Don Klein, "The Union Press," 1964, AFC Box P-57.

120. J. Ivy, "Letter to the Representative, Singapore," December 9, 1954, S-12, AFC Box P-55; J. Ivy, "Letter to Judge," December 7, 1954, AFC Box P-55.

121. See Robert Blum, "Letter to Pat Judge," February 27, 1957, AFC Box-P57; Pat Judge, "Letter to the President, HK-326," August 3, 1957, AFC Box-P57.

122. Yan Guilai, "Gei Xiongyali zhan zhong de xuesheng" [To the students at the Hungarian War], *CSW*, n.229 (December 7, 1956).

123. Hu Juren, "Xiujin tingba de changlu shu" [The strong evergreen tree], *CSW*, n.418 (July 22, 1960).

Chapter 3

1. Robert Sheeks, "To Asia Foundation President," May 11, 1956, AFC Box P-171.

2. "Opening Activities," *Far East Film News*, June 8, 1956, p.4.

3. See Christina Klein, *Cold War Cosmopolitanism: Period Style in 1950s Korean Cinema*, Berkeley: University of California Press, 2020, and especially Sangjoon Lee, "The Asia Foundation's Motion Picture Project and the Cultural Cold War in Asia," *Film History*, v.29 n.2 (Summer 2017), pp.108–137. For a different perspective, see Michael Baskett, "Japan's Film Festival Diplomacy in Cold War Asia," *The Velet Light Trap*, March 2014, v.73 n.1, pp.4–18.

4. "Survey of and Statistics on the Mandarin Motion Picture Industry in Hong Kong," n.d., AFC Box P-56.

5. "Hongkong's Theatres and the Motion Picture Industry," *Far Eastern Economic Review*, v.17 n.16 (October 14, 1954), pp.497–499.

6. M. Chase, "Conversation with Chinese Movie Man," [n.d.] 1953, AFC Box P-56.

7. See Ma Xingkong, "Guoyu pian you jiaxiang shichang liao" [Mandarin cinema has a home market now], *Xinwen tiandi*, no.766 (October 20, 1962), pp.25–26.

8. "Guoyu dianying jinri mianlin de kunnan" [Problems facing Mandarin cinema today], *Guoji dianying*, n.1 (October 1955), pp.50–51; Raymond Hsu, "Memorandum to J. Ivy," November 7, 1954, AFC Box P-56.

9. "Hongkong's Theatres and the Motion Picture Industry," p.499.

10. Ibid.

11. Grant Advertising, *A Survey of the Reading Habits of the Chinese of Hong Kong*, 1952, AFC Box P-58.

12. Chang Kuo-sin, "The Asia Picture Limited," July 15, 1953, AFC Box P-56.

13. Chang Kuo-sin ed., *Xiangang de qiantu* [The future of Hong Kong], Hong Kong: Asia Press, 1964, p.2.

14. Patrick Iber, "Anti-Communist Entrepreneurs and the Origins of the Cultural Cold War in Latin America," in Jadwiger Mooney and Fabio Lanza eds., *De-Centering Cold War History: Local and Global Changes*, New York: Routledge, 2012.

15. J. Stewart, "Letter to Thomas D. Scott," December 22, 1952, AFC Box P-56.

16. Ibid. See also "Communication Groups: Film Producers and Distributors, 1956," AFC Box P-55.

17. For a discussion of NSC-48, see Kevin Peraino, *A Force so Swift: Mao, Truman, and the Birth of Modern China,* New York: Crown, 2017, pp.250–256. "USIS Plan for Overseas Chinese in Southeast Asia," quoted from Wai-Siam Hee, *Remapping the Sinophone: The Cultural Production of Chinese-Language Cinema in Singapore and Malaya before and during the Cold War*, Hong Kong: Hong Kong University Press, 2019, pp.213–215. See also Nicholas Cull, *The Cold War and the United States Information Agency: American Propaganda and Public Diplomacy*, New York: Cambridge University Press, 2008.

18. Chang Kuo-sin, "Motion Picture Project," January 8, 1953, AFC Box P-56.

19. Chang Kuo-sin, "The Asia Pictures Limited," July 15, 1953, AFC Box P-56.

20. Charles Tanner, "Hong Kong Motion Production Project," July 14, 1953, AFC Box P-56.

21. Charles Tanner, "Motion Picture Projects—Comments," July 28, 1953, AFC Box P-56.

22. M. Chase, "Conversation with the Chinese Movie Man."

23. "Survey of and Statistics on the Mandarin Motion Pictures Industry in Hong Kong."

24. J. Stewart (for the president), "Memo: Motion Picture Project," August 21, 1953, AFC Box P-56.

25. Ibid.

26. Delmer Brown, "Memorandum to the Acting President, CFA," July 28, 1953, AFC Box P-56.

27. See L. Z. Yuen, "Memorandum to the Representative, Hong Kong," August 17, 1957, AFC Box P-172.

28. "1955 niandu xianggang shangyin shoulun guoyupian tonjibiao," [Annual Hong Kong first-run Mandarin film box-office chart], *Changcheng huabao*, n.59, January 1959.

29. L. Z. Yuan to J. Stewart, "Chinese Ex-POW Program," March 8, 1954, AFC Box P-172.

30. L. Z. Yuan, "To the Representatives, Hong Kong, Conversation with Chang Kuo-sin," August 17, 1957, AFC Box-171.

31. For *LIFE* magazine, see Alan Brinkley, *The Publisher: Henry Luce and His American Century*, New York: Vintage Books, 2011, pp.206–233.

32. For circulation figures, see Yung Sai-shing, "Yazhou chubanshe/Yazhou yingye chutan" [Preliminary study of Asia Press / Asia Pictures], in *Langzhan yu Xianggang*, pp.129–132.

33. See Christina Klein, *Cold War Cosmopolitanism*, pp.1–32.

34. J. Miller, "Memorandum to the President, CFA," June 25, 1954, AFC Box P-56.

35. Chang Kuo-sin, "Motion Picture Project," January 8, 1953, AFC Box P-56. For S. K. Chang's role in wartime Shanghai cinema and his famous big dreams, see Po-Shek Fu, *Between Shanghai and Hong Kong: The Politics of Chinese Cinemas,* Stanford: Stanford University Press, 2003.

36. Law Kar, "The Shadow of Tradition and the Left-Right Struggle," in Li Cheuk-to ed., *The China Factor in Hong Kong Cinema*, Hong Kong: Urban Council, 1990, pp.15–17.

37. Chang Kuo-sin, "Motion Picture Project."

38. Huang Jen, "Gangjiu dianying xiji shiye ziyou zonghui de jiaose he yingxiang" (On Hong Kong and Kowloon Free Filmmakers General Association) in Wong Ailing ed., *Lengzhan yu Xianggang dianying*, Hong Kong: Hong Kong Film Archive, 2009, pp.70–80.

39. Chang Kuo-sin, "Hongkong Movie Industry Faces Bankruptcy," *Hong Kong Standard*, February 7, 1956. Enclosed with Robert Grey, "Newspaper Comment on Hong Kong Motion Picture Industry," February 8, 1956, AFC Box-P172.

40. Robert Sheeks, "To Asia Foundation Representative, Hong Kong," May 11, 1955, AFC Box-P171. For Union Press intellectuals, see, for example, "Robert his," in Lo Wai-Luen and Hung Chi Kum eds., *Xianggang wenhua zongshengdao*, Hong Kong: Joint Publishing Co., 2014, especially pp.66–68.

41. Ma Xingkong, "Duli zhipian biaomian fusu" [Recovery of independents], *Xinwen tiandi*, n.663 (November 1961), pp.140–145. Charles Leary, "The Most Careful Arrangements for a Careful Fiction: A Short History of Asia Pictures," *Inter-Asia Cultural Studies*, v.13 n.4 (2012), p.551.

42. Liu Qi, "Huidao zuguo liangci" [Return to the homeland twice], *Yazhou huabao*, n.12 (April 1954), p.25. Chiang's citation, quoted from Su Tao, *Dianying nandu: Nanxia yingren yu zhanhou Xianggang dianying* [Cinema southward: Southbound filmmakers and postwar Hong Kong cinema], Beijing: Peking University Press, 2020, p.65.

43. Bureau of Cinema, Ministry of Culture, "Xianggang dianying zhipian gongsi qingkuang cankao ziliao," (References on Hong Kong production companies) 1954, quoted from Su Tao, *Dianying nandu*, p.66.

44. J. Ivy, "Letter to John Miller," May 7, 1955, AFC Box-171.

45. For discussion of the exodus, see Laura Madokoro, *Elusive Refuge: Chinese Migrants in the Cold War*, Cambridge: Harvard University Press, 2016; and Helen Zia, *Last Boat out of Shanghai: The Epic Story of the Chinese Who Fled Mao's Revolution*, New York: Ballantine Books, 2019.

46. For a different reading of *Long Lane* that focuses on the tension between tradition and modernity, see Law Kar, "The Shadow of Tradition and the Left-Right Struggle," pp. 19–22.

47. Ma Xingkong, "Duli zhipian biaomian fusu," p.15.

48. L. Z. Yuen, "To the Representatives in Hong Kong: Asia Pictures Ltd.," August 20, 1957, AFC Box P-171"; "Film Producers Urged to Come to an Agreement," *Hong Kong Standard*, February 7, 1956, attached to Robert Grey, "Letter to President," February 8, 1956, AFC Box P-58.

49. L. Z. Yuen, "Memorandum to J. Ivy," April 20, 1955, AFC Box P-172.

50. John Miller, "Memorandum to the President," June 25, 1954, AFC Box P-171.

51. J. Ivy, "Memorandum to the President, CFA San Francisco," July 7, 1954, AFC Box P-56.

52. Raymond Hsu, "Memorandum to J. Ivy," November 7, 1954, AFC Box P-56.

53. John Miller, "Memorandum to the President," July 12, 1954, AFC Box P-56.

54. C. M. Tanner, "Review, Evaluation and Proposed Project Funding for Fiction Motion Picture Activity," July 8, 1954, AFC Box P-56; Tanner, "Fiction Motion Picture Project," August 10, 1954, AFC Box P-56.

55. J. Ivy, "To the President, CFA San Francisco," July 7, 1954, AFC Box P-171.

56. G. John Ikenberry, "American Hegemony and East Asian Order," *Australian Journal of International Affairs*, v.58 n.3 (September 2004), pp.354–358. See also Akira Iriye, *The Cold War in Asia: A Historical Introduction*, Hoboken: Prentice Hall, 1974.

57. Michael Baskett, "Japan's Film Festival Diplomacy in Cold War Asia," p.5.

58. Yau Shuk-ting, *GangRi yingren koushu lishi* [Oral history of Hong Kong–Japanese filmmakers], Hong Kong: Hong Kong University Press, 2012, especially pp.52–58.

59. "8-Year Historical Highlights of Film Federation and Festival," *Far East Film News Special Supplement: Pacific-Asian Trade Lists*, 1960–1961, p.9.

60. Delmer Brown, "To the President, CFA," AFC Box P-56.

61. Michael Baskett, "Japan's Film Festival Diplomacy in Cold War Asia," pp.11–13. For TAF's relations with the federation, mainly from the South Korean perspective, see also Sangjoon Lee, "The Asia Foundation's Motion Picture Project and the Cultural Cold War in Asia," pp.108–137, and Christina Klein, *Cold War Cosmopolitanism*, especially pp.26–30, 75–78.

62. Robert Grey, "Memorandum to the President," October 4, 1956, AFC Box P-171.

63. See "The Records: William Seiter Assignment," August 24, 1956, AFC Box P-171; Sha Rongfeng, *Binfen dianying sishi chun: Sha Rongfeng huiyi lu* [Memoir of Sha Rongfeng], Taipei: Guojia dianying ziliaoguan, 1994, especially pp.119–130.

64. Frank Borzag was later known to many Chinese viewers for his 1958 romantic drama *China Doll*, set in World War II China and starring pro-Taiwan superstar Li Li-Hua. See Jing Jing Chang's illuminating study, "China Doll in Flight: Li Lihua, World Today, and the Free China–US Relationship," *Film History*, v.26 n.3 (2014), pp.1–28.

65. Delmer Brown, "Memo to the Acting President, CFA," July 28, 1953, AFC Box P-56; Brown, "Movie Distribution," September 18, 1953, AFC Box P-56.

66. "The Records: William Seiter Assignment."

67. L. Z. Yuen, "To the Representative, Hong Kong," August 20, 1957, AFC Box P-171.

68. C. M. Tanner, "Review, Evaluation and Proposed Project Funding for Fiction Motion Picture Activity," July 8, 1954, AFC Box P-56.

69. "Discussions Note: J Stewart and J Ivy, HK," August 28, 1954, AFC Box P-57.

70. Robert Sheeks, "To Asia Foundation Representative, Hong Kong," May 11, 1955, AFC Box P-171; L. Z. Yuen, "Memorandum to J. Ivy," April 20, 1955, AFC Box P-171.

71. L. Z. Yuen, "To the Representative, Hong Kong," August 20, 1957; J. Stewart, Robert Sheeks, L. Z. Yuen, and J. Ivy, "On Tuesday, February 26, the Four Met Again to Resume the Review," February 1957, AFC Box P-171.

72. Quoted from Robert Sheeks, "To Asia Foundation Representative, Hong Kong."

73. "Discussions Note: J. Stewart and J. Ivy, HK," August 28, 1954.

74. L. Z. Yuen, "Memorandum to J. Ivy"; Robert Sheeks, "To Asia Foundation Representative, Hong Kong."

75. See Lanjun Xu, "The Southern Film Corporation, Opera Film, and the PRC's Cultural Diplomacy in Cold War Asia, 1950s–1960s," *Modern Chinese Literature and Culture*, v.29 n.1 (Spring 2017), pp.239–281.

76. Glenn Iretora, "Communists Initiate Rapprochement with Movie-Makers of the Free World," *Far East Film News*, v.3 n.50 (June 1, 1956), pp.1–5.

77. See Man-Fung Yip, "The End of an Era: The Cultural Revolution, Modernization, and the Demise of Hong Kong Leftist Cinema," in *The Cold War and Asian Cinemas*, New York: Routledge, 2019, p.266; Xu Dunle, *Kenguang tuoying* (My Cinematic Career), MCCM Creations, 2005, pp.33–39.

78. J. Stewart, Robert Sheeks, L. Z. Yuen, and J. Ivy, "On Tuesday, February 26, the Four Met Again to Resume the Review."

79. "A Brief Report on Local Leftist Film Companies," March 20, 1957, AFC Box P-172.

80. Robert Grey, "Memorandum to the President," October 4, 1956, AFC Box P-171. For the founding of the Zhujiang film studio and its connection with Hong Kong, see Wang Weiyi, *Nanwang de suiyue* [The memoir of Wang Weiyi], Beijing, Zhongguo dianying chubanshe, 2006, pp.122–127.

81. "Communication Groups: Film Producers and Distributors," 1956, AFC Box-55.

82. Ibid.

83. Robert Grey, "Letter to President," February 8, 1956, AFC Box P-171; Liu Qi, "Huidao zuguo liangci," pp.22–23; Huang Ren, *Zhongwai dianying yongyuan de juxing* [Legends of Chinese and foreign cinemas], Taipei: Xiuwei chubanshe, 2010, pp.180–200; "Communication Groups: Film Producers and Distributors," 1956.

84. L. Z. Yuen, "To the Representative, Hong Kong," August 20, 1957.

85. J. Stewart, Robert Sheeks, L. Z. Yuen, and J. Ivy, "On Tuesday, February 26, the Four Met Again to Resume the Review"; "Communications: Film Producers and Distributors, Reference HK-123," March 21, 1958, AFC Box P-55; "Memorandum to the President, TAF," February 28, 1958, AFC Box P-172.

86. Charles Leary, "The Most Careful Arrangements for a Careful Fiction," p.555.

87. "Communications: Film Producers and Distributors, Reference HK-123," March 21, 1958, AFC Box P-55; Hong Kong Representative, "To the President, TAF, Kuo Phone Loan," August 3, 1960, AFC Box P-171.

88. Ma Xingkong, "Duli zhipian biaomian fusu," p.15.

Chapter 4

1. William Goodwin, "Official· Report on Shaw Organization," *Far East Film News*, 1961/2, p.25.

2. "Show Business: The Empire of Run Run Shaw," *Time*, June 28, 1976.

3. "Lee Ang," in Law Kar ed., *Transcending the Times: King Hu and Eileen Chang*, Hong Kong: Provisional Urban Council of Hong Kong, 1998, p.107.

4. For the idea of cultural entrepreneur, see Paul Hirsch, "Processing Fads and Fashions: An Organization-Set Analysis of Cultural Industry Systems," in C. Mukerji

and M. Schudson eds., *Rethinking Popular Culture: Contemporary Perspectives on Cultural Studies*, Berkeley: University of California Press, 1991, pp.313–334. See also H. Anheier and Y. Isar eds., *Cultures and Globalization: The Cultural Economy*, Los Angeles: Sage, 2008; R. Swedberg, "The Cultural Entrepreneur and the Creative Industries: Beginning in Vienna," *Journal of Cultural Economics*, v.30, 2006, pp.243–261.

5. Zhou Chengren, "Shanghai's Unique Film Productions," in Wong Ain-ling ed., *The Shaw Screen*, Hong Kong: Hong Kong Film Archive, 2003, p.21

6. Ibid, pp.18–22; Hubert Niogret, "Fangwen Shao Yifu" [Interview with Run Run Shaw], trans. Du Zangui, *Influence* (Summer–Fall 1976), pp.36–38.

7. Zhou Chengren, "Shanghai's Unique Film Productions," pp.21–23; Zhang Zhen, *An Amorous History of the Silver Screen: Shanghai Cinema 1896–1937*, Chicago: University of Chicago Press, 2005, pp.210–211.

8. For the film, see Zhou Chengren, "Shanghai's Unique Film Productions," p.21. Zhang Zheng discusses the gender question of women in martial arts film in *An Amorous History of the Silver Screen*, pp.200–206.

9. See Robin Cohen, *Global Diasporas: An Introduction*, Seattle: University of Washington Press, 1997, pp.85–86. For in-depth discussion of the overseas Chinese business ethos, see Wang Gungwu, *China and the Chinese Overseas*, Singapore: Times Academic Press, 1991, and *The Chinese Overseas: From Earthbound China to the Quest for Autonomy*, Cambridge: Harvard University Press, 2002.

10. Hubert Niogret, "Fangwen Shao Yifu"; William Goodwin, "Official Report on Shaw Organization," *Far Eastern Film News*, 1961/1962, p.24.

    "Sir Run Run Shaw: The Legend with a Golden Heart," *South China Morning Post*, January 8, 2014.

11. S. Said, "The Rise of the Indonesian Film Industry," *East-West Cinema Journal*, v.6 n.2 (1992).

12. Lao Ji, "Zhao Zuiwen yu *Gechang chunse*" [Zhao Zuiwen and *Spring on Stage*], *Dacheng*, n.18 (May 1971), pp.64–66.

13. "Shaoshi xiongdi gongsi zhaodai beng po gebao jizhe" [Shaw Brothers' enterprise press conference in Singapore], *Dianying quan*, n.63 (1940), pp.2–3.

14. Lao Ji, "Runme Shao GangJiu mai xiyuan" [Runme Shaw bought cinemas in Hong Kong and Kowloon], *Dacheng*, n.25 (December 1971), pp.62–65.

15. See Michael Baskett, "Japan's Film Festival Diplomacy in Cold War Asia," *The Velvet Light Trap*, n.73 (Spring 2014), pp.10–12.

16. Lao Ji, "Runme Shao GangJiu mai xiyuan," p.62, footnote 25.

17. William Goodwin, "Official Report on Shaw Organization," pp.24–27.

18. Ibid., p.25.

19. Delmer Brown, "Memo to the President, CFA," September 18, 1953, AFC Box P-56; see also his "Memo to the Acting President," July 28, 1953, AFC Box P-56.

20. William Goodwin, "Official Report on Shaw Organization," p.27.

21. Lao Ji, "Sanshi nian qian de Shaoshi" [The Shaws thirty years ago], *Dacheng*, n.24 (November 1971), pp.70–71; Chang Cheh, *Huigu Xianggang dianying shanshi nian* [Thirty years of Hong Kong cinema], Hong Kong: Shanlian Shudian, 1989, pp.90–91.

22. Lao Ji, *Dacheng*, n.25 (December 1971), pp.65–66, and n.26 (January 1972), pp.72–73.

23. Mei Ning, "Er zhuzhang feichi ru Tai" [Two top talents visited Taiwan], *Yinhe huabao*, n.24 (February 1960), p.15; Ma Xingkong, "Zui gou pengyou de Zhang Yang" [The amiable Zhang Yang], *Yinhe huabao*, n.24 (February 1960), pp.4–5. For plots and still pictures of Nanyang-Shaw and Sons movies, see, for example, *Dianying quan* (Hong Kong edition), nn.1–9 (July 1952–April 1953).

24. See, for example, Du Yunzhi, *Zhongguo dianying qishi nian* [Seventy years of Chinese cinemas], Taipei: Dianying tushuguan chubanbu, 1986, pp.436–446, and Chung Po-yin, *Xianggang yingshiye bainian* [A century of Hong Kong film and television], Hong Kong: Joint Publishing Co., 2004.

25. Odd Arne Westad, *The Cold War: A Global History*, New York: Basic Books, 2017, particularly pp.261–275. See also Ang Cheng Guan, *Southeast Asia's Cold War: An Interpretative History*, Honolulu: University of Hawaii Press, 2018.

26. Eva Hansson et al., "Legacies of the Cold War in East and Southeast Asia: An Introduction," *Journal of Contemporary Asia*, v.50 n.4 (2020), pp.493–510; John Dower, *Embracing Defeat: Japan in the Wake of World War II*, New York: New Press, 1999.

27. See, for example, The Editor, "Plea for Two-Way Film Traffic," *Far East Film News*, v.3 n.16 (October 7, 1955), p.3

28. William Goodwin, "Official Report on Shaw Organization," *Far East Film News*, 1961/1962, p.27; "Dongnanya zhipian shang zai Fei juxing huiyi" [Meeting in Manila], *Dianying quan*, n.17 (December 1953), n.p.; Kinnia Yau Shuk Ting, "Shaoshi guzhungpian de zhongri quwei" [The Sino-Japanese flavor of Shaw Brothers costume pictures], in Liu Hui ed., *Xianggang de 'Zhongguo': Shaoshi dianying* [China in Hong Kong: The Shaw cinema], Hong Kong, Oxford University Press, 2011, pp.188–190.

29. Eva Hansson et al., "Legacies of the Cold War in East and Southeast Asia," p.268.

30. See John Carroll, *A Concise History of Hong Kong*, Lanham: Rowman and Littlefield, 2007 pp.143–148; Neil Monnery, *Architect of Prosperity: Sir John Cowperthwaite and the Making of Hong Kong*, London: London Publishing Partnership, 2017, pp.170–175. See also Catherine Schenk, *Hong Kong as an International Financial Center: Emergence and Development, 1945–1965*, London: Routledge, 2001.

31. Syd Goldsmith, *Hong Kong on the Brink: An American Diplomat Relives 1967's Darkest Days*, Hong Kong: Blacksmith Books, 2017, pp. 120–121.

32. William Goodwin, "Official Report on Shaw Organization," p.25.

33. Law Kar, "Shaoshi Yueyu pian yu tongqi Guoyu pian, Haolaiwu yingpian bijiao" [Comparing Shaw's Cantonese productions with Mandarin and Hollywood films], in Liu Hui eds., *Xianggang de "Zhongguo,"* pp.92–98.

34. John Miller, "Memorandum to the President, CFA," June 25, 1954, AFC Box P-58.

35. For an example of the public debate, see Tang Yuan, "Yang Guifei" (Magnificent Concubine Yang), *Yinhe huabao*, n.53 (January 1961), pp.21–22.

36. Tino Bilo, "Columbia Pictures: The Making of a Motion Picture Major," in David Bordwell and Noel Carroll eds., *Post Theory: Reconstructing Film Studies*, Madison: University of Wisconsin Press, 1996, pp.420–422.

37. The Shaws managed, in just over a year, to produce eight more films than MP&GI and combined to make up 60 percent of the total Mandarin output; "Yijiuwujiu nian de guoyu pian" [Mandarin films of 1959], *Jinri shijie*, n.188 (February 1, 1960), pp.16–18.

38. "Zhao Meng, "Xianggang yinmu huaxu" [Miscellany of Hong Kong silver screens], *Jinri shijie*, n.212 (January 1, 1961), pp.28–29; Thomas Gill, *Far East Film News Annual Supplement, 1960–1961*, p.23.

39. Valuable information about Run Run Shaw's relations with his technical staff is "Shen Jiang," in *Dianying suyue zongheng tan* [Oral interviews: My cinematic life], Taipei: Caituan faren Guojia dianying zhiliao guan, 1994, v.1, pp.99–121. For Movietown, see Chung Po-yin, "Xiongdi qiye de gongye zhuanbian" [Industrial changes of a brother enterprise], in Wong Ai-ling ed., *The Shaw Screen* (Hong Kong: Hong Kong Film Archive, 2003), pp.6–9.

40. David Baird, "What Makes Shaw Run," *Far Eastern Economic Review*, n.12 (March 19, 1970), p.83.

41. Quote from I. C. Jarvie, *Windows on Hong Kong*, Hong Kong: Center of Asian Studies, 1977, p.78.

42. Pierre Bourdieu, *Distinction: A Social Critique of the Judgment of Taste*, London: Routledge, 1984, pp.358–360.

43. Chung Po-yin, "Da pianchang, xiao gushi" [Big studio, little stories], in Liu Hui co-ed., *Xianggang de Zhongguo*, pp.110–111.

44. For Raymond Chow's USIS activities, see, for example, "Robert His," in Lo Wai-luen and Hung Chi Kum, *Xiangang wenhua zhongsheng dao*, (Multiple voices of Hong Kong culture), Hong Kong: Joint Publishing Co., 2014, vol.1, pp.142–145,

45. Shen Xicheng, "Wushi niandai, Shanghi ren zai Xianggang" [Shanghainess in Hong Kong: The 1950s], *Wenhui Daily* (Shanghai), December 21, 2019.

46. See The Editor, "Plea for Two-Way Film Traffic," *Far East Film News*, v.3 n.16 (October 7, 1955), p.3; quotation from Robert Grey, "Memorandum to President," October 4, 1956, AFC Box P-171.

47. *Variety*, April 27, 1960, p.12. For alliances with Taiwan and South Korea, see, for ex-ample, Sha Rongfeng, *Binfen dianying sishi chun: Sha Rongfeng huiyilu* [Memoir of Sha Rongfeng], Taipei: Guojia dianying ziliaoguan, 1994, pp.117–126.

48. Yau Shuk Ting, *Gang Ri yingren koushu lishi* [An oral history of Hong Kong–Japanese filmmakers), Hong Kong: Hong Kong University Press, 2012, pp.75–85.

49. "Zhonggang dianyingshiye zhankai xinye" [A new chapter of China–Hong Kong film industries], *Nanguo dianying*, n.53 (July 1962), p.T2; William Goodwin, "Official Report on Shaw Organization," p.25; *Variety*, April 27, 1960, p.12. Quotation from Nationalist archive materials, see Lanjun Xu, "The Southern Film Corporation, Opera Films, and the PRC's Cultural Diplomacy in Cold War Asia, 1950–1960s," *Modern Chinese Literature and Culture*, v.29 n.1 (Spring 2017), pp.266–268.

50. Quoted from Lanjun Xu, "The Southern Film Corporation, Opera Films, and the PRC's Cultural Diplomacy in Cold War Asia, 1950s–1960s," p.266.

51. Syd Goldsmith, *Hong Kong on the Brink*, Hong Kong: Blacksmith Books, 2017, pp.80–81; William Goldwin, "Official Report on Shaw Brothers," pp.23–25; "Zhonggang dianyingshiye zhankai xinye," pp.T2–T3.

52. *Seattle World's Fair 1962*, Official Souvenir Program, https://www.state.gov/wp-cont ent/uploads/2019/04/Seattle-Expo-1962-Guidebook.pdf; "Shao Yifu zai Meiguo" [Mr. Run Run Shaw in the US], *Nanguo dianying*, n.59 (January 1963), p.62; "Shao Yifu xuanbu jinnian daji" [Run Run Shaw announced this year's big plan], *Nanguo dianying*, n.59, pp.22–23.

53. "Love Eterne," *Variety*, November 10, 1963, p.18, and "San Francisco Fest Review," *Variety*, November 13, 1963, p.17.

54. See, for example, "Yazhou mimi jingcha zai Xianggang kaipai" [Asian secret services began production in Hong Kong], *Xianggang yinghua*, n.11 (November 1966), pp.20–21; "Shao Yifu de dianying huangguo" [The film empire of Run Run Shaw], *Xianggang yinghua*, n.1 (January 1967), pp.46–49; Huang Ren, "Cong *Xianv* tan *Yang Guifei*" (From *A Touch of Zen* to *The Magnificent Concubine*), *Yinhe huabao*, n.69 (September 1975), p.87; Law Kar, "Shaoshi xiongdi de kuajie fazhan" [Shaw Brothers' transnational development], in Liao Jinfeng et al. eds., *Shoshi yingshi diguo* [The Shaw film and television empire], Taipei: Maitian chuban, 2003, pp.152–168.

55. "Show Business: Run Run Shaw Empire," *Time*, June 28, 1976, http://content.time.com/time/subscriber/article/0,33009,911822,00.html.

56. Liu Hsien-cheng, "Shaoshi dianying zai Taiwan" (The Shaw Brothers cinema in Taiwan), in Liao Jinfeng et al eds., *Shaoshi yingshi diguo*, pp.138–145.

57. Xu Dunle, *Kenguang tuoying* [Developing cinema], Hong Kong: MCCM, 2005, pp.66–69; Lanjun Xu, "The Southern Film Corporation, Opera Films, and the PRC Cultural Diplomacy in Cold War Asia, 1950s–1960s," pp.253–255.

58. "Gangjiu ziyou xiju zonghui mianlin weiji" [Hong Kong–Kowloon Freedom Film and Theater Federation in crisis], *Lianhe bao*, February 21, 1960. See also William Goodwin, "Official Report on Shaw Brothers," pp.25–27.

59. "Wushi tian zhengfeng huiyi jilu" [Fifty Days of Rectification meeting minutes], in Cheng Xiang, *Xiangang Liuqi baodong shimo* [History of Hong Kong 1967 riots], Hong Kong: Oxford University Press, 2018, pp.460–465.

60. See Aihwa Ong, *Flexible Citizenship: The Cultural Logic of Transnationality*, Durham: Duke University Press, 1999, pp.143–145.

61. "Sir Run Run Shaw: The Legend with a Heart of Gold," *South China Morning Post*, January 8, 2014.

62. The quote "grey industrial world" comes from Ian Scott, *Political Change and the Crisis of Legitimacy in Hong Kong*, Honolulu: University of Hawaii Press, 1989, p.89. On Cowperthwaite's fiscal and budgetary policy, see Neil Monnery, *Architect of Prosperity: Sir John Cowperthwait and the Making of Hong Kong*, London: London Publishing Partnership, 2017. The British colony launched "The White Paper on Social Welfare" in 1965, urging its people to follow the traditional family ideology; see Kwong-leung Tang, *Social Welfare Development in East Asia*, London: Palgrave Macmillan, 2000, pp.122–123.

63. See David Baird, "What Makes Shaw Run," *Far Eastern Economic Review*, n.12 (March 19, 1970), p.83; Chung Po-yin, "The Industrial Evolution of a Fraternal Enterprise: Shaw Brothers and the Shaw Organization," in Wong Ain-ling ed., *The Shaw Screen*, Hong Kong: Hong Kong Film Archive, 2003, pp.1–18.

64. On Governor MacLehose's reforms, see Lui Tai Lok, "'Flying MPs' and Political Changes in a Colonial Setting: Political Reform under MacLehose's governorship of Hong Kong," in John Wong and Michael Ng eds., *Civil Unrest and Governance in Hong Kong*, London: Routledge, 2017, pp.76–96.

65. Shen Bin, "Shaoshi zhipian jihua tan Xianggang dianying ye qushi" [Shaw Brothers production plan and Hong Kong film industry's future trend], *Xianggang yinghua*, n.10 (December 1967), p.61.

66. Syd Goldsmith, *Hong Kong on the Brink*, pp.80–81. See also William Goldwin, "Official Report on Shaw Brothers," pp.23–25.

67. "Sir Run Run Shaw: The Legend with a Heart of Gold."

68. "Shao Yifu xuanbu jinnian daji" [Run Run Shaw announced this year's big plan," *Nanguo dianying*, n.59 (January 1963), pp.22–23.

69. "Quan shijie zui mang de zhipianjia" [The world's busiest producer], *Nanguo dianying*, n.187 (May 1965), p.3.

70. Film advertisement for *Zhongxiao jieyi*, *Shen bao*, January 31, 1926.

71. "Quan shijie zui mang de zhipianjia." See also "Shao Yifu de dianying wangguo" [Run Run Shaw's film empire], *Xianggang yinghua*, n.1 (January 1974), p.48.

72. Lily Kong, "Shaw Cinema Enterprise and Understanding Cultural Industries," in Po-shek Fu ed., *China Forever: The Shaw Brothers and Diasporic Cinema*, Urbana: University of Illinois Press, 2008, p.43.

73. Hubert Niogret, "Fangwen Shao Yifu."

74. Sek Kei, "Movietown's 'China Dream' and 'Hong Kong Sentiments'" in Wong Ain-ling ed. *The Shaw Screen*, p.31.

75. See, for example, Peggy Chiao, "The Female Consciousness, the World of Signification and Safe Extramarital Affairs," in Wong Ain-ling ed., *The Shaw Screen*, pp.65–71. For a detailed history of Huangmei opera film, see Edwin Chen, "Musical China, Classical Impression: A Preliminary Study of Shaw's Huangmei Diao Film," in Wong Ain-ling ed., *The Shaw Screen*, pp.43–58. For analyses of the film's characters, see Siu-leung Li, *Cross-Dressing Chinese Opera*, Hong Kong: Hong Kong University Press, 2003, pp.123–129

76. See Lanjun Xu's argument in "The Southern Film Corporation, Opera Films, and the PRC's Cultural Diplomacy in Cold War Asia, 1950s–1960s," pp.258–259.

77. Qin Yamen, "Chaoyue aiqing chuanqi: xiqu dianying Liang Shanbo yu Zhu Yingtai yu xin Zhongguo de xingxiang jiangou" (Yue opera film The Butterfly Lovers and the Construction of Images of new China), *Journal of Chinese Women's Studies*, no.4 (July 2022), pp.103–116.

78. Jeanine Basinger, *A Woman's View: How Hollywood Spoke to Women*, London: Chatto & Windus, 1994, pp.8–16. See also Alson McKee, *The Woman's Film of the 1940s: Gender, Narrative, and History*, New York: Routledge, 2014.

79. "Liang-Zhu jiahua, yingtan qiji" [A *Love Eterne* Story, a movie miracle], *Nanguo dianying*, n.65 (July 1962), pp.50–51.

80. See Rick Lyman, "Watching Movies with Ang Lee," *New York Times*, March 9, 2001; Ramona Curry, "Bridging the Pacific with *Love Eterne*," in Poshek Fu ed., *China Forever*, pp.178–181.

81. See Zhang Guifeng, "Liang Zhu re" [The Liang and Zhu film craze], *World Journal*, March 14, 2000.

82. See "Liang Zhu canjia Jiujinshan yingzhan" [*Love Eterne* joins the San Francisco Film Festival], *Nanguo dianying*, n.67 (September 1963), p.65.

83. Xu Fuguan, quotes in Peggy Chiao, "The Female Consciousness, the World of Signification and Safe Extramarital Affairs," in Wong Ain-ling ed., *The Shaw Screen*, p.71.

84. Xu Dunle, *Hengguang tuoying*, pp.91–93.

85. See Zhonggong Shanghai shi Dianying ju, "Guanyu jishuchang wei Xianggang caise yingpian gongzuo de qingshi" [On developing color films for Hong Kong], December 15, 1964, Shanghai Municipal Archive, A22-1-794, 33; "Shanghai shi Dianying ju zhi xin shiwei Xuanchuan bu" [From Shanghai Municipal Film Bureau to Propaganda Department], February 17, 1965, Shanghai Municipal Archive, A22-2-1312.

86. Wai Man Lam, "Depoliticization, Citizenship, and the Politics of Community in Hong Kong," *Citizenship Studies*, v.9 n.5 (July 2005), pp.310–312. See also P. Morris et al., "Education, Civic Participation and Identity: Continuity and Change in Hong Kong," *Cambridge Journal of Education*, v.30 n.2 (2000), pp.243–262; and Jing Jing Chang, *Screening Communities: Negotiating Narratives of Empire, Nation, and the Cold War in Hong Kong Cinema*, Hong Kong: Hong Kong University Press, 2019, pp.23–48.

87. See Lanjun Xu, "The Southern Film Corporation, Opera Films, and the PRC's Cultural Diplomacy in Cold War Asia, 1950–1960s," pp.269–272.

88. David Baird, "What Makes Shaw Run."

89. See Law Kar, "The Origin and Development of Shaw's Color Wuxia Century," in Wong Ain-ling ed., *The Shaw Screen*, pp.105–118, and Po Fung, *Dianguang ying li zhan chunfeng* [Sword fighting in cinema], Hong Kong: Hong Kong Film Critics Society, 2010, especially pp.65–139. For a pioneering study of manliness in Hong Kong cinema, see Laikwan Pang and Day Wang eds., *Masculinity and Hong Kong Cinema*, Hong Kong: Hong Kong university Press, 2005. It included David Desser's "Making Movies Male: Zhang Che and Shaw Brothers Martial Arts Movies," pp. 17–34. These new-styled martial arts films initiated a new trend that developed into a global kung-fu craze in the 1970s, see David Desser, "Kung Fu Craze: Hong Kong Cinema's First American Reception," in Poshek Fu and David Desser eds., *The Cinema of Hong Kong: History, Arts, Identity*, Cambridge: Cambridge University Press, 2000, pp.15–43.

90. Man Fung Yip, *Martial Arts Cinema and Hong Kong Modernity: Aesthetics, Representation, and Circulation*, Hong Kong: Hong Kong University Press, 2017, pp.6–8, 66–73; Law Kar, "The Origin and Development of Shaw's Color Wuxia Century"; David Bordwell, *Planet Hong Kong: Popular Cinema and the Art of Entertainment*, Cambridge: Harvard University Press, 2000; and Stephen Teo, *Chinese Martial Arts Cinema: The Wuxia Tradition*, Edinburgh: Edinburgh University Press, 2016.

91. "Caise wuxia xin gong gongshi" [New wuxia in color campaign], quoted from Po Fung, *Dianguang ying li zhan chunfeng*, p.95.

92. For the significant role of Japanese directors and technicians in Shaw Brothers production, see Yau Shuk Ting, "Shaoshi dianying de Riben yinshu" [The Japanese factor in Shaw Brothers cinema], in Liao Jinfeng et al. eds., *Shaoshi yingshi diguo*, pp. 76–115. For Japanese contribution to the Shaw popular genre movies, see Darrell Davis and Yeh Yueh-yu, "Inoue at Shaws: The Wellspring of Youth," in Wong Ain-ling ed., *The Shaw Screen*, pp. 255–273.

93. Sek Kei, "Movietown's 'China Dream' and 'Hong Kong Sentiments,' " in Wong Ain-ling ed., in Wong Ain-ling ed., *The Shaw Screen*, pp.32–33. See also Man Fung Yip, *Martial Arts Cinema and Hong Kong Modernity*, pp.6–8, 66–73.

94. For different perspectives on the important question of gender politics and martial arts films in general, see Zhang Zhen, *An Amorous History of the Silver Screen*, pp.200–243, and Lai Sufen, "From Cross-Dressing Daughter to Lady Knight-Errant: The Origin and Evolution of Chinese Women Warriors," in Sherry Mou ed., *Presence and Presentation*, New York: St. Martin Press, 1999, pp.77–107. See also Siu-leung Li, *Cross-Dressing in Chinese Opera*, pp.86–102. For a particular discussion of *Come Drink with Me*, see Man Fung Yip, *Martial Arts Cinema and Hong Kong Modernity*, pp.115–136, especially 117–127.

95. Gu Er, "Cong *Yunhai yugong yuan* to *Da Zuixia*" [From *Yunhai yugong yuan* to *Da Zuixia*], *Zhongguo xuesheng zhoubao*, n.718 (April 22, 1966). See Man Fung Yip, *Martial Arts Cinema and Hong Kong Modernity*, pp.6–8, 66–73; David Bordwell, *Planet Hong Kong*, pp.245–260.

96. "Lee Ang," in Law Kar ed., *Transcending the Times: King Hu and Eileen Chang*, Hong Kong: Provisional Urban Council of Hong Kong, 1998, p.107.

97. See Gary Kar-wai Cheung, "How the 1967 Riots Changed Hong Kong's Political Landscape, with the Repercussions Still Felt Today," in Michael Ng and John Wong eds., *Civil Unrest and Governance in Hong Kong*, p.65.

98. See "Zhang Ying," in *Dianying suyue zongheng tan* [Oral interviews: My cinematic life], Taipei: Caituan faren Guojia dianying zhiliao guan, 1994, v.2, pp.428–430.

99. For discussions of Mandarin pop and Mandarin films, see Law Kar ed., *Mandarin Films and Popular Songs, 1940s–1960s*, Hong Kong: Urban Council, 1993. See also Stephen Chu, *Hong Kong Cantopop: A Concise History*, Hong Kong: Hong Kong University Press, 2017, for a well-researched study of the difference between Mandopop and Cantopop, which emerged with localization of entertainment culture in the 1980s. For discussions of Shaw Brothers' popular genre movies and their cultural politics, see See Kam Tan, "Shaw Brothers' Bangpian: Global Bondmania, Cosmopolitan Dreaming and Cultural Nationalism," *Screen*, v.56 n.2 (2015), pp.195–213; Siu Leung Li, "Embracing Globalization and Hong Kong–Made Musical Films," and Paul Pickowicz, "Three Readings of *Hong Kong Nocturne*," in Poshek Fu ed., *China Forever*, pp. 73–114.

Chapter 5

1. Xi Xi, *Wo Cheng* [My city], Taipei: Yuncheng wenhua, 1993, p.64; official English version, *My City: A Hong Kong Story*, trans. Eva Hung, Hong Kong: Renditions Paperbacks, 1993.

2. "Jiushi fengzhong Xianggang shehui wenhua shi" [Hong Kong social-cultural history in ninety minutes], file:///Users/poshekfu/Desktop/%E9%99%88%E5%86%A0%E4%B8%AD%EF%BC%9A%E4%B9%9D%E5%8D%81%E5%88%86%E9%92%9F%E9

%A6%99%E6%B8%AF%E7%A4%BE%E4%BC%9A%E6%96%87%E5%8C%96%E5
%8F%B2%20%E2%80%93%20%E7%8B%AC%E7%AB%8B%E4%B8%AD%E6%96
%87%E7%AC%94%E4%BC%9A.html, accessed on Jun 18, 2021.

3. Leo Goodstadt, "Economic Relations between the Mainland and Hong Kong, an 'Irresplaceable' Financial Center," in Gary Chi-hung Luk ed., *From a British to a Chinese Colony: Hong Kong before and after the 1997 Handover*, Berkeley: Institute for East Asian Studies, 2017, p.196.

4. See Leo Goodstadt, "Economic Relations between the Mainland and Hong Kong," pp.195–198. For Hong Kong's industrialization and GDP figures, see also Richard Hughes, *Borrowed Place, Borrowed Time: Hong Kong and Its Many Faces*, Hong Kong: Andre Deutsch, 1976, pp.23–28; and John Wong, "Constructing the Lof Governance in Hong Kong: 'Prosperity and Stability' Meets "Democracy and Freedom,'" *Journal of Asian Studies* (2022), pp.3–4, doi:10.1017/ S0021911821002230.

5. Quoted from Richard Hughes, *Borrowed Place, Borrowed Time*, p.184.

6. See *Hong Kong Population and Housing Census, 1971*, Hong Kong: Government Printer, 1972; Richard Hughes, *Borrowed Place, Borrowed Time*, p.56; John Carroll states that half of the population was under twenty-one years old; see *A Concise History of Hong Kong*, Lanham: Rowman & Littlefield, 2007, pp.161–162.

7. For the 1965 figure, see Gary Ka-wai Cheung, "How the 1967 Riots Changed Hong Kong's Political Landscape, with the Repercussions Still Felt Today," in Michael Ng and John Wong eds., *Civil Unrest and Governance in Hong Kong: Law and Order from Historical and Cultural Perspectives*, London: Routledge, 2017, p.70.

8. Quoted in John Carroll, *A Concise History of Hong Kong*, p.150.

9. The quotation is from Editorial, "Yiqie weiliao shehui anding" [All for the sake of social stability], *CSW*, n.717 (April 15, 1966). For the pro-Communist press, see Gary Ka-wai Cheung, "How the 1967 Riots Changed Hong Kong's Political Landscape," pp.66, 71.

10. John Wong, "Constructing the Legitimacy of Governance in Hong Kong," p.5.

11. Quoted from Gary Ka-wai Cheung, "How the 1967 Riots Changed Hong Kong's Political Landscape," p.70.

12. On the riots, see Cheung Kar-wai, *Xianggang liuqi baodong neiqing* [Inside story of Hong Kong's 1967 riots], Hong Kong: Taipingyang shiji chubanshe, 2000; Syd Goldsmith, *Hong Kong on the Brink*, Hong Kong: Blacksmith Books, 2017, pp.221–260; and John Carroll, *A Concise History of Hong Kong*, pp.150–163.

13. Ian Scott, *Political Change and the Crisis of Legitimacy in Hong Kong*, Honolulu: University of Hawaii Press, 1989, p.104.

14. See Christine Loh, *Underground Front: The Chinese Communist Party in Hong Kong*, Hong Kong: Hong Kong University Press, 2010, pp.118–122, and Syd Goldsmith, *Hong Kong on the Brink*, pp.231–254.

15. Syd Goldsmith, *Hong Kong on the Brink*, pp.192 and 198.

16. Quoted in Lui Tai-lok, "Flying MPs and Political Change in a Colonial Setting: Political Reform under MacLehose' Governorship of Hong Kong," in Michael Ng and John Wong eds., *Civil Unrest and Governance in Hong Kong*, p.80.

17. Murray MacLehose to Sir Alec Douglas-Home, May 5, 1972, quoted from Gary Ka-wai Cheung, "How the 1967 Riots Changed Hong Kong's Political Landscape," p.73.

18. Leo Goodstadt, *Uneasy Partner*, p.38.

19. Richard Hughes, *Borrowed Place, Borrowed Time*, p.35.

20. Leo Goldstadt, "Economic Relations between the Mainland and Hong Kong," pp.198–199.

21. John Carroll, *A Concise History of Hong Kong*, p.163.

22. Richard Hughes, *Borrowed Place, Borrowed Time*, p.56.

23. Janet Salaff, *Working Daughters of Hong Kong: Filial Piety or Power in the Family?*, Cambridge: Cambridge University Press, 1981. For insightful studies of Connie Chan's films and fan phenomenon, see Jing Jing Chang, *Screening Communities: Negotiating Narratives of Empire, Nation, and the Cold War in Hong Kong Cinema*, Hong Kong: Hong Kong University Press, 2019, pp.162–167, and Law Kar, *Dianying zhi lü* [My cinematic journey], Hong Kong: Boyi chuban jituan, 1987, pp.199–204.

24. Eric Hobsbawm, *The Age of Extremes: A History of the World, 1914–1991*, New York: Vintage Books, 1995, pp.324–325.

25. Lun Shi, "Women de dianying zai nali" [Where is our cinema], *CSW*, n.589 (November 1, 1963); see also Luk Lei, "Xin dianying: Bali, Niuyue, Xianggang" [New cinema: Paris, New York, Hong Kong], *CSW*, n.701 (December 24, 1965).

26. Leo Ou-fan Lee, *City between Worlds: My Hong Kong*, Cambridge: Harvard University Press, 2010, p.63.

27. "Loke-Lay," in Lo Wai-luen and Hung Chi Kum eds, *Xiangang wenhua zhongsheng dao*, v.2, pp.122.

28. "Law Kar," Ibid, pp.60–62 and 72 Also Personal Interview with Law Kar, August 30, 2013, June 18, 2016. For high school students' interests, see Personal Interviews with Chan Koonchung, September 2, 2021.

29. *CSW*, n.893, August 29, 1969.

30. "Law Kar," in *Xiangang wenhua zhongsheng dao*, pp.75–77; Also Law Kar, interviews with author, August 25 and September 1, 2021.

31. Hu Juren, "Xiang shumu yiyang de shengzhang" [Like a tree], *CSW*, no.470 (July 21, 1961). See also Zhiqiang, "Cong yige guer taowang shuoqi" [The escape of an orphan], *CSW*, n.586 (October 11, 1963); Ye Fengxi, "Kongtan aiguo bu yi hu" [Isn't it a shame to talk emptily about patriotism], *CSW*, n.826 (May 17, 1968).

32. "Women jiu bu aiguo ma?" [Are we not patriotic?], *CSW*, n.590 (November 8, 1963).

33. Xi, *Wo Cheng*.

34. Matthew Turner, "60s/90s: Dissolving the People," in Pun Ngai and Yee Lai-man eds., *Narrating Hong Kong Culture and Identity*, Hong Kong: Oxford University Press, 2003, pp.35–36.

35. Hugh Baker, "Life in the City: The Hong Kong Man," quoted from Leo Lee, *City between Worlds*, p.251.

36. Chan Koon-Chung, "Jiushi fengzhong Xianggang shehui wenhua shi." The term "Central District values" was coined by eminent writer Lung Ying-tai to criticize the Hong Kong government's cultural policy. See Yiu-Wai Chu, *Lost in Transition: Hong Kong Culture in the Age of China*, Albany: SUNY Press, 2013, pp.43–66.

37. Rey Chow, *Ethics after Idealism: Theory-Culture-Ethnicity-Reading*, Bloomington: Indiana University Press, 1998, pp.170–171.

38. "Shaonian yi dai dui shuangshi guoqing de renshi he ganxiang" [Young generation's understanding and feelings about the Double Tenth National Day], *CSW*, n.899 (October 10, 1969).

39. Jia Lun, "Xianggang shi women de chengshi, B.P.S. shi women de xuexiao" [Hong Kong is our city, B.P.S. is our school], *CSW*, n.909 (December 19, 1969).

40. Xi Xi, *Wo Cheng*, p.171.

41. See Yiu-Wai Chu, *Lost in Transition*, pp.121–125.

42. Chan Koon-Chung, interview with author, September 2, 2021. See also Edmund Cheng, "Loyalist, Dissenter, and Cosmopolite: The Sociocultural Origins of a Counter-Public Sphere in Colonial Hong Kong," *China Quarterly*, https://www.cambridge.org/core/journals/china-quarterly/article/abs/loyalist-dissenter-and-cosmopolite-the-sociocultural-origins-of-a-counterpublic-sphere-in-colonial-hong-kong/69EA50D5214CECFF682B61EE07D2FE27, accessed August 12, 2021.

43. See, for example, Zachery Keck, "The Senkaku Islands as Cold War Berlin," *The Diplomat*, December 2013, https://thediplomat.com/2013/12/the-senkaku-islands-as-cold-war-berlin/.

44. See Lei Jingxuan, "Xianggang de diyi ci Baodiao yundong" [The first Baodiao movement in Hong Kong], in Guan Yongqi and Huang Zicheng eds., *Women zouguo de lu* [The path we had followed], Hong Kong: Cosmo Books, 2015, pp.182–211.

45. Quoted from Law Wing Sang, "Reunification Discourse and Chinese Nationalisms," in Gary Chi-hung Luk ed., *From a British to a Chinese Colony*, p.246.

46. See Law Wing Sang, "'Huohong niandai' yu Xianggang zuoyi jijin zhuyi sichao" [Flaming decade and Hong Kong's leftist radicalism], *Twenty-First Century Bimonthly*, n.6 (June 2017), pp.71–83, Chow Lo Yat, *Xianggang: cong zhimindi dao tebie xingzhengqu* [Hong Kong: From colony to Special Administrative Region], Hong Kong: Guangjiaojing chubanshe, 1982, pp.91–119; Lai Ting Yiu, "Cong xueyun dao sheyun" [From student movement to social movement], in *Women zouguo de lu*, pp.218–222; Chan Koon-Chung, *Wo zhe yidai Xinggang ren* [Hongkongers of my generation], Beijing: Zhongxin chubanshe, 2013, especially pp.1–83.

47. Quoted from Christine Loh, *Underground Front*, p.133.

48. Leo Goodstadt, "Economic Relations between the Mainland and Hong Kong," pp.198–199.

49. See Christine Loh, *Underground Front*, pp.133–153; John Carroll, *A Concise History of Hong Kong*, pp.176–187; Julian Ho, "Xiangong hao de qianzhou" [The eve of falling to communism), June 2017, https://medium.com/@julianho/%E9%99%B7%E5%85%B1%E5%99%A9%E8%80%97%E5%98%85%E5%89%8D%E5%A5%8F-%E5%AD%B8%E7%95%8C%E6%94%AF%E6%8C%81-%E6%B0%91%E4%B8%BB%E5%9B%9E%E6%AD%B8-e49cb7ac9011.

50. Law Wing Sang, "Reunification Discourse and Chinese Nationalism," pp.250–253.

51. "Good Business Is the Best Art: Interview with Louis Sit," in Po Fung ed., *Leading Change in Changing Times*, Hong Kong: Hong Kong Film Archive, 2013, p.142.

52. See Law Kar, "Michael Hui: A Decade of Sword Grinding," and Li Cheuk-to, "Postscript," in Li Cheuk-to ed., *A Study of Hong Kong Cinema in the Seventies*, Hong Kong: Urban Council, 1984;

53. "Three Critics Sum Up the Hong Kong New Wave," in Law Kar ed., *Hong Kong New Wave: Twenty Years After*, Hong Kong: Urban Council, 1999, pp.119–122.

54. For a study of Chang-Feng-Xin during the Cultural Revolution and its aftermath, see Man-Fung Yip. "The End of an Era: The Cultural Revolution, Modernization, and the Demise of Hong Kong Leftist Cinema," in Poshek Fu and Man-Fung Yi eds., *The Cold War and Asian Cinemas*, New York: Routledge, 2019, pp.263–283. For Sil-Metropole, see Li Yizhuang and Zhou Chengren, Xiangang yinmu zuofang (The left side of Hong Kong cinema). Hong Kong: Diatomic Press, 2021, pp.246–263.

Bibliography

Archives

Hong Kong Film Archive, Hong Kong
Hong Kong Literature Collection and Database
Hoover Institution Library and Archives, Stanford University
National Archives, College Park
Public Records Office of Hong Kong, Hong Kong
Shanghai Municipal Archives, Shanghai

Interviews

Chan Koon-Chung, Beijing
Cheng Pei-Pei, Champaign
Chia LeeNi, New York
Robert Hsi, San Francisco
Kam Bing-hing, Toronto
Law Kar, Hong Kong
Lo Wai-luen, Hong Kong
Loke-Ley, Hong Kong
Qiu Ping, Hong Kong
Sek Kei, Hong Kong
Wei Wei, Hong Kong

Magazines and Newspapers:

Dianying quan
Far Eastern Economic Review
Far East Film News
Guoji dianying
Hong Kong Standard
Lianhe bao
Nanguo dianying
Ta Kung Pao
Variety
World Today, or Jinri shijie
Xianggnag yinghua
Xinwen tiandi

Yazhou huabao
Yinhe huabao
Zhongguo xuesheng zhoubao
Ziyou zhanxian

Selected Bibliography

Aldrich, Richard et al. eds. *The Clandestine Cold War in Asia: Western Intelligence, Propaganda and Special Operations*. Portland: Frank Cass, 2000.

Basinger, Jeanine Basinger. *A Woman's View: How Hollywood Spoke to Women*. London: Chatto & Windus, 1994.

Baskett, Michael. "Japan's Film Festival Diplomacy in Cold War Asia." *The Velvet Light Trap*, v.73 n.1 (March 2014), pp.4–18.

Berghahn, Daniela. *Hollywood behind the Wall: The Cinema of East Germany*. Manchester: Manchester University Press, 2005.

Berry, Chris. "Chinese Left Cinema in the 1930s: Poisonous Weeds or National Treasure." *Jump Cut*, n.34 (March 1989).

Blum, Robert. "The Work of the Asian Foundation." *Pacific Affairs*, v.29 n.1 (March 1956), pp.46–56.

Bordwell, David. *Planet Hong Kong: Popular Cinema and the Art of Entertainment*. Cambridge: Harvard University Press, 2000.

Bordwell, David, and Noel Carroll eds. *Post Theory: Reconstructing Film Studies*. Madison: University of Wisconsin Press, 1996.

Bourdieu, Pierre. *Distinction: A Social Critique of the Judgment of Taste*. London: Routledge, 1984.

Bourdieu, Pierre, and Jean-Claude Passeron. *Reproduction in Education: Society and Culture*. Beverly Hills: Sage, 1977.

Brinkley, Alan. *The Publisher: Henry Luce and His American Century*. New York: Vintage Books, 2011.

Carroll, John. *A Concise History of Hong Kong*. Lanham: Rowman and Littlefield, 2007.

Chan, Koon-Chung. *Wo zhe yidai Xinggang ren* [Hongkongers of my generation]. Beijing: Zhongxin chubanshe, 2013.

Chan, Ming ed. *Precarious Balance: Hong Kong between China and Britain, 1842–1992*. Armonk: Sharpe, 1994.

Chang, Carsun. *The Third Force in China*. New York: Bookman Associates, 1952.

Chang, Jing Jing. *Screening Communities: Negotiating Narratives of Empire, Nation, and the Cold War in Hong Kong Cinema*. Hong Kong: Hong Kong University Press, 2019.

Chang, Jing Jing. "China Doll in Flight: Li Lihua, World Today, and the Free China–US Relationship." *Film History*, v.26 n.3 (2014), pp.1–28.

Chen, Jian. *Mao's China and the Cold War*. Chapel Hill: University of North Carolina Press, 2001.

Chen, Jian, and Chen Qijia. *Xia Yan zhuan* [Biography of Xia Yan]. Beijing: China Theater Press, 2015.

Chen, Zhengmao. *Wuling niandai Xianggang disan shili yundong soumi* [Hong Kong third-force movement]. Taipei: Xiuwei zixun keji gufen, 2011.

Cheng, Xiang. *Xiangang Liuqi baodong shimo* [History of Hong Kong 1967 riots]. Hong Kong: Oxford University Press, 2018.

Cheung, Kar-wai. *Xianggang liuqi baodong neiqing* [Inside story of Hong Kong's 1967 riots]. Hong Kong: Taipingyang shiji chubanshe, 2000.

Chia, LiNee. *Xiangce li de gushi* [Stories from my album]. 2 vols. New York: Shiny Printing Ltd., 2021.

Chiang, Ching-kuo. *Jiang Jingguo zishu* [Diaries of Jiang Jingguo]. Changsha: Hunan chubanshe, 1992.

Chou, Grace. *Confucianism, Colonialism, and the Cold War: Chinese Cultural Education at Hong Kong's New Asia College, 1949–1963*. Boston: Brill, 2011.

Chow, Lo Yat. *Xianggang: cong zhimindi dao tebie xingzhengqu* [Hong Kong: From colony to Special Administrative Region]. Hong Kong, Guangjiaojing chubanshe, 1982.

Chow, Rey. *Ethics after Idealism: Theory-Culture-Ethnicity-Reading*. Bloomington: Indiana University Press, 1998.

Chu, Yiu-Wai. *Lost in Transition: Hong Kong Culture in the Age of China*. Albany: State University of New York Press, 2013.

Chu, Yiu-Wai. *Hong Kong Cantopop: A Concise History*. Hong Kong: Hong Kong University Press, 2017.

Chung, Po-yin. *Xianggang yingshiye bainian* [A century of Hong Kong film and television]. Hong Kong: Joint Publishing Co., 2004.

Cohen, Robin. *Global Diasporas: An Introduction*. Seattle: University of Washington Press, 1997.

Colby, William. *Honorable Man*. New York: Simon & Schuster, 1978.

Cull, Nicholas. *The Cold War and the United States Information Agency: American Propaganda and Public Diplomacy*. New York: Cambridge University Press, 2008.

Cullather, Nick. *The Hungry World: America's Cold War Battle against Poverty in Asia*. Cambridge: Harvard University Press, 2010.

Day, Tony, and Maya Liem eds. *Cultures at War: The Cold War and Cultural Expression in Southeast Asia*. Ithaca: Southeast Asian Program, Cornell University, 2010.

Dizard, Wilson. *The Strategy of Truth: The Story of the United States Information Services*. Washington, DC: Public Affairs Press, 1961.

Du, Yunzhi. *Zhongguo dianying qishi nian* [Seventy years of Chinese cinemas]. 2 vols. Taipei: Dianying tushuguan chubanbu, 1986.

Frohlich, Thomas. *Tang Jungyi: Confucian Philosophy and the Challenge of Modernity*. Boston: Brill, 2017.

Fu, Poshek. *Between Shanghai and Hong Kong: The Politics of Chinese Cinemas*. Stanford: Stanford University Press, 2013.

Fu, Poshek, and Man Fung Yip eds. *The Cold War and Asian Cinemas*. New York: Routledge, 2019.

Goldsmith, Syd. *Hong Kong on the Brink: An American Diplomat Relieves 1967's Darkest Days*. Hong Kong: Blacksmith Books, 2017.

Goodstadt, Leo. *Uneasy Partners: The Conflict between Pubic Interests and Private Profits in Hong Kong*. Hong Kong: Hong Kong University Press, 2005.

Grantham, Alexander. *Via Ports: From Hong Kong to Hong Kong*. Hong Kong: Hong Kong University Press, 1965.

Guan, Ang Cheng. *Southeast Asia's Cold War: An Interpretative History*. Honolulu: University of Hawaii Press, 2018.

Guan, Yongqi, and Huang Zicheng eds. *Women zouguo de lu* [The path we had followed]. Hong Kong: Cosmo Books, 2015.

Hambro, Edvard. "The Problem of Chinese Refugees in Hong Kong." *Phylon Quarterly*, v.18 n.1 (1957), pp.69–81.

Hee, Wai-Siam. *Remapping the Sinophone: The Cultural Production of Chinese-Language Cinema in Singapore and Malaya before and during the Cold War*. Hong Kong: Hong Kong University Press, 2019.

Ho, Sam. *Wenyi renwu: Xinliang qiusuo* [Literary and artistic mission: Sun Luen's quest]. Hong Kong: Hong Kong Film Archive, 2011.

Hobsbawn, Eric. *The Age of Extremes: A History of the World, 1914–1991*. New York: Vintage Books, 1995.

Huang, Ren. *Zhongwai dianying yongyuan de juxing* [Legends of Chinese and foreign cinemas]. Taipei: Xiuwei chubanshe, 2010.

Huang, Zhuohan. *Dianying rensheng: Huang Zhuohan huiyilu* [Cinematic life: Memoir of Huang Zhuohan]. Taipei: Wanxiang tushu gufen gongsi, 1994.

Hughes, Richard. *Borrowed Place, Borrowed Time: Hong Kong and Its Many Faces*. Singapore: Toppan Printing Co., 1976.

Hughes, Theodore. *Literature and Film in Cold War South Korea: Freedom's Frontier*. New York: Columbia University Press, 2014.

Ikenberry, G. John. "American Hegemony and East Asian Order." *Australian Journal of International Affairs*, v.58 n.3 (September 2004), pp.354–358.

Immerman, Richard, and Petra Goedde eds. *The Oxford Handbook of the Cold War*. Oxford: Oxford University Press, 2013.

Jarvie, Ian C. *Windows on Hong Kong*. Hong Kong: Hong Kong University Center of Asian Studies, 1977.

Jeans, Roger. *The CIA and Third Force Movements in China during the Early Cold War: The Great American Dream*. Lanham: Lexington Books, 2018.

Jin, Raoru, *Xianggang wushinian yiwang* [Remembering Hong Kong in the last fifty years]. Hong Kong: Jin Raoru Memorial Foundation, 2005.

Klein, Christina. *Cold War Cosmopolitanism: Period Style in 1950s Korean Cinema*. Berkeley: University of California Press, 2020.

Kong, Kwan-sheng. *Zhonggong zai Xianggang* [Communist China in Hong Kong]. 2 vols. Hong Kong: Cosmos Books, 2012.

Kurtz-Phelan, Daniel. *The China Mission: George Marshall's Unfinished War*. New York: W.W. Norton & Company, 2018.

Kwong, Chi Man. *Eastern Fortress: A Military History of Hong Kong, 1840–1970*. Hong Kong: Hong Kong University Press, 2014.

Lam, Wai-man. *Understanding the Political Culture of Hong Kong: The Paradox of Activism and Depoliticization*. Armonk: M. E. Sharpe, 2004.

Law, Kar ed. *Hong Kong New Wave: Twenty Years After*. Hong Kong: Urban Council, 1999.

Law, Kar ed. *Transcending the Times: King Hu and Eileen Chang*. Hong Kong: Provisional Urban Council of Hong Kong, 1998.

Law, Kar. *Dianying zhi lü* [My cinematic journey]. Hong Kong: Boyi chuban jituan, 1987.

Law, Wing Sang. *Collaborative Colonial Power: The Making of the Hong Kong Chinese*. Hong Kong: Hong Kong University Press, 2009.

Law, Wing Sang. "'Huohong niandai' yu Xianggang zuoyi jijin zhuyi sichao" [Flaming decade and Hong Kong's leftist radicalism]. *Twenty-First Century Bimonthly*, n.6 (June 2017), pp.71–83.

Leary, Charles. "The Most Careful Arrangements for a Careful Fiction: A Short History of Asia Pictures." *Inter-Asia Cultural Studies*, v.13 n.4 (2012), pp.548–558.

Lee, Sangjoon. *Cinema and the Cultural Cold War: US Diplomacy and the Origins of the Asian Cinema Network*. Ithaca: Cornell University Press, 2020.

Lee, Vivian. *The Other Side of Glamour: The Left-Wing Studio Network in Hong Kong Cinema in the Cold War*. Edinburgh: University of Edinburgh Press, 2020.

Leffler, Melvyn, and Odd Westad eds. *Cambridge History of the Cold War*. Cambridge: Cambridge University Press, 2010.

Leo, Ou-fan Lee. *City between Worlds: My Hong Kong*. Cambridge: Harvard University Press, 2010.

Leung, Mo-han. *Wo yu Xianggang dixia dang* [My life in Hong Kong's underground Communist Party]. Hong Kong: Open Books, 2012.

Li, Cheuk-to ed. *The China Factor in Hong Kong Cinema*. Hong Kong: Urban Council, 1990.

Li, Daoxin. *Guangying mianchang* [Selected works of Li Daoxin]. Beijing: Peking University Press, 2017.

Li, Hanji, and Li Minghui eds. *Xu Fuguan zawen bubian* [Miscellaneous essays of Xu Fuguan]. Nangang: Zhongyang yanjiuyuan Zhongguo wenshize yanjiusuo choubeichu, 2001.

Li, Hou. *Huigui de lichen* [The journey to return to China]. Hong Kong: Joint Publishing Co., 1997.

Li, Siu-leung. *Cross-Dressing Chinese Opera*. Hong Kong: Hong Kong University Press, 2003.

Li, Tianduo. *Taiwan dianying, shehui yu lishi* [Taiwan cinema, society, and history]. Taipei: Yatai tushu, 1997.

Li, Yizhuang, and Zhou Chengren. *Xianggang yinmu zuofang* [The left side of Hong Kong cinema]. Hong Kong: Diatomic Press, 2021.

Liao, Chengzhi. *Liao Chengzhi wenji* [Collected works of Liao Chengzhi]. 2 vols. Hong Kong: Joint Publishing Co., 1990.

Liao, Jinfeng et al eds. *Shoshi yingshi diguo* [The Shaw film and television empire]. Taipei: Maitian chuban, 2003.

Lilley, James. *China Hands: Nine Decades of Adventure, Espionage, and Diplomacy in Asia*. New York: PublicAffairs, 2004.

Lin, Hsio-ting. *Accidental State: Chiang Kai-shek, the United States, and the Making of Taiwan*. Cambridge: Harvard University Press, 2016.

Lipschutz, Ronnie. *Cold War Fantasies: Film, Fiction, and Foreign Policy*. Lanham: Rowman & Littlefield, 2001.

Lo, Wai-luen, and Hung Chi Kum eds. *Xianggang wenhua zhongsheng dao* [Multiple voices of Hong Kong culture]. 2 vols. Hong Kong: Joint Publishing Co., 2014.

Liu, Hui eds. *Xianggang de "Zhongguo": Shaoshi dianying* [China in Hong Kong: The Shaw cinema], Hong Kong, Oxford University Press, 2011.

Logevall, Frederik. *Embers of War: The Fall of an Empire and the Making of American Vietnam*. New York: Random House, 2012.

Loh, Christine. *Underground Front: The Chinese Communist Party in Hong Kong*. Hong Kong: Hong Kong University Press, 2010.

Luk, Bernard. "Chinese Culture in the Hong Kong Curriculum: Heritage and Colonialism." *Comparative Education Review*, v.35 n.4 (November 1991), pp.650–668.

Luk, Gary ed. *From a British to a Chinese Colony: Hong Kong Before and After the 1997 Handover*. Berkeley: Institute of East Asian Studies, 2017.

Madokoro, Laura. *Elusive Refuge: Chinese Migrants in the Cold War*. Cambridge: Harvard University Press, 2016.

Mark, Chi-kwan. *Hong Kong and the Cold War: Anglo-American Relations, 1949–1957*. Oxford: Clarendon, 2004.

May, Elaine. *Homeward Bound: American Families in the Cold War Era*. New York: Basic Books, 2018.

May, Lary. *The Big Tomorrow: Hollywood and the Politics of the American Way*. Chicago: University of Chicago Press, 2000.

McKee, Alson. *The Woman's Film of the 1940s: Gender, Narrative, and History*. New York: Routledge, 2014.

Monnery, Neil. *Architect of Prosperity: Sir John Cowperthwaite and the Making of Hong Kong*. London: London Publishing Partnership, 2017.

Mooney, Jadwiga, and Fabio Lanz eds. *De-Centering Cold War History: Local and Global Change*. London: Routledge, 2013.

Morris, Jan. *Hong Kong*. New York: Vintage, 1997.

Mukerji, Chandra, and M. Schudson eds. *Rethinking Popular Culture: Contemporary Perspectives on Cultural Studies*. Berkeley: University of California Press, 1991.

Nathan, Andrew. *Chinese Democracy*. New York: Alfred Knopf, 1985.

Ng, Kenny. "Inhibition vs. Exhibition: Political Censorship of Chinese and Foreign Cinemas in Postwar Hong Kong." *Journal of Chinese Cinemas*, v.2 n.1 (2008), pp.23–35.

Ng, Michael, and John Wong eds. *Civil Unrest and Governance in Hong Kong*. London: Routledge, 2017.

Ong, Aihwa. *Flexible Citizenship: The Cultural Logic of Transnationality*. Durham: Duke University Press, 1999.

Osgood, Kenneth. *Total Cold War: Eisenhower's Secret Propaganda Battle at Home and Abroad*. Lawrence: University Press of Kansas, 2006.

Pang, Laikwan. *Building a New China in Cinema: The Chinese Left-Wing Cinema Movement, 1932–1937*. Lanham: Rowman & Littlefield, 2002.

Pang, Laikwan, and Day Wang eds. *Masculinity and Hong Kong Cinema*. Hong Kong: Hong Kong University Press, 2005.

Peraino, Kevin. *A Force So Swift: Mao, Truman, and the Birth of Modern China, 1949*. New York: Crown, 2017.

Pickowicz, Paul. *China and Film: A Century of Exploration, Confrontation, and Contestation*. Lanham: Rowman & Littlefield, 2011.

Po, Fung. *Dianguang ying li zhan chunfeng* [Sword fighting in cinema]. Hong Kong: Hong Kong Film Critics Society, 2010.

Po, Fung, ed. *Golden Harvest: Leading Changes in Changing Times*. Hong Kong: Hong Kong Film Archive, 2013.

Pun, Ngai, and Yee Lai-man eds. *Narrating Hong Kong Culture and Identity*. Hong Kong: Oxford University Press, 2003.

Qin, Yamen. "Chaoyue aiqing chuanqi: xiqu dianying Liang Shanbo yu Zhu Yingtai yu xin Zhongguo de xingxiang jiangou" (Yue Opera Film The Butterfly Lovers and the Construction of Images of New China). *Journal of Chinese Women's Studies*, no.4 (July 2022), pp.103–116.

Rand, Christopher. *Hong Kong: The Island Between*. New York: Alfred A. Knopf, 1952.

Roberts, Priscilla, and John Carroll eds. *Hong Kong in the Cold War*. Hong Kong: Hong Kong University Press, 2016.

Rojas, Carlos, and Eileen Chow eds. *The Oxford Handbook of Chinese Cinemas*. New York: Oxford University Press, 2013.

Romero, Federico. "Cold War Historiography at the Crossroads." *Cold War History*, v.14 n.4 (2014), pp.685–703.

Salaff, Janet. *Working Daughters of Hong Kong: Filial Piety or Power in the Family?* Cambridge: Cambridge University Press, 1981.

Saunders, Frances. *The Cultural Cold War: The CIA and the World of Arts and Letters.* New York: New Press, 2000.

Schenk, Catherine. *Hong Kong as an International Financial Center: Emergence and Development, 1945–1965.* London: Routledge, 1990.

Scott, Ian. *Political Change and the Crisis of Legitimacy in Hong Kong.* Honolulu: University of Hawaii Press, 1989.

Searls, Guy. "Red China Switch to Love, Soft Pedal Marx to Sell Movies." *Wall Street Journal,* September 26, 1957.

Sha, Rongfeng. *Binfen dianying sishichun: Sha Rongfeng huiyilu* [Forty cinematic years: Memoirs of Sha Rongfeng]. Taipei: National Film Archive, 1994.

Shan, Dexing. *Fanyi yu mailuo* [Translation and contexts]. Taipei: Shulin chuban, 2009.

Shaw, Tony, and Denise Youngblood. *Cinematic Cold War: The American and Soviet Struggle for Hearts and Minds.* Lawrence: University Press of Kansas, 2010.

Shaw, Tony. *Hollywood's Cold War.* Amherst: University of Massachusetts Press, 2007.

Shen, Shuang. "Empire of Information: The Asia Foundation's Network and Chinese-Language Cultural Production in Hong Kong and Southeast Asia." *American Quarterly,* v.69 n.3 (September 2017), pp.589–610.

Sheridan, Michael. *The Gate to China: A New History of The People's Republic and Hong Kong.* New York: Oxford University Press, 2021.

Shi, Chuan. *Tabian qingshan ren wei lao: Xu Sangchu koushu zizhuan* [Memoir of Xu Sangchu]. Beijing: Zhongguo dianying chubanshe, 2006.

Sinn, Elizabeth. *Pacific Crossing: California Gold, Chinese Migration, and the Making of Hong Kong.* Hong Kong: Hong Kong University Press, 2012.

Su, Tao. *Fucheng beiwang: chonghui zhanhou Xianggang dianying* [Rewriting postwar Hong Kong cinema]. Beijing: Beijing daxue chubanshe, 2014.

Tang, Jungyi. *Shuo Zhonghua minzu zhi huaguo piaoling* [On the scattered fruits and flowers of Chinese people]. Taipei: Sanmin shuju, 2005.

Tang, Kwong-leung. *Social Welfare Development in East Asia.* London: Palgrave Macmillan, 2000.

Taylor, Jeremy. "'Not a Particularly Happy Expression': 'Malayanization' and the China Threat in Britain's Late Colonial Southeast Asian Territories." *Journal of Asian Studies,* v.78 n.4 (November 2019), pp.789–808.

Teo, Stephen. *Chinese Martial Arts Cinema: The Wuxia Tradition.* Edinburgh: Edinburgh University Press, 2016.

Tsang, Steve. *Democracy Shelved: Great Britain, China, and Attempts at Constitutional Reform in Hong Kong, 1945–1952.* Hong Kong: Oxford University Press, 1988.

Tsang, Steve. "Strategy for Survival: The Cold War and Hong Kong's Policy towards Kuomintang and Chinese Communist Activities in the 1950s." *Journal of Imperial and Commonwealth History,* v.25 n.2 (1997), pp.294–317.

Van Slyke, Lyman. *Enemies and Friends: The United Front in Chinese Communist History.* Stanford: Stanford University Press, 1967.

Vu, Tuong, and Wasana Wongsurawat eds. *Dynamics of the Cold War in Asia: Ideology, Identity, and Culture.* New York: Palgrave Macmillan, 2009.

Wang, David Der-wei. *The Monster That Is History: History, Violence, and Fictional Writing in Twentieth-Century China.* Cambridge: Harvard University Press, 2004.

Wang, Gungwu. *China and the Chinese Overseas*. Singapore: Times Academic Press, 1991.

Wang, Weiyi. *Nanwang de suiyue* [My unforgettable memories]. Beijing: Zhongguo dianying, 2006.

Wang, Xiaojue. *Modernity with a Cold War Face: Reimagining the Nation in Chinese Literature across the 1949 Divide*. Cambridge: Harvard University Asia Center, 2013.

Welsh, Frank. *A History of Hong Kong*. New York: HarperCollins, 1997.

Westad, Odd Arne. *Cold War and Revolution: Soviet-American Rivalry and the Origins of the Chinese Civil War*. New York: Columbia University Press, 1993.

Westad, Odd Arne. *The Global Cold War: Third World Interventions and the Making of Our Times*. Cambridge: Cambridge University Press, 2011.

Wong, Ain-ling ed. *The Shaw Screen*. Hong Kong: Hong Kong Film Archive, 2003.

Wong, Ain-ling, and P. Lee eds. *Lengzhan yu Xianggang dianying* [The cold war and Hong Kong cinema]. Hong Kong: Hong Kong Film Archive, 2009.

Wong, John. "Constructing the Legitimacy of Governance in Hong Kong: 'Prosperity and Stability' Meets 'Democracy and Stability.'" *Journal of Asian Studies*, January 24, 2022), pp.1–15, doi: 10.1017/S0021911821002230.

Xianggang nianjian 1952 [Hong Kong]. Hong Kong: Wah Kiu Yat Po she, 1952.

Xi Xi. *Wo Cheng* [My city]. Taipei: Yuncheng wenhua, 1993.

Xu, Dunle. *Kenguang tuoying* [Developing cinema]. Hong Kong: MCCM, 2005.

Xu, Lanjun. "The Southern Film Corporation, Opera Films, and the PRC's Cultural Diplomacy in Cold War Asia." *Modern Chinese Literature and Culture*, v.29 no.1 (Spring 2017), pp.239–282.

Xu, Shumei. *Zhizuo "youda": zhanhou Taiwan dianying Zhong de Riben* [Making "friends": Japan in postwar Taiwan cinema]. New Taipei City: Daoxiang chubanshe, 2012.

Yao, Souchou. *The Malayan Emergency: The Essays on a Small, Distant War*. Honolulu: University of Hawaii Press, 2016.

Yau, Esther ed. *At Full Speed: Hong Kong Cinema in a Borderless World*. Minneapolis: University of Minnesota Press, 2001.

Yau, Shuk-ting. *GangRi yingren koushu lishi* [Oral history of Hong Kong–Japanese filmmakers]. Hong Kong: Hong Kong University Press, 2012.

Yip, Hon Ming, and Choi Po King. "Zhimindi yu geming wemhua baquan: Xianggang yu sishi niandai houqi de Zhongguo Gongchan zhuyi yundong" [Colony and revolutionary hegemony: Hong Kong and Chinese Communist movement of the late 1940s]. *Journal of Chinese Studies*, v.10, 2007, pp.191–217.

Yip, Man Fung. *Martial Arts Cinema and Hong Kong Modernity: Aesthetics, Representation, Circulation*. Hong Kong: Hong Kong University Press, 2017.

Yu, Mo-wen. *Xiangang dianying shihu* [An informal history of Hong Kong cinema]. 3 vols. Hong Kong: Subculture, 1998.

Yu, Ying-shi. "Yu Ying-shih's Reminiscences of His Life and Times." Translated by Michael Duke and Josephine Chiu-Duke, unpublished manuscript.

Yu, Ying-shi. "Zhongguo ziyou zhishiren" [Chinese liberal intellectuals]. *Mingbao yuekan*, n.5 (July 2018), pp.18–20.

Yue, Qing. *Wanzi qianhong: Li Li-hua* [A sparkling life: Li Li-Hua]. Beijing: Zhongguo dianying chubanshe, 2015.

Zhang, Hong. *American Perceived: The Making of Chinese Images of the United States, 1945–1953*. Westport: Greenwood Press, 2002.

Zhang, Jishun. *Yuanqu de dushi: 1950 niandai de Shanghai* [A city displayed: Shanghai in the 1950s]. Beijing: Social Sciences Academic Press, 2015.

Zhang, Zhen. *An Amorous History of the Silver Screen: Shanghai Cinema, 1896-1937*. Chicago: University of Chicago Press, 2005.

Zheng, Yanwen et al eds. *The Cold War in Asia: The Battle for Hearts and Minds*. Boston: Brill, 2010.

Zheng, Zhuyuan. *Zhangbi zuo tianya: Zheng Zhuyuan huiyilu* [Memoir of Zheng Zhuyuan]. Taipei: World Journal LLC, 2017.

Zhou, Taomu. *Migration in the Time of Revolution: China, Indonesia, and the Cold War*. Ithaca: Cornell University Press, 2019.

Zhou, Yi. *Xianggang zuopai douzheng shi* [A history of the Hong Kong leftist resistance]. Hong Kong: Nice News Publishing Co., 2008.

Zia, Helen. *Last Boat out of Shanghai: The Epic Story of the Chinese Who Fled Mao's Revolution*. New York: Ballantine Books, 2019.

Zuo, Gueifang, and Yao Liqun eds. *Tong Yuejuan*. Taipei: National Film Archive, 2001.

Select Filmography

Air Hostess [*Kongzhong xiaojie*]. Dir. Evan Yang. MP&GI, 1959. DVD.

Blood-Stained Flower [*Bixue Huanghua*]. Collective dir., incl. Evan Yang, Wang Tianlin, and Zhang Shankun. Xinhua, 1954. YouTube, https://www.youtube.com/watch?v=j7iB m1Cfrfg.

China Doll. Dir. Frank Borzage. Batjac, 1958. DVD.

Come Drink With Me [*Da zuixia*]. Dir. King Hu. Shaw Brothers, 1966. DVD.

Father and Son [*Fuzi qing*]. Dir. Allen Fong. Phoenix, 1981. YouTube, https://www.yout ube.com/watch?v=s_m9Q06Ja90.

Half Way Down [*Banxialiu shehui*]. Dir. Tu Guangqi. Asia Pictures, 1957. Available for research viewing at the Hong Kong Film Archive.

Homecoming [*Sishui liunian*]. Dir. Yim Ho. Bluebird Movie, 1984. YouTube, https://www.youtube.com/watch?v=45P6PysLiFw.

Long Lane [*Chang xiang*]. Dir. Pu Wancang. Asia Pictures, 1956. Available at the Hong Kong Film Archive.

Love Eterne [*Liang Shanbo yu Zhu Yingtai*]. Dir. Li Han-hsiang. Shaw Brothers, 1963. DVD.

Mambo Girl [*Manbo nvlang*]. Dir. Evan Yang. MP&GI, 1957. DVD.

No Body's Child [*Kuer liulang ji*]. Dir. Pu Wancang. Kuo Phone, 1960. Available at the Hong Kong Film Archive.

One-Armed Swordsman [*Dubei dao*]. Dir. Chang Cheh. Shaw Brothers, 1966. DVD.

Peasant Takes a Wife [*Xiao Erhei jiehun*]. Dir. Gu Eryi and Da Guangming, 1950. Available at the Hong Kong Film Archive.

Princess Yang Kwei-fei [*Yohiki*]. Dir. Kenji Mizoguchi. Daiei and Shaw Brothers, 1955. DVD.

Song of the Exile [*Ketu qiuhen*]. Dir. Ann Hui. Central Pictures, 1990. DVD.

Sorrows of the Forbidden City [*Qinggong mishi*]. Dir. Zhu Shilin. Yonghua, 1948. DVD.

Soul of China [*Guohun*]. Dir. Pu Wanchang. Yonghua, 1948. DVD.

Sweet as Honey [*Tiantian mimi*]. Dir. Zhu Shilin. Phoenix, 1959. YouTube.

The Dividing Wall [*Yi ban zhi ge*]. Dir. Zhu Shilin. Longma, 1952. Available at the Hong Kong Film Archive.

The Dream of the Red Chamber [*Honglou meng*]. Dir. Yuan Qiufeng. Shaw Brothers, 1962. DVD.

The Heroine [*Yang E*]. Dir. Hong Shauwen and Evan Yang. Asia Pictures, 1955. (Lost).

The Kingdom and the Beauty [*Jiangshan meiren*]. Dir. Li Han-hsiang. Shaw Brothers, 1959. DVD.

The Magnificent Concubine [*Yang Guifei*]. Dir. Li Han-hsiang. Shaw Brothers, 1962. DVD.

The World of Suzie Wong. Dir. Richard Quine. World Enterprise, 1960. DVD.

Three Charming Smiles [*San xiao*]. Dir. Li Pingqian. Great Wall, 1964. YouTube, https://www.youtube.com/watch?v=skReZ8ZPLOo.

Tradition [*Chuantong*]. Dir. Tang Huan. Asia Pictures, 1954. (Lost).

Photo Credits

Figure 1.6 Courtesy of Jia NiLee
Figure 1.7 Yue Qing, *Wanzhi qianhong Li Li-hua*
Figure 1.8 Courtesy of Jia NiLee
Figure 2.1 Courtesy of Jia NiLee
Figure 2.2 Courtesy of Union Press
Figure 2.3 Courtesy of the Asia Foundation
Figure 2.4 Courtesy of Robert Hsi
Figure 2.5 Courtesy of Robert Hsi
Figure 3.1 Courtesy of the Asia Foundation
Figure 4.2 *Southern Screen*, n.59 (January 1963)
Figure 5.1 Courtesy of Law Kar
Figure 5.2 Courtesy of Law Kar
Figure 5.3 *70s Biweekly*, n.20 (May 1971)

Index

For the benefit of digital users, indexed terms that span two pages (e.g., 52–53) may, on occasion, appear on only one of those pages.
Figures are indicated by f following the page number.